The Congress of Vienna

The Congress of Vienna

AN EYEWITNESS ACCOUNT

Edited and with an Introduction
by Hilde Spiel

TRANSLATED FROM THE GERMAN BY RICHARD H. WEBER

Chilton Book Company

PHILADELPHIA   NEW YORK   LONDON

Contents

21394

eigns"—Money trouble—Meeting on the May Field—Napoleon after the battle of Waterloo—Last letter to his wife

FINALE

THE FUTURE   303

"German affairs must be put in order"—The Italian problem—
The Bourbon dynasty—Dalberg's precarious position—A letter
from Paris—Dark fears in Austria—Count Stefan Széchenyi's
prophecies—The noble robber chieftain Grasel and his gang—
Preparing the minutes of the Congress—Napoleon goes aboard
the "Northumberland"—Grasel's execution

Introduction

Very often, world history is shaped under theatrical circumstances. Apocalyptic visions foreshadow the doom of an age; amidst thunderclap and lightning the epiphanies are born. Out of the depths of Germany came the murderous horsemen who overswept the crumbling Greco-Roman empire. Papal anathemas and the stake accompanied the onrushing Reformation. Christopher Columbus in his *Santa Maria* reached for the New World over mighty billows. And the dethronement of the Most Christian of Kings, the downfall of feudalism in France, proceeded along a gory path, lined with lopped-off heads and ravished bodies. But, once the curtain had fallen over the Empire, the most proper manners were once more observed at that conference of princes and politicians in Vienna. Dress swords clanged, not chains, and ladies swept past at the side of elegant statesmen who, a few hours hence and, as it were, by-the-way, would nonchalantly and with deft fingers redraw Europe's new borders, without fanfare, without the whooshing noise of the guillotine, without dramatic posturings. The Congress of Vienna was no thriller-diller but a social event, enacted against a marvelously splendid background and played by the foremost actors the world stage afforded.

The first Treaty of Paris had provided for a meeting of ruling statesmen for the purpose of ratifying a series of territorial and other international decisions, made as early as the end of the

Wars of Liberation of 1813–14. Whereas the Paris Treaty had fixed the relationship with *France*, the purpose of the Congress of Vienna was to discuss and reach agreement among victors, vanquished, and neutrals on a new *European* order. And in fact, with the sole exception of Turkey, all European Powers sent delegates to Vienna between September 18, 1814, and June 9, 1815. Originally, no thought had been given to a general reconstruction of existing conditions. The uniqueness of the conference is, that in the end precisely such reconstruction did come about, a reconstruction largely based on the *status quo ante* 1792.

Structurally, the Congress of Vienna is perforce of a pattern with the series of conferences of mutual discussion, of tidying up, of parading, which occurred ever more frequently at this turning point in history: the fruitful dialogue between the forces of progress and the forces of retrogression. This series begins with the ill-fated Congress of Rastatt and, via Tilsit and Erfurt, leads straight to Vienna, without, however, ending there. Indeed, the pragmatic task of the Congress of Vienna is best defined by considering it merely the first in a series of conferences—Aachen, Carlsbad, Troppau, Laibach, and Verona—organized by the Philistines to gently thwart attempts at change. But how different, how far more fateful were the effects resulting from the Vienna meeting of emperors, kings, and diplomats! It seemed as if the vast, complicated, and many-faceted struggles with the Corsican giant had required a final denouement, befitting the latter's stature. From the very outset, this denouement developed and followed its own logical pattern. In scope and range of interests, as well as in the myriad ramifications of its grandly conceived course, the Congress seemed comparable only to the ecclesiastical conferences of the fifteenth and sixteenth centuries, in particular to the Council of Constance.

In the sense of modern totalitarianism, Napoleon had not been a monolith. In this, despite all cruelty, lay his humanity. He was the last antique man; he was the first modern man enthroned. Against him who achieved and killed the Revolution, who, together with Danton, conceived and conquered nationalism, against him, the Antichrist and Superman—as Nietzsche rightly saw him—had risen those who, as has often happened in the course of history, and with good reason, had donned the mask of Christians and Crusaders. And it was indeed this seemingly defeated, invisible foe who presided at the Congress. It was thanks to him and in consonance with an ancient wisdom inborn in truly conservative circles that caused the duped French people, who had served the Corsican genius as instrument, to be treated with the velvet glove of tolerance. Talleyrand's role was an easy one at a conference table where peace terms as such were no longer debated.

To be sure, this Congress was unique in its conciliatory spirit towards the former enemy, thereby causing a change in fronts. This resulted from the complete restoration of conditions as they had existed before 1792, even before 1789, and as they had only recently been brought about by Napoleon himself. That differentiation between the leader and the led, which came under severe attack in the latter part of the nineteenth century, and which our own era again at least postulates, was taken entirely for granted in the Vienna of 1814 and 1815. Souls were bartered at the Congress and new borders scissored out in the best of tradition. An attempt was made to create "the best of all possible Europes" along the lines of a Leibnizian universe. The edifice raised remained immutable, until forty years later East and West were at each other again. But even though this slightly antiquated building, shored up by Metternich and the Bourbons, by Talleyrand and the Hapsburgs, rested for a long time on sound foundations as the dwelling place of the mighty, the worm was distinctly and noticeably in the woodwork. Yet, the dynastic forces were still sufficiently strong, and had provided so well and so lastingly for peace, that all uprisings in the *Stürm und Drang* years of 1848–49 were doomed to fail. Granted, raising legitimacy to the role of guiding principle at the Congress presupposed its prior violation. The age of feudalism had paid no particular heed to the concept of legitimacy. Any opponent of the established order was conscious of being a rebel, and he who would drive out local rulers or behead kings considered himself a divine instrument in the service of exterior or domestic, but at any rate religious, powers. But this time the principle of legitimacy and the so-called "reac-

tionary forces" had so thoroughly prevailed, that the laws of dia-
lectics seemed abrogated. The youthful iconoclasts among the
student organizations which met at the Wartburg festival of 1817
were mentally, spiritually, and politically of a cloth with Lützow's
Black Rifles [1] and Schill's [2] officers, even with Pichegru and
Moreau, the generals who broke with Napoleon. In Vienna, however, at the Congress, the ancient principle ran into a cul-de-sac.
Here, the Napoleon-made kings kept their throne and even that
Friedrich August I of Saxony, who had fought on Napoleon's
side as late as 1813, only lost two-fifths of his domain plus 850,-
000 souls, not so much in punishment, as because Prussia had to
be rewarded. As Franz II good-naturedly put it, it was "simply
too terrible to throw a legitimate ruler off his throne." Inevitably,
though, the blind alley of legitimacy eventually blended into the
landscaped garden of the petty bourgeoisie, which, in contrast to
the *ancien régime*, felt the nagging of an almost frivolous, but at
bottom pious, twinge of a conscience ill at ease.

The famous bon mot of the Austrian field marshal Prince de
Ligne that "the Congress dances but it does not march" pinpoints
the salient characteristic of the meeting. The policy of the velvet
glove prevailed and diplomacy became a function of social activities. Above all is the meeting linked with the name and person of
the Austrian statesman Prince Klemens Wenzel Lothar Nepomuk Metternich—called "Metternich the Butterfly" by his
detractors. To some extent, of course, the festive mood of the
Congress resulted from the Austrian emperor's desire to "put on
the dog" in order to prove that his and the House of Hapsburg's
star was far from setting, that, despite the national bankruptcy
three years before, there was no need at all to be tightfisted and
frugal. Metternich, on the other hand, made a personal bent into
a collective art. He carried on the intrigues, plans, chessboard
moves, and parleys of statecraft "with other means" and contin-

[1] A volunteer corps led by the Prussian officer Adolf Freiherr
von Lützow in daring exploits against Napoleon I in 1813–14.—
Transl.

[2] A Prussian patriot who organized a volunteer corps against
Napoleon I.—Transl.

ued the diplomatic war even beyond the official meetings to the ballroom floor, in front of the buffet, even into the boudoir. Everything was planned, everything "calculated in." That he often overshot the mark, even his most ardent admirers never denied. Metternich, next to Talleyrand and Russia's Alexander I, the most dominant and influential figure of the Congress, was an eighteenth-century feudalist who treated each case and solved each problem strictly on its own merit, without principle or grand concept. Like a butterfly he fluttered from one person to the next, promising and foreswearing, lying or telling the truth, savoring to the fullest the freedom that remained largely denied to the peoples he administered. At heart he didn't care a hoot for ideals. His daring, conceit, and insouciance carried him through the toughest situations; critical contemporaries believed to notice in him as well "indolence, inattention to duty, and a proneness to dally." His first guests at the Congress were served from plates that had been presented him by Napoleon I during his Paris ambassadorship. "What is to be expected," Talleyrand wrote his new king, "of a man who spends the most serious moments with trifling things and who thinks nothing of staging a rehearsal of *The Pasha of Suresne* in his own home?" Of course, Metternich might have objected that production of this silly musical had been ordered by Her Majesty, the Empress Marie Louise herself. Actually, "trifling things" did not exist for Metternich at all, for everything fell into a pattern with the plans he had conceived with cunning nonchalance. Through a whirlwind of amusements to mollify, divert, and in the end wear down both friend and foe— and who was not a friend, not a foe?—was part and parcel of Metternich's system of negotiation. Besides, he delighted in surrounding himself with princes, diplomats, and beautiful women.

Metternich, and Austria's Lord High Steward, Prince Trauttmansdorff, accordingly had set the stage by throwing huge parties, very soon to be followed by a plethora of amusements and diversions. Vienna was in honor bound to live up to its reputation as a city of the easy life, of banquets and balls and of carriage rides in the Prater. Still, voices arose that claimed a capital to be an ill-suited place for a conference, and here and there sighs were heard in worry over "these everlasting fetes" or fears expressed that "this indefinitely extended presence of foreign sovereigns in Vienna will make an extremely bad impression on Vienna itself and on all of Germany."

Not only did the upper strata of society find the new diplomacy-through-entertainment difficult to understand. After a while, even the Viennese man in the street lost enthusiasm for the super show. Initially, the people had joyously welcomed the Congress and the foreign visitors within their city gates. But when the entertainment program stretched beyond the originally planned months of October and November and there seemed no end to the chain of court concerts, theater performances, masquerades, hunting parties, military parades, court and private balls, tournaments, sleigh rides, and carriage drives, the Viennese fell into their customary grumbling. Only those deriving profit from the merry-go-round of foreigners and fetes refrained from complaining: the innkeepers, lodging-house owners, theater managers, art dealers, trinkets merchants, and ladies of easy virtue. Though these exceptions numbered many, the great mass of grousers was more numerous. It was they who footed the bill, since in those days court expenses were financed through direct public revenue. The huge sums spent for the foreign potentates and kings, who were in no hurry to go home and who were billeted and largely also fed at government expense, caused a fifty percent trade tax to be imposed on everybody. Small wonder there were shouts from the ranks of onlookers during the famous royal "sleigh rides" in January, 1815: "There goes our fifty percent!"

In any case, the concept of "politics-through-excitation-and-partial-gratification-of-all-conceivable-physical-and-spiritual-sensations-of-pleasure" had caused a drastic change in Vienna and its inhabitants, indeed in the character of the Congress itself. Nor was this so strange in view of the sheer bigness and variety of all the events and happenings. In a manner never before experienced, quantity had become transmuted into a quality, unknown heretofore, and never again reached. According to a somewhat daring estimate, the populace of Vienna had swelled by one-third. Five emperors and kings, eleven ruling princes, ninety plenipotentiaries,

and fifty-three non-invited representatives of European powers
had come to the city. First to arrive were those who came from
abroad, the principals being accompanied by their servants, secretaries, scribes, personal physicians, and father confessors, in
addition to all manner of soldiers-of-fortune, improvisors, and
charlatans. This itself created a demand for service personnel in
Vienna, causing a second invasion from the provinces and the
city's suburbs. The chanceries needed office personnel, the cuisines
cooks, the ladies hairdressers, the gentlemen mistresses. Lace sellers
and milliners, lackeys from the country, Hungarian grooms,
Italian singers, French and English portrait painters, purse
snatchers, swindlers, itinerant preachers from everywhere, all
these had assembled into a gigantic, exotic, and free-for-all
mélange.

Though the Viennese mocked and sneered, railed and
grumbled, the fact was, they hugely enjoyed the spectacle in
spite of its drawbacks and, as the one hand paid the special tax
imposed, the other assiduously strove to make hay while the
political sun shone. They were a special breed, these Viennese,
full of self-mockery, envy, laziness and cunning, but also forever
ready to play the comedy of their own lives, and watch themselves
doing it. If on top of it there was an honest-to-goodness czar and
his czarina to be admired, as well as his two grandducal sisters, the
"clubfooted devil" Talleyrand, and a king so gross of paunch a
hole had to be cut in the table for him, why, this only added
spice to the general fun. But sneer as they might over the parsi-
monious English lords, or with a sure instinct for the apt phrase
call the King of the Danes the "King of the Dance," the Viennese
sold themselves, their city, and their royal house by no means
cheaply. It may well be that the dubious inference of the phrase
"the easygoing Viennese" dates back to these days.

One had one's pets among the foreign princes, yet homegrown
"Papa Franz" remained the most popular of all. But though the
foreign dignitaries found favorites among the ladies of Vienna,
it was the foreigners, among them the three princesses from
Courland, the Duchess of Sagan in the lead, who were most in
demand in the salons and alcoves. This Congress was for a fact, as

later anecdote or operetta depicted it, indeed of the stuff that a Richard Strauss envisioned for an opera and that a Hofmannsthal would indignantly reject. Love largely wielded the scepter—at least what the age considered as love. A rococo cupid, half Eros, half cherub, a messenger of pink billets-doux and a purveyor of secrets, dispatched shaft upon shaft from his quiver. Metternich himself, inventor of the new parlor-and-bedroom politics, was frequently deeply involved in affairs of the heart. Spheres of interest touched and commingled and many a matter moved from the diplomat's dispatch case into the pocket of the gallant swain, causing Gentz, secretary of the Congress, to comment to the Courland princesses about the talkativeness of his minister, Prince Metternich: "It is simply unbelievable what gets known."

What plethora of history! What hustle and bustle on the streets and in the highways and byways of the "inner city," that conglomerate of houses surrounded by bastions which, in the manner of the Middle Ages, hugged the Imperial Palace and St. Stephan's Cathedral! At all hours of the day and night, carriages and state coaches blocked the roads, sedan chairs became motionless in the melee, horses pranced, and the "Graben nymphs" traipsed along the sidewalks. Which part belonged to world history, which to the gossip of scandal? Food for the imperial table came to 50,000 guldens daily and the total cost for entertainment during the five months of the Conference amounted to forty million francs. Yet, behind this gay façade, and often unbeknown to the casual observer, the most serious matters were at stake. Foremost among the problems were the border questions of Poland and Saxony. In addition, many decisions, ranging from indemnifying the German rulers west of the Rhine to the abolition of slavery, had to be made. These matters did not much concern the average Viennese. What did interest the man in the street was Prussia's future role. Memories of the Silesian Wars, not more than fifty years back, still stirred, as did the thought of Prussia's part in the Treaty of Basel (1795), or that nation's attitude during the battles of Aspern and Wagram, those purely Austrian campaigns of 1809. An undefinable feeling of dread towards the successors of Frederick the Great had remained, a fear that, with the extinction of the Wettin dynasty, Prussia would become Bohemia's northern neighbor. Even Archduke Johann, the courtly knight and brother of Emperor Franz, touching on the business of Poland and Saxony, wrote in his diary the revealing words: "How typically Old Prussian!"

But how was one to take a congress that had not even been formally convened? The only authentic documentation extant concerns its final session which was at the same time its first and last official meeting. Those ceremonious consultations, originally planned to take place in the huge ballroom of the imperial palace, never were held. The real work was done in committees and non-public conferences at the ministry on the Ballhausplatz, by the committees of the "five" and of the "eight," in private conversations or at social gatherings, in the ballroom or at the banquet table. Small wonder then that official business moved at a snail's pace. Talleyrand himself, wirepuller par excellence, though carefully keeping in the background, once complained to his master in Paris that two full days had lapsed with not a single conference held, one having been devoted to a hunt, the other to a party. It is to be assumed, however, that such to-ing and fro-ing, such "temporizing" and "artful cuning" were part of Metternich's method. Gentz, the latter's secretary and, as it were, professional optimist, emphasized that, contrary to former congresses, there was to be no standing on protocol and formalities in Vienna. Nor can there be any doubt that, despite all frivolous festivities, those directly concerned, that is, the emissaries and representatives of participating countries, never lost sight of the purpose of their being there. The Prussian delegation was by far the most matter-of-fact one, hardly surprising since it had most at stake. The deafness of the one representative, Hardenberg, and the happy marriage of the other, Humboldt, were no doubt conducive to serious work but hardly to pleasure-seeking. Not only the Prussians, however, but everyone took his mission most seriously.

And yet, the element of the tragic was absent from the Congress, certainly from its participants and idle observers. Despite a number of untoward and sad events that occurred in those months, the tragic muse made no appearance. The time and the place—Vienna's easygoing atmosphere and the spirit of the frivolous rococo, by no means dead—held sway, at least for the time being. Thus the death and especially the burial of the nearly eighty-year-old Prince de Ligne failed to evoke the tragic strain. Nor, on the other hand, was there any premonition of the unhappy fate that was to befall the then three-year-old son of Napoleon I. But anyone with a keen ear and a sharp eye could have detected omens of dire events soon to come to certain participants at the Congress. Already, the skids were being greased that were to send Czar Alexander crashing from the heights of his Olympian seat as Europe's arbitrator down into the miasmic regions of a misunderstood Christian mysticism. Also, Metternich's German policy foreshadowed the same danger to Austria as did the voluntary disinterest of the House of Hapsburg in the German imperial crown and its simultaneous turning toward the Italian sphere.

Missing at the Congress was above all that concept of a world based on Christian ideologies which for centuries had been the mainstay of the power and mission of Austria's ruling dynasty. The relationship with the papal court was anything but friendly. By no means had all traces of the enlightened reforms of Joseph II (1741–90) been eradicated at the Imperial Palace. Metternich was a Freemason and agnostic. Nor did the second dominant figure at the Congress, Talleyrand, believe in unification under the banners of a universal Catholicism. Although he had made some effort to have a requiem mass celebrated at the anniversary of Louis XVI's death, he was *persona non grata* in clerical circles. The married Bishop of Autun, notorious for his impiety, had long since departed the society of the brethren of Jesus. Small wonder that Cardinal Consalvi, the Vatican's delegate, who was specially interested in the return to church control of the North Italian Papal States and who was annoyed with Austria's lack of cooperation, should ironically comment in public that the Holy Father had been compelled to appeal to the Turkish sultan and to the King of Sweden for help. The subsequent course of the Congress had a salutary effect on Metternich, however. The Papal States were in the end returned to the Vatican, which netted the princely Freemason, who earlier had confirmed Murat's rule in Naples and even left him to hope for some of the Papal lands, a signed portrait from Pius VII in token of appreciation. From the Bourbon Ferdinand, when the latter became King of Naples, Metternich not only received an annuity of 60,000 francs but was created Duke of Portella to boot.

The Congress of Vienna forever buried the rivalry between the Hapsburg and Bourbon dynasties. But another deep cleavage, running straight across Europe, was only temporarily healed. This was the struggle for supremacy in Germany which, though already ominously apparent, was still being held in check by Russia's controlling influence in all German matters. Alexander's Polish ploy, as well as the Saxon trade in souls, had caused an acute war crisis in November and December, 1814. Open conflict over both questions was avoided through England's realignment, following a change in government. There nonetheless were days and nights of extreme tension in the Ballhausplatz and the *salons*; there even came the moment when the otherwise phlegmatic Franz, aroused by the constant threat to kick his brother-in-law, Friedrich August I, from his Saxon throne, darkly hinted: "If that happens, by God I'll shoot." With the alliance of Austria, France, and England against Russia and Prussia toward the end of the year, the crisis considerably abated. The question of Saxony was satisfactorily solved, however, on February 10, 1815, when Austria accepted the Russo-Prussian proposals. The spirit of compromise once more had gained a victory at the very fountainhead of compromise.

Indeed, in its love for the conciliatory deal, as much as in its sophisticated worldliness, Vienna proved to be a highly suitable locale for the Congress. For centuries the city had served as residence of an international ruling dynasty that had gathered civil servants from Lower Austria and France, architects from Italy, and artisans from the Slavic countries. Internationalism was also the keynote of the Congress, as it was the binding link among the dynastically interrelated European sovereigns and a consanguineous European nobility—in contrast to the awakening nationalism of the *bourgeoisie*. Again and again during the course of the Congress examples of changes in national allegiance appear. Karl Freiherr vom und zum Stein, Prussian councilor and statesman and in a certain sense the creator of Prussia, was born in the Rhineland, as was Austria's leading minister, Metternich. England's first delegate, Lord Castlereagh, was Irish. Even Russia, then considered the very fountainhead of nationalistic strivings, was international to the very tailfeather of the "Eagle of all the Russias"—its most prominent representatives were the Alsatian Anstett, the Corsican Pozzo di Borgo, and the Corfiote, Capo d'Istrias. And the great adversary of them all, Napoleon I, Emperor of the French, was a Corsican of Italian descent who never learned to use the French language correctly.

Little wonder, then, that international plans and tasks should to a high degree occupy the Congress. Its openmindedness in world affairs found expression in the indemnification program for the reapportioned territories west of the Rhine, in the agreements concerning the Ionic islands and Malta, in the shipping regulations on Danube and Rhine, as well as in discussions on global abolition of slavery. To be sure, there is a difference whether such "internationalization" proceeds from below or is enforced from above. The author of the reactionary Metternich system nevertheless in his memories came out in favor of a so-called "European concert," a more inclusive community that appears progressive even by today's standards. "Politics," he wrote, "is the science of a nation's vital interests in the broadest sense of the word. Since, however, an isolated country no longer exists, it becomes necessary to consider the *community of states* an essential precondition of the modern world. The great axioms of political science are applicable to the true political interests of *all* nations and it is this community of interests that guarantees their existence. The essentiality of political policy in our day is the bringing about of international ties, mutually supported and based on the respect for the rights of others. . . . Diplomacy is merely the daily execution of this policy."

All these postulates, compromises, and provisional decisions caused the Congress more and more to resemble the furious activity of an anthill, a simile that in a frantic manner took physical shape with Napoleon's return from Elba. But in all fairness, who could possibly have reconciled the myriad claims? Who could have expected the formerly sovereign princes, already sadly plucked by the Regensburg Diet of 1803, to acquiesce in all decisions? Were these not forced on them by powers that from the very outset fought a diminution of their own territories and a whittling away of their own sovereignty in favor of some feudal anachronism? Could the princes of Thurn und Taxis, of Loewenstein—Wertheim—Freudenberg really count on entering the German Diet, side by side with their powerful dynastic brothers whom Napoleon had raised to high places? By and large, however, order was finally restored amidst the panic caused by Napoleon's return, an order that was accepted, not because it was what had been hoped for, "the best of all orders," but because it was the best one available. During months of frenetic rounds of conclaves and *salon* intrigues, of dances and theatrics, messengers at midnight, boar hunts during daylight, musical assemblies, whisperings in the alcoves, missteps and *Te Deums* in the cathedral, a new Europe had been constructed with the aid of old concepts. Papa Franz' forty million francs had been well spent.

Yet, were it not for eyewitness reports of a special kind, it would be impossible for a later age to reconstruct the events of this politico-diplomatic gathering whose work was done almost entirely behind the scenes. For, in contrast to the average historian who still selects his source material more from extant state documents and protocols than from contemporary contributions of a private nature, he who would depict the Congress of Vienna is forced to use other sources. These are the reports of the Austrian emperor's secret police, of those *confidants*, trusted members of the upper class, agents, and other auxiliary forces available to the emperor and his officials—not to mention the snoopers in the service of a Metternich or Gentz, or those of foreign ministries and missions. This apparatus had been created by Joseph II. Though only moderately used by Leopold II, Franz II, his son, put new life into it and made it into an important instrument of governmental policy. "The police is charged with preventing as far as possible all disruption of public and private tranquility."

Here is already in evidence a shift in scope and an enlargement of an authority that had initially envisaged only the protection of the individual citizen as stated in the phrase that it, the police, would serve in support of "the authorities in the direction of welfare, morals, order, and personal protection." As the welfare state of enlightened absolutism changed under the pressures of revolution, war, and national uprisings into a police state, the safety of the individual took a back seat to the security of the state as a whole. Not only the means, the very mission of the police became different. The nephew of the "reform emperor" in his struggle with a revolutionary France, which itself had created no mean secret and public police service, employed similar measures to save his own skin.

In 1785, Joseph II had appointed Count Johann Anton von Pergen, Secretary of State for Internal Affairs, to head the security apparatus for all non-Hungarian territories. Already, as president of the Lower Austria provincial government, Pergen headed the Viennese police. Now the governors of the other provinces as well turned to him in all matters relating to secret police activities. In 1793, Franz II even created a new "Ministry of Police" of which Pergen became the first incumbent minister. His power grew, censorship fell under his control, and privacy of the mails was officially violated. Baron Sumerau, who succeeded Pergen in 1803, was the first to recommend the recruiting of "trusted members of the upper class" whose identity was to be safeguarded. The heyday of the secret police began. Like many fathers, "Papa Franz" was consummately curious. Only the most detailed knowledge about his subjects, it seemed to him, would enable him to best look after their welfare as emperor and chief authority. To look after his compassionate police interests, Francis employed Baron Hager von Altensteig, the "ostensible head of the imperial police and censorship office." Report has it that this official enjoyed "a very good public reputation," that he was considered "a very loyal and just man who does not at all really like espionage nor engage in it."

The apparatus was extensive, intricate, and far-flung. There was a headquarters, containing the codes files. In addition there were "mail cubicles," cubbyholes at the major provincial post offices where mail was monitored and decoded. Suspicious letters were intercepted, opened, copied, sealed again, and delivered. These copies were called "intercepts." Added to the secret police's official staffs were agents of the foreign service, who constituted the actual foot soldiers of the secret service that included several men in high position. Also used were servants and lackeys, room attendants and chancery employees, but especially innkeepers, by law required to act as informants, and those letting private lodgings.

Great interest was shown in the contents of wastebaskets and open fireplaces. Here, the proverbial Viennese slovenliness came to the aid of politics, for, in one way or another, the well-informed government would later take care of those who burned insufficiently or destroyed carelessly. The contents of these wastebaskets and fireplaces, wherever possible, were sent directly to the Ministry of Police. Here, a painstaking attempt was made to reconstruct the original missive, whether letter or rejected draft. Such resurrected documents were called *chiffons*. And all this, the reports, intercepts, and *chiffons*, arrived daily on the desks in the imperial police headquarters where they were first studied by Hager and his trusted helpers and a précis composed, to be used at the next briefing of the omniscient, all-caring monarch.

Confronted by this huge apparatus, one is apt to suffer a moment of vertigo. The firm ground seems to undulate, solid figures to distintegrate. A vice is here sanctioned by the state, and out of disorder and chaos is created an order that for sheer bulk and uncontrollability is itself threatened by chaos. At a comparatively early period a degree of public surveillance was achieved that today requires the use of expensive machinery. Man can still out-perform a tape recorder. If one chooses to be silent, no automatic device can record one's thoughts and opinions to be played back in the courtroom. Confidants, on the other hand, who observe and analyze the total personality, are able to perform a yet better service for their masters and for an inquisitive posterity. The historian may indeed doubt if the reports contain more than mere gossip, gossip that obscures rather than reveals the important events. Undoubtedly, information of little value takes up the bulk of the space and it is more the human actors and their background, rather than the action itself, that serves as this book's theme. But out of the plethora of trivia there is apt to arise the revealing fact, out of latrine rumors emerges a historical figure.

We learn that Lord Castlereagh in his rented palace on the Minoritenplatz keeps in physical trim through daily dancing sessions, with wife or sister-in-law if they are at home, but with a chair if they are not. This slightly ludicrous fact stems from the report of a parlor maid, whom the secret service had been able to install despite the lord's precaution of hiring his own servants. Alexander, Czar of all the Russias, each morning, we hear, rubs face and body with ice. No doubt this information also was not easily obtained, for the secret police had infinite trouble gaining access to the Imperial Palace where the czar resided—the palace personnel being resentful of serving any other than their own master. But what use can a historian make of such information? Should it be summarily rejected as aberrations, as eccentric traits, or may it not afford us an immediacy in observing these figures that could scarcely be duplicated? Does not the British foreign minister's solitary dance with the chair contain a hint of that English isolation which, though openly mocked and sneered at in Vienna, was secretly feared? Does not the czar's morning ritual admit of similar symbolic interpretation if one visualizes the great liberator of Europe by the grace of his Cossacks daily administering to himself the barbaric baptism with a chunk of ice?

We are indeed indebted to the conscientious informants, to the stupid, indiscriminatory zeal and blind faith of Franz' trusted subjects, who have enabled us, after a century and a half, to relive the Congress of Vienna with a clearness that no other documentation can approach.

The Congress: Whence, Why, Whither?

Battles and conflagrations, weddings and deathbeds have their eyewitnesses. Even love scenes and conspiracies are spied upon, and gossip as well as intrigue may be evaluated. But to find one's labyrinthine way through as complex a matter as that of the Congress of Vienna, the mind's eye must, as it were, open inward. Research must turn detective and hunt down the intimate knowledge that hovered over the contemporary scene to register and comment on each and every event. The early days of the Congress especially are shrouded in conjectures, however, that, correctly placed, become keystones in the jigsaw puzzle of history. The cautious German historian August Fournier, expert interpreter of the period, writes about the Congress: "(It) grew out of a scheduled meeting of two foreign sovereigns, Czar Alexander and the King of Prussia, who had suggested the conference to the Austrian emperor at the Battle of Leipzig." Fournier's contemporaneous source is a newspaper, the Berliner Zeitung *of October 26, whose account is reprinted in a special supplement of the* Österreichisch-Kaiserlichen privilegirten Wiener-Zeitung Nr. 153 *of November 5, 1813:*

Events of October 19, Tuesday:
. . . . . in the meantime, General Bennigsen's corps had also mounted an attack at the *Peterstore* and this decided the issue.

The Crown Prince of Sweden now entered (Leipzig) by the *Grimmaische Tor*, Count Langeron by the *Hallische Tor*, and General Bennigsen by the *Peterstore* . . . . . Within the city, the victors were received by the German contingents from Saxony, Baden, and Darmstadt, which now came over to their side, with Prince Emil of Hesse-Darmstadt of the Darmstadt, and Count von Hochburg, son of the recently deceased grand duke, of the Baden contingent. As the Swedish crown prince dismounted in the market square, the Russian czar and the king of Prussia also arrived, all three embracing under emotions appropriate to the importance of this victorious moment. A half hour later, the Austrian emperor likewise appeared on the scene but, after a talk with the two Allied monarchs, left again for his own head-quarters near Leipzig. The other two sovereigns lunched with the Swedish crown prince.

During the winter campaign 1813–14 the Allies on several occasions still suffered Napoleonic maulings that left them disunited and in disarray. During the unsuccessful peace talks between Napoleon I and his opponents at Châtillon-sur-Seine in February–March, 1814, conducted on the French side by the Foreign Minister Caulaincourt, Duke of Vicence, there appeared a rift that was subsequently to deepen: Austria on the one side, conditionally supported by England and opting for leniency toward the vanquished, even toward the Napoleonic dynasty; on the other hand, a warlike and expansive Prussia and a victorious Russia, conscious even then of a role as Europe's mediator.

Archduke Johann, the Austrian emperor's younger brother, friend of the Alpine peoples, democrat and idealist, was at the Allied headquarters at the time. The diary entry of March 12 reads:

Today, the 12th, peace was to have been concluded. Caulain-court had instructions to sign everything short of the turnover of Paris. My emperor was in agreement, but the czar wanted to enter Paris, topple Napoleon from the throne, and—oh good God—offer the crown to the Bourbons. Thus the chance was missed, never to return. Later, the battles of Montmirail and Langres. We are at Troyes, from us an ultimatum, demanding less than that which Napoleon was willing to accept (concern over the future). Napoleon is still solidly entrenched.

A letter, which Metternich had addressed to Caulaincourt as late as March 18 and which unluckily fell into Talleyrand's hands, was highly compromising and could readily be employed at the Congress to put the Austrian statesman under pressure:

You are of course familiar with our aims, our principles, and our wishes. The first are entirely European in nature and therefore pro-French. The effects of the second show Austria's interest in a flourishing France. The third concerns a dynasty, intimately linked to our own.[3] I have full confidence in you, my dear duke. . . . I will exert every effort to detain Lord Castlereagh a few days. Once the minister has left, peace is out of the question. Peace still lies within your master's power.

But the peace treaty of May 30, 1814, that followed Napoleon's abdication depended of course on a different set of men. And it was this treaty which, having disposed of French matters as scheduled, in accordance with Article 32 set the stage for the Congress of Vienna, there to consider European affairs, in particular German matters, Saxony and the Duchy of Warsaw especially:

Within two months all powers that participated on our side or the other in the current conflict will dispatch plenipotentiaries to a congress to be held in Vienna in order to arrive at decisions that shall spell out the provisions of this treaty.

The opening of the Congress is at hand. All the world knows about it, with the capital city of Vienna probably the least well informed. Thus, in September, 1814, we read in the highly popular contemporary Viennese publication Letters of the Newly Arrived Herr Eipeldauer to His Cousins in Kakran: [4]

[3] Napoleon was married to a daughter of Franz II.—Transl.
[4] These letters were purportedly written by an unlettered rustic from the Eipel region in Bohemia come to Vienna to gawk at the Congress and earn some easy money, allegedly working at one of the chanceries. They were actually composed by the newspaper's editors.—Transl.

4 The Congress of Vienna

Blest be the Lord, but here with us in Vienna the birds they're shouting it from the rooftops we're to have a peace conference at last at which all big and little potatoes will come to and also the Russian emperor and king of Prussia have given our most gracious Monarch their parola as Cavaliers they will put a visitation on him in Vienna.

From the very start the Congress gazed at itself as in a mirror. Both the diplomats, grown skeptical during the war years, and the irony-prone people of Vienna approached this peace congress with a mixture of suspicion, mockery, and wide-eyed wonder. The bookdealer and publisher Carl Bertuch had initially come to Vienna from his native Weimar to lobby for the abolishment of censorship and for a ban on copyright infringements. The diary he kept and his correspondence with his father are most revealing in their ingenuous observation. On October 4, 1814, he writes to Weimar:

The secret affairs of the Congress, of which glimpses may be had now and then through confidential sources, are of the utmost importance. There is a great jockeying for position by the vested interests and everything is still in flux. Poland and Saxony are the focal points of movement, with the latter gaining great support.

The Abbé Giuseppe Carpani, poet, musician, and friend of Mozart, had a professional interest in the Congress: he was in the pay of the Austrian secret police. From the very outset his was a pessimistic view of the general situation:

There's trouble in the air. . . . Russia begins to pout: she wants Poland. Europe is unable to go along in this. France is annoyed over the union of the Belgian Netherlands with Holland and Talleyrand is trying to revoke this concession to England. Denmark demands indemnification for Norway, and Prussia wants Saxony. Castlereagh has submitted a note indicating England will oppose Russian annexation of Poland. The Pope will never give up his claim to the Papal states. Spain is adamant about the Etrurian kingdom or its equivalent, as it is about the return of Naples to the Bourbons. Campochiaro, on the other hand, is circulating a note in which he proves Murat to be as legitimate a king of Naples as all other sovereigns who recognized him, and that it is in the interest of all to retain him. Things are confused and nothing moves and after all that's been done, said, and promised, the resumption of war is not quite so inconceivable.

The second-ranking Prussian delegate, Baron Wilhelm von Humboldt, about the same time arrived at similar skeptical thoughts:

For the evil to be eradicated cleanly and decently, the war should have been fought and concluded differently. There is a twin of this war, and sooner or later it will come, but it may well in its turn destroy all the good gained. For only a very few have seen the light. Nothing is, nothing will be, done cleanly, whatever patchwork results, not the war, not the Paris Treaty, not this Congress.

According to an agent's report of October 8, 1814, Prince Talleyrand expressed his own general views about the Congress to his second in command, Count Goubernet de la Tour du Pin, in these words:

. . . . . a) a capital is no place for a congress; b) there never yet was a congress without a mediator, from Münster and Osnabrück to Teschen; c) today, a mediator is more urgently needed than ever; d) only France could serve as mediator, since it is the only Power without claims; e) the current Congress will bear no fruit whatever; it looks as if there will be no agreement on anything.

Count Karl von Nostitz, former adjutant of Prince Louis Ferdinand of Prussia, now a staff officer in Russian service, made the following diary entry for January 16, 1815:

From a distance, doubtlessly everything looks meaningful and important and each new day offers new insights, each gathering, each conversation seems to shed new light. On the contrary: at first, the woods are not seen for all the trees, and then, both woods and trees are gone. Poor, dear Congress! One hardly knows, has it begun? In Leipzig, at least the bells are rung at every mass. Here, nothing. Will there be pealing at its conclusion? Probably not. . . . The big results of the bighearted Congress will be nought but bartering of souls, just like the Regensburg and Augsburg Diet meetings, at which, in the wake of the Treaty of Lunéville, territories were bandied about like so many scraps of paper. Nothing that is done improves on Napoleon, because everyone is caught in the selfsame dilemma of self-service, narrow-mindedness, and stupidity. Rotten, mediocre ministers who conduct demoralized politics and who override the needs of their peoples with their own worm-eaten personalities. And capping all these ills is an ingrained slothfulness . . . that makes the Peace of Westphalia a model of devout zeal and concern!

The Austro-German problems above all are approached with a certain desperate, albeit painfully slow, tenacity. According to a confidential agent's report of October 24, 1814, the Bavarian delegate, Field Marshal Prince Karl Wrede, had this to say on the subject:

Our conference is not progressing at all. Nothing is decided, nothing is agreed on. And in truth, who would be dictated to in his own country? To boot, far too few meetings are held, the whole time being consumed with these nauseating, never-ending fetes. The sovereigns won't be able to get away before the end of November. The rest of us will be here till the end of the year, with a possible postscript in France. Consalvi plagues us with his *Concordat Germanique.* Bavaria and Württemberg will not be treated highhandedly.

Confidential Agent analyzed Austria's position on October 31, 1814, the day following the official Congress opening, in these words:

So the situation at the opening of the Congress on November 1 is that Russia militarily occupies all of Poland and threatens our Galicia; Prussia occupies all of Saxony and threatens

our Bohemia; in South Germany we are trying to force a constitution on Bavaria and Swabia that neither government wants
and expressly rejects; in Italy we must support a large army
with cold cash, straining the Viennese money market since gold
and silver must be purchased locally before it is sent to Italy;
in the Italian provinces that we occupy, the people to a man
declare: "We did better under Napoleon than presently under
Austria!" This is what the Italians in Vienna say; this is what
the letters arriving from Italy contain; this I even read in an
article printed by the *Moniteur*, an article Baron Thugut takes
pleasure in pointing out; this, in private, even Baron Wessenberg
admits. The situation is as follows: the emission of some 500
million new promissory notes which is what the visiting rulers
cost the court; the belief that Count Stadion supports Count
Karl Zechy's paper-money system; the opinion that this paper-
money system must sooner or later come to an end, necessitating
a second finance reform; that the conditions in Southern Germany,
in Saxony, in Poland, even in Italy, are such that not two years
hence there is bound to be another war; that after the Congress,
Austria cannot disarm; that Austria must be on its guard in Italy,
in Galicia, in Bohemia, and on the Inn; [5] that these armies are
bound to utterly ruin our finances, our credit etc., etc.! All this
is plainly in evidence, is firmly believed by everyone, is an open
secret . . . . the Congress of Vienna is no more than the calm
eye in the great tragedy of our current epoch, of our *bellum
omnium contra omnes* ["war of all against all"]. . . . These
are the jeremiads heard today, the eve of the Congress. . . . Lord
Stewart, the English ambassador, has pinched the *derrières* of the
Misses Kohary at a ball, demeaning himself by such and similar
boorish actions in the eyes of high society.

*This dissatisfaction with the way things were going at the
Congress was brought out even more sharply in a report of Confidential Agent, who appears to have gained access to the circle
around Count Stadion, Metternich's predecessor in the foreign
office and now his bitterest foe:*

[5] i.e., On the border between Austria and Bavaria.—Transl.

8 The Congress of Vienna

I hear it said: "The current meeting of the bigwigs in Vienna should be called *rendezvous* not *congress*. An emperor [6] who has neither a good heart nor a good head but wants to play the despot in France and Austria as well as in St. Petersburg; a king [7] out to sell German freedom and the balance of power in Europe to Russia; in Vienna a ministry at once unscrupulous and lazy, one that disavows in December what it has agreed to on October 22, one that inherently lacks confidence and trustworthiness: how can the work of this Congress prosper? Are these the ingredients likely to bring the heterogeneous interests, that lack natural cohesion, into balance?" These are the latest views about our interminable Congress, whose end is nowhere in sight.

This backbiting Cassandran cry was uttered several days before conclusion of the secret triple alliance between England, France, and Austria, an alliance that was the first step in solving the Saxon problem. This solution, a compromise par excellence, was not universally admired. Thus, Carpani had this to say:

Although, in general, satisfaction is shown over the progress made, everyone is nonetheless unhappy with the settlement. The Austrians, because they now lack a buffer state in the north and because the king of Saxony will become a Prussian puppet. In Vienna, Metternich is blamed on all sides. Prussia is disappointed over the smallness of its booty, and the king of Saxony laments that the settlement pays no heed to his rights.

Time and again, the wailing voices echo moral scruples and pity over the plight of the impotent peoples in the hands of their rulers and diplomats—which is not without irony, when the voice is that of a secret agent such as the self-knighted "Chevalier" Giovanni Ludovico Freddi-Battilori ("as well known in Italy as on the Bosporus and the Orontes"). Towards the end of the Congress he wrote:

At the "Golden Sun" café the results of the Congress are discussed. The Hanoverian diplomat Franz von Reden com-

[6] Czar Alexander.
[7] Of Prussia.

mented: "If the partitions, condoned by the potentates without regard to geography, to the mores and the practices of nations, or to the inalienable rights of peoples, are any criterion for judgment, it looks as if the rulers have done some horse trading by arbitrarily annexing strips of land to suit their own taste."

But on June 13, 1815, four days after the signing of the final document that ends the Congress, five days before the Battle of Waterloo, "Confidential Agent" reported:

It is contended that, on the whole, the Congress in its eight months of meetings has performed a tremendous task and never has a congress achieved more meaningful or grander results. For centuries to come, this Congress will glorify the reign of Emperor Franz II. And the majority of people now are saying: "The minister of foreign affairs has reaped honor from his work, from the conception and execution of the idea of the Congress of Vienna, and from the meeting of the sovereigns in consequence thereof."

If glorifying the reign of Franz II is still considered the finest achievement of the Congress in June, 1815, history's judgment is based on other criteria. In 1856, G. H. Pertz, Baron vom Stein's biographer, wrote shortly after the outbreak of the first major conflict since the Congress of Vienna, the Crimean War:

The merit of the Congress of Vienna, in brief, is that in implementation of the Treaty of Paris it replaced the vanquished Napoleonic tyranny and hegemony with the return to a confederacy of coequal sovereign states. This work of a wise and grand political strategy, though imperfect in part, will yet remain the only sound and lasting basis of European existence. And if the latter was later warped and stunted, it is not the Congress that should be blamed, but lesser men that followed and a deterioration in the times.

A deeper study of the far-reaching, albeit veiled, effects of the Congress is offered by the first-rate Italian historian Guglielmo Ferrero in his work Reconstruction: Talleyrand in Vienna, *published in 1939:*

It is our duty to acclaim the Congress of Vienna a great success. The solutions it found to the most urgent problems were not always the best. Many of them were mediocre and created new problems, the German and the Italian, for example, that have not ceased and will not cease for a long time to come to plague the world. But the Congress freed Europe of a deep fear and this is to its everlasting, shining credit. In the century from 1815 to 1914 the fear that shakes the race of man and gives it nightmares was lessened in Europe. It was a century in which Europe had the greatest confidence in the present and in the future. And this, after all, is the quintessence of every true civilization.

The Grand Political Strategy

*At the beginning of the nineteenth century politics remained
still the prerogative of the upper and lower ranks of nobility.
Even if this was at times a doubtful prerogative, it had the
advantage that the interest in the political events of the day
had not, as it has today, palled through routine. In those days,
the adepts at politics, both the professional and the dilettante,
though weak in number were strong in expertise and background.
Thus, despite the huge amount of diplomatic activity, these
custodians of the common weal usually found time and inclination
detachedly to view events as "history-in-the-making." Count
Nostitz, in his cynical way one of the most zealous of observers,
in his diary entries of December, 1814, has passed on to us a
rather extensive situation report on the Congress and its participating nations:*

Beneath the misleadingly smooth surface of the ostensibly
inspiring spectacle that this meeting of sovereigns is to represent,
one finds unspeakable intrigues where there ought to be openness,
envy instead of amity, pettiness instead of liberality. It is hardly
remembered why the monarchs are met here. Some say it is to
restore the royalist principle, and in consequence thereof the
restoration of the illegally deposed masters of their countries.

This principle is to regain Friedrich Augustus his throne. To this Russia counters: ". . . if there is to be trouble, better over a dynasty than over a country." The Prussians contend the question is not only over the regent, but over the country as well. Saxony's geographic location, they say, demands union with Prussia once the loss of South Prussia has robbed the country of its topographical center, on which the security in both north and west depends to equal parts.

Humboldt makes no bones about this politico-military reasoning. Hardenberg and the king are of the same opinion, and the Prussian people are so firmly in favor of possessing Saxony that a petition, recently got up in the country, offers the king every support in his claim for Saxony.

The Russian emperor in his odd willfulness firmly supports Prussia. . . .

The naïve comment of Emperor Franz to all this political backing and filling is: "It's a rough thing to do to push a regent off his throne."

The fight over Poland is just as intense and even less decisive. One would love to let Prussia take a big bite out of this country, if only to separate Russia from the West. Rather than allow Metternich to achieve his real, secret, diplomatic goal, this conflict of interests has united Russia and Prussia in strong opposition and in their demand that Prussia get Saxony and Russia, Poland.

"What tremendous role might not the Russian emperor here play, what lasting monument set himself, if only he would consummate the grand compromise and not haggle over a few acres of land." Thus shouts Austria, hoping of course to achieve its own goals.

The small powers, too, have demanded admission to the conferences over Germany, a demand granted for all but the more important decisions. Germany will not prove immune to the demands of the ruling *Zeitgeist* and if matters are not settled peaceably, they will come to a head in explosions for which political discontent will furnish the spark.

On the German question, especially on Saxony, France is in unshakeable opposition, the secret purpose apparently being to be won over by concessions in other areas. Russia and Prussia probably rightfully condemn these politics as forgetting that it was the Allies who pushed Bonaparte off his throne, that therefore the Confederation of the Rhine had been dissolved and a Bourbon king could no longer represent the princes of the Rhenish lands.

In this tangled web England plays the role of brakeshoe. By means of its newly founded (1814) kingdom of Hanover, it develops a continental system which Count Münster through his intermediary, Baron von Gagern, . . . is linking with Holland, Brunswick, and Hesse into a Hanoverian-German confederation. The personal animosity between Czar Alexander and the British Prince Regent that has developed in England, as well as the latter's dislike of the majority party, has caused an anti-Russian stance in the British cabinet. England still sanctions politically Russia's expansion into Poland but puts into opposition against Prussia all those German states that are controlled by it through Hanover. Austria, on the other hand, largely thanks to Metternich's skillful handling, has gained much favor in an England where Czar Alexander has made foes and King Frederick William no friends. This, in Northern Germany, has created an association inimical to Prussia because of the latter's close ties with Russia.

Bavaria is not interested in a confederation that might cramp its political style in a larger Germany. On the contrary, by claiming more territory she attempts to become a major European power and is ready to fight in any direction where she is opposed. Hers is a politics of rawest belligerency that, at the moment, strongly inclines towards Austria. Württemberg, on the other hand, feels deeply offended by Austria. The crown prince is inspired by Minister Stein, his mentor, with ideas that make him the tool of Prussia and Russia. . . .

France probably makes overtures to England only to regain access to the seas, in the wake of peace. Thus, there are so many divergent interests at loggerheads here at this long-awaited peace conference that the most marvelous realignment combinations occur with each new note of disharmony. In this crisis of strange political bedfellowship, Metternich has lately achieved a tremendous bargaining advantage in that Lord Castlereagh unexpectedly joined his side. A stern dispatch from the Prince Regent clearly instructed Castlereagh to adhere to the principle of legitimacy and not permit any currently popular ideas of a revolutionary trend to gain a toehold. This has caused a complete turnabout in the noble lord which, though it came as a surprise, entirely delighted Metternich. Czar Alexander, who as his own foreign minister had habitually conducted the negotiations in direct talks with Metternich, called for the latter. Metternich, emboldened by Castlereagh's conversion, argued so vehemently that the resulting altercation could be heard in the antechamber. . . .

Wherever one looks, contradiction and confusion, with nary a chance for change. How wise of Gentz, who all alone opposed the congress idea!

Daily the pile of claims is increasing, as ever more evil spirits appear when the conjuring sorcerer has forgotten the magic word. He who demands and does not receive gets dissatisfied and turns mean.—Even those installed by Napoleon have sent their delegates, and the marshals impertinently request return of their estates in Germany.

Archduke Johann, Emperor Franz' brother whom the national interest kept tied to Vienna, had heavy thoughts about the ticklish situation caused by the question of Poland and Saxony. On December 21, 1814, he confided to his diary: [8]

[8] Translating from Austrian-German is at best a difficult task, caused by untidy habits of thinking and writing, as well as by an extensive use of colloquialisms and foreign phrases. In Metternich's day the Viennese, including their emperor, spoke a patois more closely related to Bavarian dialect than to Prussian German. It is particularly troublesome to reduce the Archduke's curiously involved, stultified yet simplicistic language to reasonable meaning and manageable sentences. —Transl.

I went to see Prince Metternich to tell him all I knew. I found him extremely affable (unfortunately the antechamber is full of ladies, bent for romance!). He spoke quite openly on all matters . . . and gave me the exchange of notes between Austria and Prussia to read. From all this I deduct the following: Metternich has posed two problems, one concerning Poland, the other, Saxony. The first he considered to be the more important one and feels here there must be no wavering. It seems to me that for this reason Prussia was given backing and even hopes (I cannot believe firm promises) for Saxony. Prussia didn't take the bait or at least didn't want to take any active part, only look after its interests. Thus the matter kept dragging on. England took a weak stand and Austria was not about to start anything alone. After prolonged haggling, it seems to me the matter of Poland was dropped, if only not to make matters worse. Saxony is the important question that must be settled and, since Prussia is adamant in its claim to the territory, Russia's active support should be sought by yielding on the Polish question. The second question was the integrity of Saxony, which must be maintained if the Polish solution is not feasible.

Czar Alexander, who practically gave Saxony to Prussia, now is asked to force the latter to relinquish its claim, which he understandably refuses to do. He is sympathetic to Saxony's plight but, I believe, he really doesn't want to leave Prussia in the lurch. The ticklish matter—concerning Poland—whereby Austria confines its claim, as in 1808, to East Galicia including Krakow leaving West Galicia to Russia, was settled with Alexander. Prussia was to keep the Polish territory up to the Warta and Nida rivers, as well as the city of Toruń. The Austrian note that informs Prussia of this expresses Austria's happiness over everything Prussia can get out of Russia.

However, it seems to me not yet sure that Austria will get Krakow, and if this does not happen, Russia is to guarantee not to fortify the city, as was the provision.

Hardenberg's note, an answer to the one that seeks Prussia's collaboration in the attempt to persuade Russia to give up its plans concerning Poland, clearly expresses Prussia's inability to wage war without outside help. Yet, at the same time, it contains proposals at a future date to take advantage of the first opportunity unfavorable to Russia (how typically Prussian!). The personal attachment of the king to the czar at the moment precludes any action disagreeable to the latter. Everything reveals a desire for mischief. To risk nothing, but in boundless selfishness to covet Saxony's territory. Starting point was the status of 1805, when Prussia withdrew from an active role concerning Poland, with England at the time still soft-pedaling the issue. Thus, the Polish matter was dropped and all effort directed towards Saxony. In the friendliest of words Austria offered Prussia full indemnity and even threw some 300,000 to 400,000 souls into the bargain, such as a part of Lower Silesia, Hildesheim, Münster, Paderborn, etc., also the area between the rivers Meuse, Moselle, and Rhine. Prussia refused. Angered by this and by Austria's coming to terms with Russia on the Polish question, the Prussians show two Austrian notes and a private memorandum of Metternich to the czar. This of course exposed Metternich's plan of using Saxony as bait in trying to get Prussia to use its influence with the czar in the Polish matter, and, by yielding in Poland, to win Russia, get Prussia to desist from its designs on Saxony. In high dudgeon, Alexander confronted our sovereign who, taken aback, called Metternich on the carpet and ordered him to open all files to the Russian czar. These are the files he also showed me and which revealed to me our grave error but, fortunately, also Prussia's malicious, false game. This in itself supplies us the means for sweet revenge. My advice to Metternich was, after I had told him all that is being said about him (no sense pussyfooting here), to tear the mask off Prussia's face. This might cause an angry Russia to drop Prussia and leave us to settle Saxony with that state alone. Metternich thought he could not reveal everything since this would alert the czar, in regard to Poland, to some weakness in his own state, which caution forbade.

I disagreed with this. I believe it is better to throw the most revealing light on the whole matter and to show who after all is the better thinker.

Sad to say I miss the straightforward path, for it is rotten politics that strays afield. How false to posit the strength of a politician in his cleverness, his ability to deceive, etc. To me, true political strength lies in the accuracy with which a given situation is gauged, consequences calculated, appropriate decisions made, and the most effective means of carrying out these decisions chosen. He who here sees most clearly has the upper hand. Here, honesty is the best policy.

Matters having progressed thusly, I begged for firmness toward Saxony. Here, honor, advantage, in short everything, is at stake. My advice was to go the limit, not give an inch, which may be done without danger since Prussia cannot move without money and the money, by the way the English now talk, is on Austria. Russia would have its hands full with Poland, besides being beset by internal troubles like any other state, and England, by blockading the harbors and threatening the capital, could make war very unpopular. In this, Austria would be supported by France, the Netherlands, England, the German Confederation, the voice of all peoples. Under these conditions everything might be dared. It is impossible to listen to Prussia's demands in regards to Mainz, Luxembourg, border fortifications, and a kind of hegemony in Northern Germany. The true political situation, the interest of Germany itself, demands a strong Prussia that may serve to protect but not swallow Germany. Prussia must be made to see that it cannot isolate itself from All-German affairs and every effort must be bent towards preventing a concentration of power. By pushing Prussia as far west as the Rhine, it must be forced actively to participate on Germany's side in the impending war (this it doesn't want). Metternich thought likewise, but I fear he will yield in the end. It would be a dastardly thing for Austria to abandon Saxony with a mere protest.

What good is our 600,000-men army and how equally terrible if this Congress should dissolve without having achieved anything? This would spell the end of all respect for our country. Germany would be irrevocably lost and what great unrest and chaotic conditions would not then become the order of the day!

It was quite natural that this unique gathering of monarchs, statesmen, and aristocrats should never lose sight of its own role. Thus was created a political climate that is a curious mixture of cynicism and a sense of hopelessness which, nevertheless, admits of no genuine seriousness. Only those who had retained a child-like ingenuousness and who partook in the new trends of nationalism and democracy showed a more positive attitude. Friedrich von Gentz, the "Secretary of the Congress" and renegade from the Prussian cause, Viennese by choice, partly gray eminence, partly the widely known exponent of Austrian politics, commonly serves to typify the feudalistic or pseudo-feudalistic weariness, the sorrowful-sarcastic wit that was the hallmark of the cleverest of statesmen at the Congress. As early as September 30 Gentz wrote in his diary:

Conference of the ministers, initially among the five, then with Talleyrand and Labrador. The interference of the latter two has badly disorganized and overthrown our plans. They protested against the form of our procedures in a scene I shall never forget. At half past three the prince went to his gardens with me to check on the preparations for the party on October 18. The prince is not as aware as I am of the awkwardness, even frightfulness, of our situation.

Or somewhat later:

Dinner for eight at my house. Prince Metternich, Prince Talleyrand, Prince Louis Rohan, Floret, and Fontbrune. Everyone was entranced with my food and my lodgings. Everyone stayed till nine o'clock. It was a remarkable day.

I contributed little to the conversation, which was led as usual by Metternich and Talleyrand. Meanwhile, I was struck more forcibly than ever with the futility of human affairs, the weakness of the individuals who hold the world's fate in their

hands, even with my own feelings of superiority, but all this only
in a semiconscious state and as if in a fog in which the inane
twaddle of my dinner guests had warped my brain.

*In contrast to Talleyrand, Gentz is not avaricious, only
pleasure-seeking and frivolous. His diary entry on New Year's
Day, 1815, reads:*

The general outlook is sad indeed, not, however, because of
the frightfully threatening hordes hovering over our head as in
the recent past, but because of the poor caliber and stupidity of
nearly all actors. Well, I have nothing to blame myself for, and
so the detailed knowledge about all this pettifoggery and all these
small creatures that rule the world does not burden my soul but
rather amuses me, and I enjoy the whole spectacle as if it were
given for my private pleasure. For me, the year 1815 starts under
rather favorable auspices. As concerns politics, I am fully aware
of the futility of believing it capable of fulfilling the hopes the
enthusiasts put in it, hopes I have forever abandoned.

*The waggishness of the common folk, though limping some-
what behind the caustic wittiness of the aristocracy, also pokes fun
at the Congress' cumbersome procedures.*
In the March, 1815, issue of the Eipeldauer Report *we read:*

Now it's black on white, my dear cousins, the Cungress has
begun, for already all newspapers they say the four plenipotentiary
ministries that have underwritten the peace in Paris last year,
that is: Austria, Russia, France, and Prussia, they have opened an
office here at the state chancery where we now check the cre-
dentials of all the ambassadors that come from all the other great
and little courts, and from upper and lower Rhine, and from the
Meuse, and God knows from where else, and now the Viennese
they think sure, they'll get going with this Cungress—ha, but
wait a bit! I've spoken to the gent about it who's such a fancy
pants Latinist, and he said to me first it is Congress not Cungress
as we call it in Eipeldau, and then he really puts me wise—says
he: "Dear, dear, the people they're not no longer comprehending

even the littlest Latin word, for if the Congress was a case of *sitting* together then it should of been called *Consess* which in German would be sitting together, but since it's called only a Congress, it is only a *going* together, for that's the meaning of Congress in Latin."

The idealist Archduke Johann at about the same time uttered entirely different sentiments in his diary. His Hapsburgian virtuousness discovered distinct goals in the offing:

Napoleon has introduced the highest type of despotism. Under him, all other states became tools, the nations objects of barter, nothing honored, nothing kept, pressure everywhere, intolerable. Greed introduced a methodical system of remorseless exploitation. The resulting impoverishment aroused the various peoples who saved the day, because the sovereigns were forced to turn to the masses and to the arising nationalism as the last and only resort. Armed, the peoples expressed the spirit of revolution, but in a just cause. What there was of nobleness, wisdom, and strength rose to the top, there was general cooperativeness, everything fell automatically into a pattern. The princes, though numerous, were too weak to rule. They let the current run, being myopically incapacitated to look into the future and prepare the measures now that would one day be needed to prevent those ills that would inevitably arise out of the achievements of the past. The evil spirit had been exorcised, but, as is usual, the extremes are prone to touch: the liberal followed on the heels of the despotic spirit. The peoples had become conscious of their power, they felt rescued from danger and, aware of the causes of their former plight, they appreciated the futility of sovereigns and the power of their new masters. No longer did the nations want their weal or woe exposed to, and misused by, the arbitrary actions of individual ministers. This is the situation today, only the Congress, keeping everything in suspense, still holds back. But everywhere there is foment and it is no longer in the power of the princes to contain the flood they themselves once released for their own safety.

THE BEATEN FOE

The principle of legitimism had caused dynastic fronts to cut squarely across national boundaries. This, to some extent at least, explains the mild conditions imposed by the Allies in Paris on Bourbon France, a kind of treatment which, thanks largely to Talleyrand's virtuosity, was continued in Vienna. But in addition there was a certain civilized humaneness in evidence that even found expression in the Eipeldauer *publication:*

On the whole, the enemy looks to me like he's a wounded boar that blindly rushes from the underbrush, not knowing which way to turn, and such an animal, in its thrashing about, might well still tear off a limb from this or that hunter, until all hunters gang up on him and give him the death stroke.

And again in a similar vein:

Ever since the Great One gave up, one field marshal and one corps after the other goes over to Louis the Eighteenth and the tyrant stands there all woefully alone, everybody is swearing the oath of loyalty and Louis' dear brother is mighty kind to everybody, he's put the old and new nobility into a melting pot, everyone wins because of Bony, all Europe gets what it's hankered for this many a year—only he alone, he all alone is in a pickle and soon there won't be a trace left of him, in a few years not even a good-for-nothing vagabond will mention him. His statue is already tumbled down and the statue of peace will take his place. Everything that's remindful of him is rubbed out, even his gold pieces are done over again, so the poor people are not frightened no more with the memory of their misery, and in twenty years—when, as is bound to happen, there'll be mentioning him (likely on Good Friday for repentance)—the little ones will ask their parents: "Say, Mama, who was this Bonaparte?"

From the very start Napoleon's former foreign minister, the great Charles Maurice, Prince of Talleyrand-Périgord, Duke of Benevent, former Bishop of Autun, now again in the service of the French king and chief delegate at the Congress, knew how to defend the rights of France as a co-equal partner with the other participating powers. He himself reported to his present sovereign Louis XVIII about an invitation extended to him alone to attend a meeting of the Big Four on September 30, 1814:

Prince Metternich gave me a memorandum to read, signed by himself, Nesselrode, Castlereagh, and Hardenberg. Every paragraph of this document contained the word "Allies." I picked this expression up, declaring that it forced me to ask if we were still at Chaumont or Leon, if peace had not yet been concluded, if there was still some point of argument and what it might be. . . . I then called the protocol Metternich had read a skein of metaphysical sophistry, meant to support claims, based on treaties that are unknown to me and the discussion of which, I claimed, would lead to endless debates. I felt it incumbent upon me to refute the whole thing with an unbeatable argument. I read several paragraphs and said: "This I do not understand." Then, with the mien of a man trying hard to get at the meaning of something, I slowly reread the same paragraphs, declared that they still made no sense to me, and added: "To me there are two dates between which nothing has happened: May 30, when the calling of a congress was decided on, and October 1, when it is to convene. Everything that happened in between is alien to me and does not exist for me." Discouraged, Metternich put the protocol aside and Gentz tore up the rest. The plenipotentiaries then withdrew the memorandum, which Metternich put permanently into the files and which was never mentioned again.

RUSSIA, THE COLOSSUS

All sides soon became aware that the real danger to the balance of power in Europe lay primarily with Russia. The Duke of Dalberg, the German renegade whom Napoleon had ennobled but who in the meantime had turned turncoat again for the Bourbons, summarized this a week after Talleyrand's grandstand scene before the Big Four:

The real crux is the grand duchy of Warsaw, is the Polish crown given to Russia, is Saxony ceded to Prussia. . . . They well realize that Talleyrand, Labrador, and I would return to Paris the moment they confide this secret to us. We do not understand Metternich's policy. If he hands Poland's crown to Russia the latter will drive the Turks out of Europe in less than fifteen months. Russia will become a greater danger to Europe than Napoleon ever was. Prussia surrenders to Russia, which, however, its geographic situation might force it to do. But why doesn't Austria, instead of collaborating in preventing Russian hegemony, openly side with France in common cause against the Russian colossus that one day will utterly destroy Austria and all other powers?

Archduke Johann expressed similar views.

This trading in lands and peoples is disgusting! We rightfully denounced Napoleon and his system because he debased mankind. Yet, the very princes who sought his overthrow are now following in his footsteps. Which means it was he as a person who was resented, not his system. Russia pushes westward—can this be tolerated?

Prussia does nothing against it, is for the moment content with Saxony, and pursues its customary policy of greed, having learned nothing from the bitter lessons just received, capable of defending its booty, if need be ready to join Russia against the others, against even Austria which always honestly advocated the partition and which, together with Russia and Napoleon, could have wiped Prussia off the face of the earth with a mere nod of the head. . . .

A purblind Prussia does not look ahead and will live to rue it, for Russia will show no gratitude. . . . Prussia wants Germany up to the Rhine and Main rivers. It is she who divides the nation, who has never ceased to covet all of Germany. This is her true aim. . . . Austria, England, and France must remain firm. They will be joined by all German princes and Holland, all of whom will defy the others and no one will dare start an unpopular war, exhausted as their lands are. In Russia this might well cost the czar his life; in Prussia the estates might arise and ask the king the whyfors and cut his wings. Now or never. The coming century is at stake, ours and the peace of our posterity, therefore we must be firm if victory is to remain ours.

AUSTRIA'S BANKRUPTCY

Despite the grand-scale festivities and hospitality which the Austrian imperial court lavished on all sovereigns staying at the Imperial Palace, there was an ominous cloud which spread and would not move but hovered over everything, and this in spite of patriotic fervor and the knowledge that a great war has just been won. This cloud was the memory of the national bankruptcy of 1811, the effects of which were still reflected in the worst imaginable state of national finances and in the weak position of the Austrian gulden. The very fountainhead of disaster seemed to lie here. Based on a report of the confidential agent von Leurs, Küster, Prussian ambassador to the courts of the South German princes, commented:

The French emperor treated Austria even less intelligently than Prussia. The conditions of the past several years have weakened Austria as no other European country, leaving it at the mercy of any clever conquerer. The majority of civil servants is underfed, oppressed, and treated beneath their dignity. Better to be a shoemaker or a tailor than a captain or a councillor. It is the sheer willpower of the civil servant that protects the country, not the nation as such. If the invading French emperor had begun, in the very first provinces he entered, to pay all wages and salaries in Convent money, the state would have crumbled, with everyone turning to the new master.

The imperial finances suffered not least because, despite the Treaty of Paris and the convening of the Congress, much of the armed forces must be kept on a war footing, especially in Italy:

Yesterday, at the Arnsteins' and at other homes, there was much talk about the latest article in the *Wiener-Zeitung*, which dealt with the currency question and made mention of the frequent court fetes. Arnstein himself explained the currency deterioration as follows: "Each and every foreigner present in Vienna for the Congress has bought up all Austrian paper money prior to his departure from home. There are today roughly two million guldens-worth of certificates and promissory notes abroad which, on the whole, is not much. But these certificates and promissory notes entered Austria all at one time. Our imperial court buys up these reimported instruments to keep its army in Italy on a war basis. Meanwhile, the foreign sovereigns, ambassadors, etc., currently in Vienna are living on our reimported currency, supplying no foreign exchange of their own. This necessarily devalues our currency, our paper money. It will not be easy to stabilize our economy permanently, but merely a return to peaceful conditions that do away with the fear of war, a reduction in the armed forces, and a recall of the promissory notes will, without recourse to any other financial manipulations, greatly improve the monetary situation and bring back prosperity."

But there was great lamentation when the rate of exchange kept climbing from 200 to 300 guldens at the opening of the Congress to 320 guldens for 100 guldens silver in early February:

The latest currency quotations are renewing the complaints and grumblings against the stock exchange and paper money at all levels of the Viennese public. The bankers are not happy and the general public is in a foment as never before.

THE PRUSSIANS

Bankrupt Austria feared Prussia as much as it disliked it, the sovereign excepted. France might still have shuddered at the thought of Blücher's not always well-disciplined soldiers: in Austria the Prussians were blamed for the Saxonian vexatious politics that one would be gladly rid of but for which Russia surely deserved equal blame, with the one small difference: big Russia was possibly feared even more than its smaller partner. At any rate, France (Talleyrand) and Austria (Metternich, and von Gentz) agreed that Prussia's greedy designs for more German territory must be contained at all costs. Already in September Talleyrand had formulated his views in a memorandum:

Side by side with the general principles of justice, the more practical interests of France must be taken into consideration. What serves the interests of the smaller states also serves France. Each wants to preserve its existence; in this we must aid them. . . . In Italy, Austria's desire to expand must be counteracted. In Germany, Prussia is the danger. The very shape of this monarchy necessitates territorial ambitions. Prussia will use any pretext, it has no scruples, right is what best serves its purposes. . . . Its overweening ambition has not at all been cured by the terrible debacle it caused. At this very moment Prussian agents and supporters are in Germany, are actively painting France as planning ever new attacks and claiming Prussia to be the only power capable of defending Germany, wherefore the latter ought to be turned over to and saved by Prussia. Belgium it would have liked to have. Everything lying between France, the Moselle, and the Rhine it covets. Luxembourg it wants. All is lost if it doesn't get Mainz. Its security is gone if it doesn't get Saxony. The Allies are said to have agreed to its pre-1807 boundaries, to ten million inhabitants, that is. But if it gets its way, it would soon have twenty million and all of Germany would be under its heel. This drive must be blocked.

The traditional friction between Austria and Prussia which in the older generation very often was born of memories of the Silesian Wars is frequently also in evidence at the social level. To separate the private individual from world events is hardly possible in such an epoch and at such a place:

Prince Hardenberg last Tuesday at the Arnsteins' remarked that his stay in Vienna was highly distasteful to him and was daily becoming more so. Fanny Arnstein's comment was: "I am very sorry Hardenberg and Humboldt are no longer happy here. At first they used to like it. But it is truly a pity the attempts that are made to rekindle the old enmity between Prussia and Austria. Unfortunately, that was the purpose of the odious pamphlet *Saxony and Prussia,* which contains much that is true but nothing that is new. Why rekindle memories of a Prussia that once forgot to be German? Have not they atoned for this, done penance, and cleared the slate with wondrous deeds and an undeniable devotion to the whole, to Germany's deliverance? There's no gainsaying that their territorial ambitions are suspect and worry us. Yet, a cool appraisal of their situation clearly points up the inevitability of having to furnish this scattered, elongated state that has no depth with a greater compactness. Let us hope, though, that this was reasonably accomplished by the gain of the two Silesias and Wittenberg and that therefore a respected dynasty need not be stricken from the roster of crowned heads. . . ."

When toward the end of December the crisis over Saxony deepened, anti-Prussian sentiments become louder in Vienna:

When the rumor suddenly sprouted early this week that the Polish matter had been settled between the sovereigns, and that therefore Saxony would not be handed over to Prussia but retain its independence, it was again the Prussians that were loudest in complaint. Now there was no one imbued with more loyal and humane thoughts and principles concerning the common German good than Prussia. Prussia, so she said herself, had never given a thought to aggrandizement and conquest, had never desired more than what the treaty signed at Paris had promised her, that is to re-establish the population figure of 1805. Much incense was wafted in Austria's direction for that country's own noble and charitable stand, but by means of many a prettily turned hint and phrase it was pointed out that Prussia smelled no less sweet as a rose. In general, Prussia, probably realizing that she is all but detested in the whole of Germany—for having shown her claws too soon—is busily backpedalling.

In Southern and Western Germany especially there was keen interest in what Prussia was up to:

All embassies of the erstwhile independent petty principalities are decidedly anti-Prussian. They claim: "In 1813, Prussia waved the flag of German liberation to gain support; in 1814,

Prussian greed is in evidence on all fronts. Prussia firmly sticks to Russia, has concluded a secret convention with Russia which it does not reveal. Prussia is a traitor to the European cause and to the balance of power. The storm flags of Europe and of Germany must be raised against Prussia and Russia. . . ."

The Dutch representatives likewise expressed great animosity:

The Dutch mission is anti-Prussian, saying: "The Prussians are like the Jews, always out for a deal. They are your true cut-purse, industrial pirates, soldiers of fortune, risking little, wanting all. Each eye looks in a different direction, like the eyes of Baron Humboldt. The Berlin ministry today is more false, more evil, more cunning than ever before. The leading dupe of this soldier-of-fortune coterie is the weak, silly king. Humboldt is appointed minister of state and gains the upper hand. The Duke of Weimar and the Ernestinian Line [9] are Prussian to the core and will be amply indemnified when the Albertinian Line is deposed."

When the Prussian compromise offer, perforce made under pressure of the sub rosa alliance of Austria, England, and France, was finally accepted by the opposing side on February 10, thus settling the Saxon question at least, there was at first disappointment in Prussian ranks that was soon, however, succeeded by a degree of satisfaction. In this vein Humboldt wrote his wife Caroline:

The solution arrived at doesn't exactly hurt Prussia. We are slowly getting somewhere and the other part of Saxony will come some future day and we shall certainly prevail in Germany . . . For us, the present arrangement, though not the best possible, is far too advantageous not to prefer it to war or even a prolonged period of uncertainty. . . . Had we gained the whole of Saxony, the Rhenish Palatinate would obviously have become not only smaller but, since the king of Saxony was at any rate to receive part of Westphalia in compensation, would also have been torn apart. . . . Our king was very disappointed we didn't gain

[9] The older line of the House of Wettin, compared to the younger or Albertinian line.—Transl.

Leipzig, but really only as a point of honor. Actually, he is quite right in this, only the others wouldn't have signed without this concession.

THE GERMAN PROBLEM

The struggle over Germany, the battle over the form of government and constitution which at the same time was also a battle over German supremacy, was fought on several fronts. It was a battle at once domestic and external, between the weak and the mighty, between the satiated and those greedy for compensation, between those petty princes who lost their sovereignty and the Big Five (Austria, Prussia, Bavaria, Württemberg, and Hanover). First to be considered was a sample constitution, submitted by Prussia and drafted by the moving spirit behind All-German unity, Baron Stein, foe of absolutism and of Metternich, Prussian reformer, for many years an exile, now Czar Alexander's unofficial advisor. This first draft constitution provided for a division of Germany into five large regions, each to be administered by a "regent" and none coinciding with historic German boundaries or peoples. According to a confidential-agent report, the delegate from Hesse-Darmstadt, Baron Türckheim, had this to say about the matter on October 31:

We are frequently invited by Talleyrand, in particular we, who are much in the news, the delegates from Saxony, Baden, and Darmstadt. We don't enjoy going because it attracts the attention of Austria, Prussia, and Russia. The five regions and their regents suggested by Prussia please neither Talleyrand nor me. Talleyrand very seriously advises us minor states not to accept the constitution when it is submitted for approval by the Congress. And so it will happen and the proposed constitution will be rejected. We want one emperor, not five. We want Austria as emperor.

In the conflict between the Big Five and the smaller states, but also between Austria and Prussia on the one hand and Bavaria and Württemberg on the other, the tug-of-war over "people's rights" played an important role. Here, internal political concessions to constitutionalism were to a large extent used as weapons against the more reactionary governments of Prussia and Austria. In this business, the cunning King Frederick I of Württemberg repudiated the Congress powers:

Yesterday, January 16, 1815, everyone at the Prussian court and embassy was highly alarmed by what happened in Stuttgart. The address with which Württemberg's king submitted the new constitution to the assembled states was depicted as the product of the most dangerous democratic principles. With this constitution the king is said to have relinquished all royal prerogatives, without exception, to the control of the people's representatives. He has not only released the people from allegiance to the royal successor, should he refuse to swear to uphold the constitution, but has even left the royal budget to the generosity of the states. It is admitted that this step is particularly odious to the Prussian monarchy in which is to be found not a trace of constitutional government. . . . Some take it particularly amiss that the king in his address patently disavowed all responsibility towards the Vienna Congress, putting his own and the defense of the new All-German constitution in the hands of the people.

Circles close to the crown prince of Württemberg are reported to see this royal act as directed against the heir to the throne. The king is said to be highly displeased with his behavior in Vienna and allegedly had him closely watched.

Once the case of Saxony was settled, democratic sentiments emerged in the most unlikely quarters:

Among the Prussians forgathered at the café Kleine Landskrone on Wildpretmarkt the Court councilor Butte (a Bavarian) remarked that shortly there would be close friendship also with Southern Germany, all things pointing in that direction. . . . Human rights would now no longer be at the mercy of monarchs, England and Holland had led the way, Prussia, also, had done much of which more would become known. There is secret agreement that within ten years, at the most, there will be

upheaval in Germany in which Freemasonry, under British influence, will play a prominent part. Butte is not in Bavarian pay
but is probably on a secret mission. He is thoroughly pro-Russian.
They are all Masons and are in the habit of passing the signs,
even at table.

*The importance of international movements such as Free-
masonry in furthering the cause of unity on a democratic basis
to the contrary notwithstanding, the difficulties arising out of
confederate disunion were enormous:*

It is the German confederate system as embodied in the
All-German constitution and in the individual states, as well as
the German Confederation, that offers a wealth of material to the
malcontent and serves as breeding ground for intrigues and
rumors. Those sovereigns who were mediatized want to be
reinstated, and those German monarchs and rulers, whose
sovereignty the Austrian accession treaties confirmed, are not
giving up an inch. The old ruling houses, mainly those in
Northern Germany and within the new Prussian boundaries,
seek Austria's protection in order not to be swallowed by Prussia.
These relics of the defunct German Empire, the mediatized
sovereigns and isolated princely dynasties, are in fact foreigners
who are most vociferous and rail loudest against our government.
The Prussians and Bavarians, experts at their trade, who desire
nothing more than to bull the ousted sovereigns, to "snow them
under with paper" as the saying goes, give them constitutions
that seem to quite satisfy their desires. But the malcontents
are so unfair as not to see that they owe these favors to the
Austrian government from which in all honesty they cannot
expect more. Who is so naïve as to believe the Austrian government is to expose, is to compromise itself on behalf of the mediatized rulers!

The locals say: "Those princes who lost their sovereignty
have been bulled in too much false hope and illusions. It won't
be easy to awaken them out of their dream world!" They say:
"Bavaria should not reap all the benefit in Southern Germany,

Austria must come to an understanding with Prussia and Hanover. . . ."

Concerning the question of German hegemony, whether, that is, Prussia, the Kingdom of the North, or Austria, the imperial and royal monarchy in the South, was to fall heir to it, Baron Stein, Prussia's reformer and champion of German unity, in his memorandum on the subject opted for Austria since it alone, after the surrender of its West German possessions, like no other dynasty offered the surest guarantee against any possible territorial claims in the Reich:

Let us admit that Austria is less interested in Germany than is Prussia, that there are even internal forces straining for separation. If despite this it is believed to be vital to Germany and in Europe's best interest that the two countries be united, then it follows that a constitutional modus vivendi must be found which reunites Austria with Germany in a manner that the former is assured of a dominant influence, an influence, however, based on responsibility and mutual benefit.

Talleyrand, needless to say, saw German unity with entirely different eyes. As early as October, 1814, he wrote Louis XVIII:

To the Germanomaniacs, German unity is the battle cry, the doctrine and religion they defend with the utmost fanaticism. Who can calculate the results if a mass like the German, amalgamated into a single whole, should turn aggressive? Who can tell where such a movement would stop?

The result was the German Confederation, that product of the Congress of Vienna laid down in Articles 53 through 63 and, on Metternich's special behest, added to the final protocol as signed June 9, 1815. This confederation was provided with a constitution, a Bundestag, an assembly composed of sixty-nine representatives, the ruling princely houses, and the four free cities. Members of the Bundestag included three foreign sovereigns: the kings of Great Britain, Holland, and Denmark. The dominant power in this Bundestag was, however, Austria after all.

THE FATE OF THE MEDIATIZED PRINCES

That the mediatized princes were highly dissatisfied with the final protocol was revealed by an intercepted letter sent by the representative of the deposed sovereigns, Gärtner, to Count Solms-Laubach on June 9, 1815:

This morning I expect to at last discover how matters stand with the constitution, for yesterday's is to have been the concluding meeting. What a noise there will be about the final protestation! I've already made two drafts, both rejected for being too mild. If Baron Vrints is not able to douse this fire, there's nothing for it but utter separation.

Baron Vrints represented the mediatized house of Thurn und Taxis:

Does the end of this war presage a better future? I doubt it. Only a thorough upheaval could effect a permanent change. And then the cure may be worse than the illness, may be a reform in reverse.

THE ITALIAN QUESTION

Similar dissatisfaction and confusion obtained at the Congress —and in Italy itself—when the Italian question was discussed. In Vienna, not only did the former viceroy of Italy, Napoleon's stepson Eugène Beauharnais, assiduously cultivate the Czar of all the Russias, but the kingdom of Naples even had two delegations at the Congress: the one, headed by the Duke of Serra-Capriola, on behalf of the legitimate Bourbon, the later Ferdinand IV; the other, under the Duke of Campochiaro, for Joachim Murat, the usurper king, Napoleon's former cavalry general and still Austria's ally. At the Congress there existed strong antagonism between the champion of legitimism, Talleyrand, and Metternich, who was charged by the Congress with a pro-Murat policy. On November 11, 1814, Talleyrand reported to his king on a conversation with Metternich:

I told Metternich: "The Congress must decide the matter of Naples. Get Italy politically organized and Murat will lose all following. Put an end to this intolerable interim arrangement. Circumscribe exactly who owns what in Northern and Central Italy. There should not be an acre of ground under military rule between Naples and the Alps. Everywhere, the legitimate rulers should be in power and an orderly administration in force. Put the matter of the Sardinian succession in order and dispatch an archduke to head the Milan administration. Recognize the queen of Tuscany and Umbria, return the Papal states you presently occupy. Do all this, and Murat will lose all influence with the people and will be no more than an Italian bandit."

This program, however, was easier to conceive than to carry out. Fate at last came to the aid of the legitimists. With Napoleon's return from Elba, Murat thought the hour had come to throw the mask away. He sided with his great brother-in-law, attacked Austria, and was decisively beaten, a defeat that eventually cost him both throne and life. Now the matter of Naples was settled in favor of the Bourbons in the final protocol:

Yesterday, at the Zichys', much was made of Sweden's refusal to acknowledge Ferdinand IV as king of the two Sicilies and to hand the crown of the latter to the Bourbon dynasty, both of which actions were to be made part of the final Congress treaty. Sweden based its objection on the pretense that the 1814 Treaty of Paris had made no mention of the Sicilian crown and that the 1814 Congress of Vienna should not treat of matters not initially included in the Treaty of Paris.

In the rest of Italy, however, the voice of the people was against the legitimists whose administrative manipulations were in fact dictated more by reaction than sound common sense. Cardinal Consalvi reported on the matter to a friend in Rome, a city which meanwhile had been returned to the Pope:

The Prussian councilor Bartholdy told me he had dined with Cardinal Consalvi yesterday. The latter had expressed his despair over not being in Rome, where matters were being

handled badly and all was being ruined. Thus everything has
returned to the old happy-go-lucky Italian style, with the Jews
being molested and street lighting and other sensible improve-
ments abolished. Wealthy Jews were leaving Rome, money and
provisions had become scarce, taxes were ineptly reduced from
a total of ten to two, leaving the Holy Father in dire financial
straits. In short, to bring back the old order in everything is
considered both untenable and inexcusable.

THE MAJOR PROBLEM: SAXONY-POLAND

*The Italian problems even played a certain role in the
major question of finding a solution to the matter of Saxony
and Poland. At one time the proposal was made to indemnify the
deposed King of Saxony with the so-called Papal states (Ferrara,
Bologna, Romana). At the end of November the confidential
agent Lewis succinctly summed the current stand of the Saxony-
Poland question this way:*

I have it from a trustworthy source that everything the
Russians and Prussians propose now is based on an agreement
concluded between them at the time of their alliance in Kalisz.
In a secret codicil to this agreement Prussia agreed at a future
date to cede its portion of Poland to Russia, but to be indemnified
by Saxony once Germany had been freed of French occupation.
At the time Austria joined the common cause against France, this
codicil is said not to have been fully known. When subsequently
it did become known, the armies of the Allies had already advanced to the Rhine and Metternich for sound reasons did not
consider it wise to object to the mentioned codicil, all the less
since it was to be feared Prussia would turn about and return
home. Afterwards, the matter was mentioned in Paris and
London. While there was objection, things in the main were
allowed to drag on. Still, at one point the Czar is said nearly to
have decided not to come to Vienna, yet to have taken the
precaution of concentrating troops in the Warsaw area and
dispatching his brother Constantine from Paris to set up the

so-called "Poland." This is said to have been the situation up to the Congress of Vienna. When the Congress openly began to discuss this matter, Hardenberg well recognized the hopelessness of Prussia's cause, being roundly opposed as he was by his own colleagues, especially by Humboldt, Stein, the generals Knesebeck and Jordan, and others. The Czar, quite determined to uphold the treaty with Prussia, was deaf to all counterproposals made by Austria and France, believing as he did to end the matter with a *coup d'état* by a definitive turnover of Saxony to Prussia. But when this decision led the other powers to speak in no uncertain terms of impending war, the opposing faction was all the more embarrassed when Hardenberg, roughly handled before in the same matter by the Czar, let it be known that he intended to ask his king for his dismissal. . . . Despite his petition, however, Hardenberg was not dismissed.

After war had been averted by the secret alliance between England, France, and Austria, secret agent C. K. sent a special report to the Imperial Palace under the heading "Clarification of the Confusion between the two Parties":

As reported on January 9, the secret conference between the two imperial majesties did in fact take place behind the locked doors on this date. The meeting lasted three hours but occurred without the reported two ministers. Yesterday, the two emperors held a grand council, at which the debating ministers were Prince Metternich, Viscount Castlereagh, Prince Talleyrand, and Count Razumovsky. There is every reason to be satisfied with the results. The hope now is to dispose of Prussia with like speed, all the more since Humboldt no longer has a voice and Hardenberg is left to carry on alone. Count Razamovsky is credited with having dispelled the Czar's hostile attitude against Prince Metternich, an attitude nurtured by the low cabals and tale-bearing of minister Nesselrode, in cahoots with Humboldt and for a long time hurtful to the good cause. The whole court was happily forgathered at the Burg and Kärntnertor theaters yesterday, something that hasn't happened for quite a while.

But in May there were second thoughts:

I hear the following argument: is it conceivable for the Kingdom of Saxony, reduced as it was, to take any action against Prussia or Russia, or to assist either? Is not the reduced kingdom of Saxony, be it ruled by a Saxon or Prussian dynasty, dependent on Prussia? Totally under Prussian influence? Has Europe had the least diplomatic gain from all this stir about Saxony? Would not Austria long since have achieved its Inn River boundary, including Passau and Wasserburg, had the Saxon dynasty been sacrificed as planned in the 1814 Treaty of Paris? Would this not be far better for the monarchy than carry the weight of the Saxon dynasty on its back? Is our government bent on being the generous giver, on playing the thankless role of providing asylum for sinners? If our government doesn't begin to emulate Prussia and start grabbing things, we shall forever remain unsuccessful, forever get shortchanged!

A week later, there was a report from the West that cast a pall over the impending struggle with the exiled Napoleon:

At the homes of the Arnsteins' and Eskeles' a great to-do is made over the news that at Liège troops of the King of Saxony have smashed windows in the homes of Wellington and Field Marshal Blücher.

ENGLAND: THE BALANCE WHEEL

England was the balance wheel. Of interest here was the interplay of many factors. Domestically, there was the change in governments in England, causing Wellington's replacement of Castlereagh on February 1, 1815, and also the inherently democratic character of all British governments. On the foreign policy front there was the peace concluded with the United States on December 24, 1814, which in the final analysis makes possible the secret alliance between France, Austria, and England and, therefore, the resolution of the Saxon-Polish problems. On January 4, 1815, Talleyrand reported to Louis XVIII:

The coalition is dissolved, undoubtedly for good. France is no longer isolated in Europe but proceeds side by side with the two major powers and the three secondary ones, Bavaria, Hanover, and the Netherlands. Peace with America, the arrogance of Russia and of Prussia, all this has changed Castlereagh's mind and I take advantage of this mood to insist on the agreement I have discussed with him for some time past. He came along far enough to suggest he write down his thoughts on the matter. The day following our last talk he sought me out and I was pleasantly surprised when I saw he had arranged his thoughts under separate headings. . . . He begged me to study his plan carefully, together with Prince Metternich. That same evening, after we had carried out several formulatory changes, we accepted it in the form of an agreement. Several articles might have been composed somewhat more carefully, but with people of [Castlereagh's] weak character one must act with dispatch to reach an end, and so we all signed [the agreement] tonight.

In the political arena a touch of the ludicrous clung to the English, also of envy and jealousy. Nonetheless, it was England's sea power that had won the Napoleonic wars, a factor not easily forgotten. Two weeks after the above letter, Talleyrand furnished a further account of events at Vienna:

After Castlereagh, Metternich, and I had come to a full understanding on the legitimacy principle, it becomes necessary now to reach agreement on the balance of power question in order for us to offer a joint proposal. Initially, Prince Metternich stood ready to make limitless concessions. I convinced him of the folly of this, pointing out how his leniency would endanger his monarchy and thus redound to his own discredit. Now, he fights passionately for what he was ready to give up. I advised that some of his best-informed military men attend our conferences to give us the benefit of their thinking and reasoning. To get him to agree to this I declared I would repeat in public what I had advised him to do were he to ignore my advice. Prince Schwarzenberg is to have a talk with Lord Stewart and day after tomorrow will bring several of his officers to discuss matters with us.

Talleyrand had a very low opinion of the British delegates, especially of their knowledge of geography. Truth to tell, Castlereagh was said to have been greatly surprised when he accidentally discovered Leipzig to be a city in Saxony. Talleyrand wrote about this in the above letter:

Castlereagh is astonishingly ignorant of military topography or even of the most rudimentary Continental geography. I might even say his ignorance in these things is total, so much so that the most elementary matters have to be explained to him, no easy task in view of his lack of knowledge.

A talk between a highly placed informant and the Russian advisor Capo d'Istrias threw light on the balance of power problem in Europe in relation to England:

The moment the subject was mentioned, Capo d'Istrias asked me if I was satisfied with the current status of affairs. I said: "Yes, as concerns the past, but not enough as to the present." "Very well, I feel the same. Too much time has been allowed to lapse. Somehow there will be agreement eventually but neither on a decent nor sound basis." He bases his contention primarily on the fact that the situation calls for a great statesman who is nowhere in sight, is certainly not in the forefront. . . . "One has forgotten that this war was a war of nations, not of rulers. Since Napoleon's overthrow, one has lost sight of national interests, being busy with the interests of the rulers as in past wars. And now confusion again reigns supreme, conflicts of interest clash, and to satisfy everybody has become quite impossible." My reply was that I saw only one possibility for an honorable way out, that of creating a kind of balance among the major powers. "Fine," he answered, "but how is this to be achieved since one single major power is mistress of the seas? Is there any other sea power except England? Can one be formed? No, and therefore farewell balance of power. One wants major powers, but these must have common borders and will for this reason always find reasons for conflict. What is needed are small states to act as mediators." I didn't want to bring up the knotty question of Poland since he had told me that now, with all danger of being wiped out gone, all powers were currently only thinking of aggrandizement. "If only justice had been made the basis of action, if only the people had been imbued with it, won over to it, made quiet by its magic charm! But the people see justice on one side, injustice on the other, they mull over this and widen the gulf between them and the rulers."

THE RETURN FROM ELBA

At this critical juncture of the Congress the all-important question was whether legitimacy was to fade back once more into limbo and Napoleon re-emerge and rule again, or whether, contrariwise, the adventurer would himself be legitimized by his return. With his escape from his comfortable prison of Elba, England's sea rule was put in question. Why had he been permitted so close to the shores of France and Italy in the first place? But this being done, why had he been guarded so carelessly? Such reflections were rendered academic for the Allies by the rush of events: flight, landing near Cannes, mockery and scorn, malicious joy and panic. Was all this, the absence of Elba's governor, the alleged visit of the Austrian General Koller with the emperor, merest coincidence, or was it a plan, a trap set, the web of an agent provocateur, spun after the Bourbonic intent of heaping guilt on Napoleon's head so that the incurred punishment now justified banishment of the outlawed brigand to the isle of St. Helena? We don't know. The first report of his escape, rendered by the British commander Campbell to the British general Bentinck, was reprinted in translation in the Leipziger Zeitung:

Porto Ferrajo, February 28 [1815].

General! I have the honor to inform you that Napoleon has left Elba Sunday evening, together with his loyally devoted troops and chevaliers. He has left the former mayor Lapé, one of his chamberlains, as governor in the rank of brigadier general behind.

The latter, asked if he would defend the island against the Allied Powers, declared he would turn it over only to Napoleon or on his orders. Napoleon has left some Corsicans on the island, as well as the unarmed national guard. His mother and his sister Pauline have remained in Porto Ferrajo. He took with him several cannons, some horses, and food for several days, as well as the brigantine *L'Inconstante*, the gunboats *La Stella* and *Caroline*, and four feluccas for his troops. Yesterday afternoon this small flotilla was lost sight of north of Capraja, leading me to believe he intended to sail for the Antibes or make for the neighboring coasts of France or Piedmont.

The next report is sent by the Turkish ambassador in Paris to the Turkish foreign minister on March 8. On its long journey to Constantinople, the letter was intercepted in Vienna and brought to the attention of interested agencies:

Napoleon had left Elba with several ships on February 26, when an English frigate espied him from a distance. Unable to stop or overtake him, this frigate immediately returned to Leghorn and from there informed the British minister at Florence of the matter. The minister at once dispatched couriers to Vienna and to here. . . . Subsequent news is such that it has calmed the excitement here. All cities on Napoleon's route of march have refused to admit his emissaries. In Digne, his heralds were chased from the city in the nude. Napoleon himself went past many cities, showing neither fear nor care. In Gap, he appeared at first to be heading for Grenoble but pulled back and took the road to Italy, where he is now believed to be in the Piedmont mountain region. None of the cities or villages have shown the least attachment to him. It is precisely this which sets the present government up in great hope. The King during yesterday's assembly told the diplomatic corps in quiet serenity to send their courts a firm assurance that the peace of neither Europe nor, especially, of France would be in the least disturbed by this event, the rebel being known everywhere and sure to be rebuffed by all.

Many years later, Metternich in his memoirs described the arrival of the news of Napoleon's escape from Elba:

The first news of Napoleon's escape reached me in the following manner. There had been a conference at my house between the plenipotentiaries of the "five" during the night of March 6 to 7 which lasted till three in the morning. In view of the lateness of the hour, I had left orders not to be awakened should there be dispatches arriving later that night. Despite this order, my valet woke me at six in the morning with an urgent message that had just arrived by relay rider. Reading on the outside envelope the words "from the imperial consulate general at Geneva" and having been abed only three hours, I put the unopened message on the night table and tried to go back to sleep. But, once awake, I could not return to sleep and at about half past seven decided to open the message. Its six-line content read that the Englishman Campbell had just arrived in the harbor seeking information if Napoleon, who had disappeared from Elba, had not arrived at Genoa. Receiving a negative answer he had returned to sea in his frigate.

I was dressed in a few minutes and was with the Emperor before eight o'clock. He read the report and with the cool calmness he always showed in moments of stress he said: "Napoleon seems bent on playing the adventurer, which is his pleasure. Ours is to preserve the peace of Europe which he has disturbed for years. Go at once to the Czar and to the Prussian king and tell them I am ready to order my army back into France. I do not doubt the two monarchs are of a mind with me."

At eight fifteen I was with Czar Alexander who wholly agreed with my emperor, as did King Frederick William III, whom I saw at half past eight. By nine o'clock I was back at my house where I had already asked Field Marshal Prince Schwarzenberg to meet me. At ten, the ministers of the four powers arrived at my request. At the same hours messengers had been posted in all directions to order home-bound troop units to halt.

All this was decided on in less than an hour. When the ministers arrived they were still unaware of the momentous event. Talleyrand was the first to enter. I gave him the report to read. He showed no emotion and the following laconic exchange took place between us:

Talleyrand: Do you know Napoleon's destination?

I: The report says nothing about it.

Talleyrand: He will land somewhere on the coast of Italy and fall into Switzerland.

I: He proceeds by the most direct route to Paris.

This is the story in all its simplicity.

Most immediately hit by the news were Napoleon's wife, Marie-Louise, with her little son, currently the Prince of Parma, l'Aiglon, and all Frenchmen in Vienna, especially the diplomatic corps of the Bourbon king, Talleyrand himself at the head. A report from Schönbrunn read:

Yesterday, nothing was heard at Schönbrunn about today's news of Napoleon's escape. Young Montesquiou, the secretaries Ménéval and Mihaud, and the clerk Forestier composed doggerel rhymes about the Congress.

Talleyrand had had a "very gay" four-hour session with the Sicilian ambassador Ruffo on March 7:

Talleyrand said: "I have no idea where he might turn, certainly not to France. He is finished with us, it is too late, there is nothing left for him to do." Then, turning to the Czar, he very loudly proclaimed: "There you have it—the laggardness and the inane debates of the Congress."

Two days later, a report from Schönbrunn:

Yesterday, March 8, Mme. Montesquiou at an early hour went to Her Majesty, the Empress Marie Louise, to deliver the news about her husband. The empress listened without the least comment, went into her bedroom, and there cried for some time so that her sobs could be heard in the antechamber. She then reappeared and gave strict orders to all servants, including the coachman who usually takes Count Neipperg to the city, not to mention a word about the matter. Mme. Montesquiou's story was that Napoleon had fled Elba February 24; that the British had discovered this only February 26; that the claim was Napoleon had gone to America; and that many but not all of his guard had joined him.

An informant at the French Mission learned:

I can't find out anything else except that the Duke of Bénévent,[10] when he heard the news, calmly declared: "There is a real masterpiece for you. I shall concern myself with it, have already written the king about it. Bonaparte's efforts will be in vain but will not fail to create confusion, which will of necessity prolong our stay in Vienna."

A similar source reported:

Among the French and the Russians, confusion took over the moment news of Napoleon's escape arrived. The calmness shown by the Duke of Bénévent was only skin-deep, yet, by dint of his great self-control, he gave no outward sign of worry. Only those in his immediate circle are able to follow his thoughts. Thus, at Pressburg,[11] he confided to the Princess of Lorraine his great worry and doubt about the loyalty of Marshal Soult, the minister of war. But his confidence is reviving, especially since the refusal of Antibes to allow Napoleon to land has proved that the latter roams abroad as an adventurer and without a well-prepared plan. The Duke of Bénévent is said to have said that this person, not content with a tragic end, will now find a farcical one.

Gossip rode high in all Viennese circles:

Amazement is expressed in social circles that the Russian czar still counts Beauharnais, La Harpe, and Czartorisky among his intimates. Count O'Donell [sic] related at the Pufendorfs' yesterday: "On the wall of the Paris Louvre the following was seen February 25:

[10] Talleyrand.—Transl.
[11] Now Bratislava, Czechoslovakia.—Transl.

Question: Why does the king wear gaiters?
Answer: Because it's cold in February.
Question: What will he do in May?
Answer: He'll be on his uppers, being on the way down."

"Congress has broken wind."—"Congress has laid an egg."—
thus do the Viennese wags spoof Napoleon's escape.

Yesterday at Metternich's, Count Vaigemont commented
on Napoleon's escape: "I have just seen Talleyrand who said
to me: Napoleon has gone to ground in the Dauphiné woods
where he plays the pirate. It won't be long before he is caught. . . .
I am no friend of political sentimentality and it is precisely such
sentimental politics that has brought back Napoleon, who will
only plunge us back into the misery of revolution and war."
Countess Colloredo-Crenville said yesterday: "I now go every
day to the Empress Marie-Louise, who expresses no opinion but
is sad. . . ." Countess Lichnovska said: "If only Czar Alexander
knew, but every Pole is heart and soul for Bonaparte again ever
since his reappearance in France. . . ." Concerning Napoleon's
escape, the Czar is reputed to have said: "It is nothing if we
consider it to be such."

*Not only the Poles in Vienna were "heart and soul for
Bonaparte":*

Everywhere there is speculation about his landing. Now it is
Naples, now Imperia or Nice, now Toulon. From here he is seen
as marching straight and unopposed to Paris. The nuncio, as
well as the Portuguese and Spanish ministers, have assured me
there is a sizeable number of partisans in France, that there
is even fear of a conspiracy of which the government is not unaware and which is the reason General Dufour and others were
arrested today, making it plausible for Napoleon to enter France
and encourage his party to stir up civil war in order for him
to reascend the throne. Others believe he is headed for Italy,
where there is said to be a veritable hotbed of malcontents, and
where, together with Murat, he would invade the whole peninsula.
He would massacre the Austrians and forever free Italy from

the yoke of the barbarians—this is at least the claim of the Italians in the café on the Michaelerplatz.

In Vienna, levity counterbalanced abject fear:

The uneasiness into which Napoleon's hazardous undertaking had thrown the city's populace has given way to a premature calm and to raised hopes, all the more since the public press has published details and put the facts in their true perspective. Bets are being made on Napoleon's capture or death within fourteen days. There is so little confidence in the chimerical adventurer that the Count Triangi's 100 to 1 bet that Napoleon would be either captured or dead in half a month finds no takers. The number of congenital pessimists who seem to fear catastrophic results is small. The Poles, contrariwise, believe their fortunes to be on the upswing.

Prince Koslovski told me no one is more aroused and alarmed than the Bavarian king, who has bitterly berated the Russian czar for his excessive leniency towards the French by releasing 150,000 French prisoners of war, all graduates of the Napoleonic school and currently the bitterest enemies of the Bourbons.

With the damage done, the mocking voices were soon heard from:

The leniency, some call it indolence, exhibited by the allies in April, 1814, as well as the criminal indifference shown towards Napoleon's Elba imprisonment, are subject of acrimonious complaints and commentaries against the governments of all Powers. The story was told yesterday, March 10, at Mme. Wieland's, wife of a Swiss delegate, of a caricature showing mice poking fun at a caged cat but scattering wildly when the cat forces the cage. At the Zichys' and at many other houses, great annoyance was expressed yesterday that, despite the most ominous recent events, an imperial fete and a carriage promenade have been announced for the Augarten today, and that the insane rounds of fetes had not yet been stopped.

And how did the person chiefly concerned by all this, how did Talleyrand react to this series of evil tidings? An informant in servant's disguise reported on this March 18:

The morning of March 18 when, as usual, I asked for my instructions, the Prince told me: "My dear friend, my days of instruction are over. Let me have only one more courier from Paris who tells me all is peace and quiet there, this is all I ask for and nothing more." This the Prince uttered in deep emotion and then in a melancholy manner began to scratch his head with both hands. Baron Gagern arrived at one o'clock with the news. I am told that the King had left Paris for Holland. At two a courier from Paris reported all quiet there, adding that on his way he had seen the guards, stationed at Nancy and Metz, in disciplined fashion go over to Bonaparte, whose entry into Lyon is reported to have been peaceful and orderly. According to Secretary Roiren, Napoleon took the post chaise at Lyon and, under cavalry escort, is said to have started for Paris.

The Prince spent afternoon and evening at the chancery. He is reported to have commented that even if he could do nothing further for the King, he would still serve his country to the best of his ability. Today, four secretaries are returning home to Paris—in the wake of the Prince's statement of wanting to reduce his household. They are Roiren, Sens, Dawons, and Saint-Marc. Labesnardière will follow in a few days. It is really very touching, considering that the Prince (really the best of men), until recently all but directing the show, is now all but infamous and abandoned. If what I hear is true and the Prince is going to reduce his household to one servant and one valet, then matters must be in dire straits indeed and quite hopeless.

But the old fox had far from abandoned the desperate battle. Already two days earlier he had written the French ambassador in Constantinople a letter that was "intercepted" soon after:

Ever since I learned of Bonaparte's attempt I kept thinking that a unanimous declaration of all sovereigns against the usurper would, in addition to all other advantages, by removing all hope of success serve as a check to those deluded and criminal elements tempted to join him. The proposal I made was accepted with the greatest possible unanimity. The result is the declaration of which several copies are enclosed and which was signed on

the thirteenth of this month by the plenipotentiaries assembled
in Vienna for the Congress.

*The declaration in which the allies proscribed Napoleon
read in part:*

The powers, signatories to the Treaty of Paris and now in
Congress at Vienna assembled, have taken notice of the escape
of Napoleon Bonaparte and of his armed invasion of France.
They owe it to their own dignity and to the interests of the
social order to set forth in a formal declaration the emotions
aroused in them by this event.

By abrogating the contract that designated the island of
Elba as his place of residence, Bonaparte has destroyed the one
and only legal title to his existence. By stepping on French soil
with the avowed intent of causing unrest and disorder, he has
deprived himself of all legal protection and has revealed for all
the world to see that with him there can be neither peace nor
an armistice.

Therefore, the powers declare that Napoleon Bonaparte has
removed himself beyond the pale of decent social intercourse
and, as enemy and disrupter of world peace, has bound himself
over to the public courts of law.

They further declare their firm intent fully to carry out the
conditions of the Treaty of Paris, both as already decided and
as still to be formulated and agreed on, and to apply every means
and direct all mutual efforts in such manner that the general
peace, the goal of all Europe, as it is of this Congress, shall not
be disturbed anew but shall, on the contrary, be safeguarded
against all wanton attempts of throwing the peoples once more
into the disorders and miseries of revolution. And, even though
fully convinced that France, united behind its legitimate ruler,
will in short order send this last bold venture of a culpable and
impotent madness back into limbo, the sovereigns of Europe,
inspired by like emotions and guided by like principles, nevertheless unanimously declare their readiness, in case of some
unexpected danger arising out of this event, to furnish every
support to the King of France, to the French nation, as well as

to any other government, necessary to the reestablishment of public order, and to make common cause against those who might be tempted to disturb this order.

Above declaration is to be included as such in the protocol of the meeting of March 13, 1815, of the Congress assembled in Vienna and is to be publicly proclaimed.

Vienna, March 13, 1815.

The signatures of the signatory governments follow in alphabetical order (after the French original):

Austria:	Metternich, Wessenberg
Spain:	Labrador
France:	Talleyrand, Dalberg, Latour du Pin, Count de Noailles
Great Britain:	Wellington, Cathcart, Stewart
Portugal:	Palmella, Saldanta, Lodi
Prussia:	Hardenberg, Humboldt
Russia:	Razumovsky, Stackelberg, Nesselrode
Sweden:	Clan-Löwenhjelm

The text as finally adopted was drafted by Secretary Gentz. Only the original text was penned by the unforgiving and vengeful Talleyrand. At the behest of the Austrian emperor, this text, because of the "impropriety of its expressions," was toned down. Humboldt wrote to his wife about this:

Emperor Franz found the appeal to the general public to kill Bonaparte like a mad dog distasteful. He had this phrase changed to read that only those attached to his government, etc., are free to slay him. The English, also, objected to making the slaying of a tyrant a matter of private sport. Thus, the entire part that made the whole so particularly appealing to me was omitted.

But not even during the debate over the declaration and especially afterwards were the ranks against the disturbers of the peace at all closed. Gentz, who very often anticipates Met-

ternich's opinions, though he might formally formulate them only later, said:

I must add, though, that the Congress is far from united in this first step. Several of the most level-headed ministers consider such a step as being too precipitate and wrong. Yet no one is eager to speak his mind on this most ticklish question because, under Europe's present condition, all states without exception see in a general war a terrible and incalculable misfortune.

Czar Alexander, too, had weighty objections which he made no attempt to hide:

If despite all these discussions the current French situation is still fraught with dangerous possibilities, it still must be admitted that, no matter what the superiority of the Allied armies, the war for which we are preparing is nonetheless exposed to the vagaries of ill-fortune and it behooves us to weigh one against the other.

These misgivings tally exactly with those of Gentz, who rather pessimistically noted:

An important consideration against this war lies in the uncertainty over final aims and in the differences of opinion even now prevailing in the cabinets of the Allied powers concerning the decisions to be made in case of victory. Basically there is unity on only one point: to get rid of Napoleon. Beyond this, nothing has been settled, nothing decided. . . . To the Czar, Napoleon's great and unforgivable sin lay not in his personal character, nor in his methods of conquest, nor yet in his bent for absolute power, but in his marriage, which puts the French throne within reach of the Austrian emperor's grandson. But to the question of who is to take Napoleon's place, there is only silence. Despite all his cleverness and experience, Metternich as yet lacks a clear conception of what is to be proposed or tried in case of complete victory over Napoleon. Prussia, for its part, is equally ignorant and, what is worse, non-concerned about the matter. Its sole goal is to consolidate the gains made and to prepare for new ones. . . . Wonderful ingredient for a coalition indeed!

Nor had Napoleon remained idle in the case of his arch-enemy Talleyrand, about whom he commented in March, 1815, in Paris:

He is still the man most familiar with this century, with the world, the cabinets, and the peoples. He has left me; I myself gave him an unkind dismissal. . . . We were not always of the same mind but he was able more than once to give me sound advice.

Nothing if not consequential, Napoleon soon dispatched the Count Casimir de Montrond, "Casimir the Handsome," as ambassador extraordinary to Talleyrand in Vienna, who, in no way surprised by Napoleon's action, was not impressed, however. He told de Montrond:

You are too late. Europe has already made its decisions. So have I.

This rift among the leading politicians was of course reflected in the top echelons of Viennese society. The salons take an anti or pro stand, according to their background and tradition. An informant reported on an incident, occurring in the salon of the well-known and well-liked Fanny Arnstein, a Berlin lady who had married the Jewish banker Arnstein of Vienna and who maintained an open house during the Congress in which the most exalted of personages are frequent visitors. She was an outspoken, almost fanatic, critic of the French and of Napoleon and a thorough Prussophile. A secret agent—probably Abbé Carpani—in a previous report had quoted Napoleon's stepson Eugène Beauharnais as declaring at the salon of Princess Bagration his failure to understand why the allies did not come to terms with Napoleon. Surely, should Napoleon be content with the current French boundaries, one could easily come to an understanding with him. This same agent reported to Hager, the minister of police, on March 31:

Méjean, Beauharnais' secretary, says even much worse things. Day before yesterday a scene occurred at Frau von Arnstein's that was witnessed by a large number of people including, among others, General Degenfeld, Count Scherr, and the ladies de Bruce and Fossati. The matter was related to me by Mme. Eskeles and Abbé Rauen, who had it straight from the lips of Frau von Arnstein:

Frau von Arnstein mercilessly berates Napoleon and is enraged about what has just occurred. After she has just effusively greeted M. and Mme. Méjean, she says to the former, after he has barely sat down: "Well, monsieur, are you not ashamed to be a Frenchman, after all that has just happened? And those traitors Ney and Suchet!"

Méjean replies he has always been proud of being French and that he has an even greater respect for France, now that it has come out for its emperor, even as those brave marshals who had always remained loyal to their emporer.

Frau von Arnstein told him: "So you do not blush in shame when you honor this faithless man?" To which she adds whatever innuendo her anger supplies.

Mme. Méjean thereupon assures Frau von Arnstein in German that her husband didn't mean it that way but, on the contrary, appreciated those who kept faith, etc. In this manner she tries to undo the damage and gives her husband a sign to stop this talk.

Frau von Arnstein answers in French: "No, madam, you are mistaken. I understand exactly what he said. . . . Do you want proof? Well, monsieur, repeat your words, if you have the courage!"

Without any hesitation Méjean repeats his statement and everyone is indignant over the audacity of this Frenchman, who was not only well received and liked, but who had even married a Viennese and who was fully familiar with the declaration of the Congress.

All this so excited and disconcerted Frau von Arnstein that she had a nervous breakdown, could not sleep, and is still in ill health. However, she took prompt revenge. Following the scene, General Degenfeld and other military people talked about Austrian troop movements. Both the Méjeans were still present. Frau von Arnstein, having listened to the conversation from a distance, raised her voice and said: "Gentlemen of the military, you are ill advised to discuss such matters here. One should make sure only trustworthy people are around." Méjean swallowed the pill without comment.

In its seriousness and patriotic fervor the attitude of the Prussian Jewess was somewhat in contrast with the general mood of Vienna, a mood partly resulting from the "demeanor" that was de rigueur *in the leading circles, and partly based on the congenital inability seriously to become* engagé *in anything. We are indebted to Count Auguste de La Garde for a deep insight into the collective Viennese soul. His sketches, though they are often criticized for their apparent superficiality, rather accurately reflect the mental image of Vienna at the time of the Congress. De La Garde opens his sketches of those by-gone days with a report he ostensibly had received from Prince Koslovski:*

There was no doubt that Napoleon had left Elba. Europe's master and its prisoner, as he has been called, had, armed with only his fame, flown the coop and had entrusted "Caesar and his fortune" to a fragile bark.

"The news," Koslovski said, "has arrived here by a courier whom Lord Burghess had dispatched from Florence. The latter had it from the British consul in Leghorn. Lord Stewart, the addressee, has informed Metternich and the sovereigns. The ministers of the big powers were also immediately informed. No one knows which direction Napoleon has taken. Has he gone to France? Is he, as some think, out to woo the United States? There is a surfeit of speculation. But who is going to protect him from the gathering storm, what good fortune prevent the bolt from striking?. . . . The high and mighty arbiters of the Congress wanted to suppress the news until they had been able to take some action in line with the gravity of the situation."

Whether it was this secrecy or that the momentum of

amusement had hid the horror, the city of Vienna retained its customary face; the walls and the Leopoldstadt that led to the Prater were crowded with strollers, eager to catch the sun's warm rays. Nothing as yet presaged the coming thunder. Everywhere nothing but carefreeness and joy.

In the evening, a private showing of *The Barber of Seville* and, if my memory serves right, of a vaudeville piece much in favor at the time, called *The Interrupted Dance*, was to take place. Prince Koslovski had asked me to accompany him. Being eager of the chance to study high society, and also in hope of obtaining some tid-bits of this great social event, I had accepted his invitation. The social gathering was up to its customary glitter and size. But somehow the usual carefree calm was disturbed, some ever so light clouds in evidence. Here and there, groups had formed; there was eager debate over the likely results of that escape.

"Impossible for him to evade the British cruisers," said one.

"Senor Pozzo di Borgo has assured us," declared another, "let Napoleon but set foot on French soil and he will be strung up on the nearest tree." Thus everyone seemed to have his own antidote to reality.

"How lucky for us," said some Bourbon partisans in Sicily. "Surely Bonaparte did us a great service. Now he'll invade Naples and the Congress will be forced at last to take action against Murat, the puppet usurper."

Meanwhile the Austrian empress had given the sign. Everyone took his seat and the curtain rose.

"We shall see," I remarked to Prince Koslovski, "if this event that no one has in the least foreseen will not shake up these high personages somewhat."

"Hardly. Unless the enemy is before the gates of Vienna and the sound of cannon heard in the city, they will not wake from their stubborn sleep. M. de Talleyrand received the news this morning even before he arose. Mme. Edmond de Périgord sat at the foot of his bed and was engaged in lively conversation with him when a message from Metternich was delivered. 'I suppose,' said the prince, 'I am being told the hour that the Congress will convene.' The handsome countess mechanically opened the letter, looked at it, and read the momentous news. This was the day, by the way, that she had planned to visit the wife of Metternich, there to hold a rehearsal of the farce *The Deaf One or the Inn without Room*.

" 'Napoleon has left Elba,' she cried. 'Oh, uncle, my rehearsal. . . . !'

" 'It will take place, madam,' the diplomat calmly replied.

"The rehearsal *did* take place. . . ."

For nearly five days Vienna was without further news, but the festivities and amusements went on as usual. Slowly the cloud of apprehension seemed to lift. But, in the end, the truth came out with thunderclap effect: Napoleon was in France. Not only did the French people hail the adventurer, as Pozzo di Borgo had dared to call him, but the soldiers flocked to their general and nothing opposed his triumphal march. The giant's fall, once considered inconceivable, aroused less surprise than his return to power. The news hit the social world like a bolt out of the blue and the thousands of taper candles seemed suddenly dimmed.

The news spread with lightning speed. The waltz stopped; in vain the orchestra played on; one gazed in disbelief; questions were asked. The four words: "He is in France!" were like Ubaldo's shield which, as soon as seen by Rinaldo, dispelled Armida's magic charm.

The Czar approached Prince Talleyrand: "I told you before, this couldn't last." Without a change of expression, the French ambassador bowed and said not a word.

The King of Prussia beckoned the Duke of Wellington and both left the ballroom. Soon after they were followed by the Czar, Emperor Franz, and Metternich. The greater part of the guests slowly disappeared. Only a few groups remained in the various rooms, conversing in worried tones. Prince Koslovski, whom I met at the *soirée*, had no further news.

"Now," he said, "the troubador gentlemen have a splendid chance to present us with a second performance of that lovely farce *The Interrupted Dance*. Count Pálffy, who did so well in the Wasner role, might very well sing:

> " 'At last, see, the dance is interrupted;
> What is one to make of this incident?'

"Only I fear the refrain will soon be accompanied by the roar of battle." It would be difficult indeed to paint the face of Austria's capital as it now appeared. Vienna seemed like a person who, sweetly asleep with dreams of love or ambition, is rudely awakened by the night watchman's hoarse cry or the alarm bells, informing him his house is on fire. The numerous guests from all parts of Europe all too vividly recalled every phase of the recent past: twenty-five bloody war years of ravished cities, corpse-strewn battlefields, paralyzed trade and commerce, mourning families and nations—all this passed before their mind's eye. And all these terrible images were thrown into garish relief by a Moscow aflame. Yet, there had been vengeance too in the recent past, and the allied troops' entry into Paris had furnished sufficient proof that a conqueror is not necessarily unconquerable. But all this only heightened their fears. To bring down the colossus had required such confluence of circumstances and, more important, such harmonious collaboration among so many divers peoples that the resulting whole had increased the strength of the individual tenfold. Now they gazed at each other and the only certainty there was was the present misery they had thought themselves forever free of.

THE JEWS

The sovereigns and lords at the Congress of Vienna did their best to solve the European question. With bold words, sharp scissors, and cocked weapons they managed the current affairs of this small continent as though they dealt with the whole world. Intrigues, sacrifices, threats of war, alliances, and now the imminence of war caused by the enemy's return. All this becomes the object of a politics that lays claim to being all-embracing. In the final analysis, however, everyone thought, talked, and acted in an area, if not exactly small, at least of limited size. At the time, the equation "European politics–world politics" was no more than a metaphor, a pat phrase, a logogram. But in the wings there stood two powers that had no longer or had not yet a part in this politics-of-the-moment. The one was a great power of the past, of tradition—a suffering power, a power of the intellect. The other was an enormous power of the future, of freedom from tradition—an active power, a power of the will. The first was Judaism: the second, the United States.

The law guaranteeing to the Jews every equality before the law was passed by the French Constituent Assembly in 1791 and was never repealed by Napoleon, even in his later, less Judeophile years. Now, as the Allied armies "liberated" the French-occupied Rhenish provinces, pre-Revolutionary conditions were re-established as a matter of mechanical routine. Thus, as Rome lost its French-introduced streetlights, the Jews lost their newly acquired rights. At the very least, this was the prospect they were faced with. It was for this reason that the Frankfurt Jewish community, as early as October, 1814, had appealed to the Congress of Vienna for a reaffirmation of Jewish rights. Prince Metternich, on June 9, 1815, sent the following message:

To the Jewish deputies of the city of Frankfurt, the Honorables Baruch and Uffenheimer.

In reference to the petition which the Israelite deputation of the city of Frankfurt sent to the High Congress on October 10, 1814, and which requested confirmation of the treaty concerning the civil rights of members of the Jewish faith that was concluded December 28, 1811, with the then Grand Duke of Frankfurt, be it made known to you that the document of the ninth of this month which grants Frankfurt the status of a free city binds the magistrate to respect all documented rights of every class of citizens and asks it to avoid all ex post facto measures.

This ruling ought also to serve to reassure the Jewish community of Frankfurt-on-Main, since by it the legal claims justly based on a prior agreement are completely safeguarded.

In a similar, though a far more detailed and pleading, manner the Jews of the Austrian emperor's patrimonial dominions in a direct appeal to Emperor Franz asked for equal legal status with the rest of the citizenry:

To His Imperial and Royal Apostolic Majesty!

On behalf of all members of the Jewish faith within the imperial and royal German lands, their authorized agents most respectfully submit the following plea and petition:

This is not the first time the subject matter of this most respectful petition is brought before Your Majesty's most illustrious throne. Your Majesty has deigned to receive earlier pleas of similar import with such outstanding favor and kindness that the undersigned feel confident of receiving an equally gracious understanding today.

The time chosen by the representatives of the Jews in Your Majesty's imperial German domain to dare once again to express their wishes seems especially propitious to their cause for more than one reason. There is not only the most urgent desire for a material improvement of their condition, but the progress they themselves have made in the past twenty years under conditions heretofore often repressive and burdensome, the obvious advantage that accrues to the state from precisely those measures the Jews seek, and, not least, the enlightened attitude of a large segment of their Christian fellow citizens, has not only caused a general weakening and dissipation of ancient anti-Semitic prejudices but has gained the Jews many friends and protectors in the higher ranks of society, among the confidential advisors of the rulers of many lands, and of many top-ranking statesmen. Not a shred of doubt can remain against the essential justice, fairness, and feasibility of their petition and of the oneness of the latter with the commonweal.

We owe this happy turn of events to the fact that the High Congress currently assembled in Vienna has been petitioned from several different quarters to grant complete equality before the law to Jews and members of other faiths and, as is reported, this same Congress in its deliberations over the future German constitution is seriously concerned with this subject matter.

It is not for us to say in how far this hope is well-founded and what shall be the results, in legal terms, of this Congress' deliberations. But we should be joyful over any improvement in the fate of our fellow believers in Germany. But for us in particular, who have the good fortune of living under a monarch whose wise and time-tested parental principles leave us to face the future in complete equanimity, and whose all-embracing love for his loyal subjects needs no external nudge to reveal itself in its full splendor—for us all these steps are of import only because they offer us a decent and opportune occasion to submit to Your Most Gracious Majesty once more these immediate concerns of ours that on previous occasions were so kindly received.

Your Majesty has kindly deigned to interpret the edict of August 3, 1797, pertaining to the Bohemian Jewry to mean that the legislature is enjoined to abrogate any difference in treatment, as heretofore practiced, between Christian and Jewish subjects.

These comforting words shall forever live in the memory of our posterity, even as that law itself shall remain one of the most wonderful of monuments to the justice and wisdom with which Your Majesty has ruled over and blessed your peoples.

Most worshipful Emperor and Sire!

The members of the Jewish faith have lived up to Your Majesty's expectations. The facts as known attest to their skill in all kinds of useful trades. In many of the monarchy's provinces there is evidence of their diligence, and their great factories and far-flung foreign trade connections leave no doubt as to the use to which they have put their energies and their capital under a liberal and equitable legal system. Whenever they have been asked, or only permitted to, they have gladly done service in the public interest, and in their love of country and loyal devotion to their beloved monarch, they are at least on a par with their Christian fellow citizens. They have proved the preconception that they are unfit for military service as baseless. True to the call of their sovereign, they have freely pledged their persons and their lives during the past years of bitter warfare and, as it behooves all good citizens, have shed their blood for the safety and honor of their common country in the joyous hope that now at last this country will cease treating them as stepchildren. They have spared neither effort nor money to better the education of their youth. All this has been verified to Your Majesty by unanimous reports from all administrative levels. We have met every test. If there still exists a humiliating borderline that separates us from other citizens, this is because of antiquated opinions or blind and groundless fear of competition that may seem dangerous to the petty private interests but is of obvious benefit to the good of the whole. In Your Majesty's generous soul this borderline has long since disappeared.

May we here be permitted to point out that on occasion there appeared to be reasonable doubt if the moral condition, the habits and inclinations, as well as the bourgeois changes undergone by a segment of the Jewish nation did not put in question their fitness for certain branches of the food industry or other fields of endeavor. But the real roots of such fear lie solely and exclusively in precisely those unfortunate barriers that have been raised between the Jews and other classes of the citizenry. And those who would deny the Jews civil equality under the idle pretext that they are not yet deserving such equality are in effect trying to block the road to equality by permanently depriving the Jews precisely of those chances they need to prove themselves fit for full citizenship. No matter how well-intentioned or how well-endowed by nature, a people oppressed by unequal and peculiar laws can reveal its true character only if the pressure under which it suffers is removed. All we ask is the chance to show the world that we are worthy of the same benevolent protection as are all others. Given this chance, we shall soon dissipate every objection against us. Let there be equal opportunity and equal justice for us and the quality of our citizenship shall be of equal measure.

We are quietly confident in the serene hope that the goal

toward which we have struggled so long is near at hand and that
in one form or other the fate of our fellow believers, be it in all
German lands, be it at least in Your Majesty's royal domain, will
be favorably and satisfactorily decided.

We are confident that the High Congress here assembled
will, in its deliberations and decisions under Your Majesty's most
powerful influence and guided by the noble humanitarian basic
principles that have ever enjoyed Your Majesty's protection, bring
these matters to a successful conclusion. This is our most fervent
wish, partly because we should like to owe the benefits that we
are to receive to Your Majesty's grace and kindness alone, but
partly also because we are convinced no European sovereign has
a fairer claim than Your Majesty to the glory of having achieved
a major improvement in civic government and legislation, and
of having liberated a large class of citizens from prolonged and
undeserved oppression.

Should time or the pressure of business or other obstacles
prevent the Congress from debating this most important matter, we should nonetheless be obliged if Your Majesty, in the
fullness of Your grace as father of the country, would deign to
look kindly upon our wishes and needs and speak that one mighty
word that shall forever elevate us and make us happy. All prep-
aratory investigations have been concluded. Every result on every
side has been in our favor. The justice of our petition admits of
no doubt, nor is Your Majesty's decision for the betterment of
Your own subjects linked to any alien influence or foreign concern. And should there be some more information required on
this or that point, information that would surely only bear out all
previous research in the matter, we should in the meantime consider ourselves fortunate indeed if only the bright promise of
1797 were carried out, if only the general principle that puts the
Jews on an equal footing as concerns ownership of property, free
choice of profession, and unrestricted trading opportunities with
the members of all other faiths were declared the law of the land
by Your Majesty.

We fervently beseech Your Majesty in the name of our fellow believers, our children, our posterity, in the full knowledge

of the love Your Majesty bears all subjects and of all those virtues for which Your Majesty is admired by the people and by the world, to no longer withhold from us those reassuring words. We at the same time raise our voice to God, who will not leave this noble deed unrewarded, to visit every blessing on Your Majesty's sacred person and on the state, which may for years untold prosper and flourish under Your Majesty's wise and mild scepter. We remain Your Majesty's most deeply respectful, most humble, and most loyal subjects.

Vienna, April 11, 1815

Signed on behalf of Vienna's Jewish Community:

> Nathan Freiherr von Arnstein
> Bernhard Ritter von Eskeles
> Leopold Edler von Herz

On behalf of the Jewish community of Bohemia:

> Simon Ritter von Lämel

On behalf of the Jewish community of Moravia:

> Lazar Auspitz

No action was ever taken on this petition. But in the years following the Congress, the condition of the Jews progressively improved in the Austrian imperial lands, even though the theoretic equality before the law had by no means become legally established.

Under the same date of June 9, 1815, when Metternich sent his message to the Free City of Frankfurt, the Congress directed a letter to the "Jews in Germany," addressing it to the representative of the German Jewish community, the Honorable Dr. Buchholz of Lübeck:

The high powers here in Congress assembled, ever concerned with the well-being of the individual, have decided that the members of the Jewish faith within the German Confederation shall enjoy the full benefits of common civic rights. The timetable has not permitted the matter to be fully settled by the Congress in Vienna. As an interim measure it is directed in the Constitution of the German Confederation that the Ger-

man Diet, sitting in Frankfurt, shall deliberate in what manner
the common civil rights are to be offered the Jewish communities in Germany and that, until conclusion of such deliberations,
those liberties and rights presently granted the Jewish communities in the various German states shall remain in force. This information is furnished the representative of the Jewish Communities in Germany, the Honorable Dr. Buchholz from Lübeck,
in answer to the latter's petition to the Congress of December 9,
1814, and as a reassuring reminder for the communities that the
Diet will most actively support the move of granting civil rights
to them and to protect the interests of the Jewish communities.

*That Jewry, the power of the past, could not implicitly trust
futurist assurances, from whatever quarters these might come,
soon became evident. The constitutional article that was to guarantee retention of those civil rights already guaranteed, the one
that Humboldt had initially written, was amended in the final
version of the constitution to read:*

But those rights that have heretofore been granted to the
members of this faith by the several German states shall be retained.

*This in effect abrogated again those rights gained since the
French Revolution, for the German Wars of Liberation had re-
established pre-Revolutionary conditions. One reason for this lay
in the general ideological atmosphere at the Congress where,
with the notable exception of Wilhelm von Humboldt, Jewry
had very few friends but many enemies, as, for example, Gentz.
Not to mention the official Austrian police agencies, whose very
black-and-yellow bones [12] since time immemorial have been
steeped in anti-Semitism. Thus Police Chief Göhausen reported
to his superiors about the Jewish delegation from Frankfurt:*

Attached report from Herr von Weyland clearly confirms
that the Frankfurt Jewish deputation is here solely to engage
in secret cabals. The mentioned Idzstein, formerly head of the
police force, later President of the Law Courts, is known for a

[12] An allusion to the Austrian imperial colors.—Transl.

dirty protector of Jews. The Free City of Frankfurt, once it has consolidated its administrative authority, is sure to get rid of him. The authorities ought seriously to consider removing from here this deputation, made up of these people Gumprecht and Baruch. To which should be added that according to a most reliable source this Gumprecht has not yet even bothered to pay a courtesy call on the municipal councilman, Syndikus Danz, who does not have the slightest knowledge about such a mission.

THE CONTINENT OF THE FUTURE

Seen only as through a cloudy haze lay the land of the future: America. Since the opening of the Congress, the German-American doctor Justus Erich Bollmann had been in Vienna. Not only did he prove to be an intelligent political observer, untainted by any hint of informant activity, but he had a head full of bold and at times abstruse ideas, to which latter category certainly did not belong his project on the "operation of a ship by means of steam" on the Danube. Fully a decade earlier Robert Fulton had demonstrated a steamship model before Napoleon on the Seine which the Emperor, blind in this direction, had laughingly brushed aside. Doctor Bollmann, whose numerous letters of introduction had opened many Vienna salons to him, had also appeared at the home of Secretary Gentz on an evening when, among others, Prince Reuss XIX, Wilhelm von Humboldt, Prince Ferdinand of Coburg-Gotha, Count and Countess Fuchs, and Lieutenant Varnhagen, had also gathered there. We owe a report of this visit to Varnhagen:

Soon everyone fell silent to listen only to Bollmann's wondrous tales about the United States of North America. The prolonged maritime war has estranged that country from us. Even stranger was the thought of such a republic, whose evolution presented the marvelous, even frightening, example of a common citizenry achieving a might and a greatness that we Europeans are wont to associate only with the nobility and royalty. Urged along by the ingenuous questioning of a fellow guest, whose curiosity was insatiable, the talk assumed more and more the nature of a well-rounded, well-documented lecture on republican basic principles and precepts, such as one would least have expected at this Congress of monarchs. The very weight of the argument deeply disturbed and oppressed Gentz, who felt as if an assassination had been attempted in his presence.

Time and Place of the Action

The backdrop to all this was baroque Vienna, the capital and residential city of the Hapsburgs, the city of Johann Bernhard Fischer von Erlach and of Lucas von Hildebrandt, the city of the Belvedere castle and of St. Stephan's Cathedral, a city with its suburbs newly built not more than a hundred and fifty years before, its imperial summer palace of Schönbrunn, and its Prater park. Bedded in open green spaces, Vienna hugged the slopes of the Vienna woods, lay enfolded within the Danube's grassy plains, a city of richly decorated palaces, whose interiors resembled the diamond's cold glitter. Now it was filled to bursting with visitors to the Congress, in addition to its own ebullient population, its "primary" and "secondary" social levels. There was a feeling of momentous change in the air, of the end of an epoch that had begun with the Renaissance and its breakaway from the Christian way of life and reached its peak in the appearance of the conqueror whom the last representatives of feudalism and the first of nationalism had just laid low in defeat. The minuet had given way to the waltz, and once more the ancien régime appeared in full splendor; but inflation was eating away the national patrimony and a plainer style of living was in the ascendancy. The love of ostentation, of refinement, of unfettered love itself, hallmarks of the eighteenth century, was now replaced by the heartier joys of the cup and the table. The quietly idyllic Bieder-

meier slowly engulfed the tremendous ruins of a dying age. In this period of change, of momentous upheaval, Vienna remained cool, serene, beautiful.

At half past ten at night Czar Alexander hired a public fiacre, accompanied only by his Russian personal valet. He returned after midnight, a matter of frequent occurrence. The Czar goes to the palace belonging to the princely dynasty of Palm in the Schenken-strasse, where the Duchess of Sagan and the Princess Bagration have their apartments on the second floor. A countess Cl. and several other cocottes seek Alexander's favors but are kept at a distance by his aide-de-camp, Volkonski. The Czar is quite happy in Vienna, saying that in all his travels he has not had so much fun. His Russians are nothing new to him, and in the countries he visited during the recent campaigns he had found much misery and many discontented people. England he had found too overcrowded. Austria alone he found to possess the essential ingredients of true amusement, embodying as it does the golden mean of all nations and in its demeanor neither too extreme nor too provincial.

This paean of praise was echoed by Carl von Varnhagen:

A Vienna day seemed made of special stuff and what it touched, it made part of its own self-contentment. What to most is but a daily chore—the eating, drinking, strolling, gazing about—is here the style of living, irresistibly made into a matter of joy and pleasure.

There was first of all the city's panorama, its houses and gardens, its belt of green vistas—engagingly portrayed in the diary of Carl Bertuch, bookdealer and publisher from Weimar, from his vantage point at Schönbrunn:

We stroll towards the Glorietta. All is quiet and very pretty, the panorama superb. The view of Vienna creates a feeling of great serenity. The white, wide buildings, the red gables, St. Stephan's mighty pile darkly rising skyward. The cheerful domes of the Karlskirche, the chain of mountain ranges and the Leopoldsberg.[13] The row of houses stretching as far as Schönbrunn, on the opposite side the townships of St. Veit and the two Brühls. Behind Laxenburg: the plains, with the Hungarian mountains in the background. The initial plan of Fischer [von Erlach] called for the palace to be built on a plateau with terraced slopes.

Dined well in Hietzing today. . . .

At ten to the Diana baths, where the lowers are one florin and twenty-four kronen and the uppers two florins. Furnishings and service are good, bathrobe and several towels are supplied. . . .

April 5: visited the Kahlenberg.[14] Ligne's [15] grave behind a wood fence, a great wooden cross marking the site. Fräulein Traumwieser, a lovely girl, rests by his side.

A howling wind brought rain, and we made our way through several empty houses of this abandoned colony until we came at last to a restaurant where we dined well but expensively. After that to the Leopoldsberg. The lowering sky picturesquely limned by the white buildings, lying as though on an isthmus. . . .

April 23: lunch in the Prater. Incomparably beautiful, the massy foliage with its stalls underneath. Russian swings, merry-go-rounds, other popular entertainment, accompanied by brassy music, deafen the ear. A street minstrel with a harp, sitting on some boards together with two women, sings patriotic songs and curses Bonaparte. All this stretches on up to the great Prater promenade, where the elegant world passes to and fro. The coach-and-fours, whose coachmen in buckled shoes and hose sit negligently sideways on the driver's seat. Or light chaises with two grooms in the rear, wearing surcoats equipped with colorful collars, cuffs, and trimmings. The hats accoutered with rattles and bows.

Focal point and showplace of the city was the Imperial Palace, whose Spanish Riding School became the scene of the

[13] A small mountain near Vienna.—Transl.

[14] Part of the Vienna Woods.—Transl.

[15] Charles Joseph, Prince de Ligne, Austrian field marshal celebrated for his cosmopolitanism and wit, had died during the Congress.—Transl.

more magnificent spectacles. On this Eipeldauer had the follow-
ing to say to his "cousins in Kakran":

At the moment they're at it converting the hulking Riding
School, that's already quite big enough with its king-sized upper
and lower balconies for 7–8,000 people to whoop it up in, into
a splendiferous dance palace that, combined with the big and
the little masquerading halls (that ordinarily have enough room
for from 4–5,000 people), will allow nigh onto 12,000 people to
dance, eat, drink, and make merry in. . . .

You've got no idea for what this Riding School has not already been used for, first the lottery drawing that has always
taken place there, then there were even those rope dancers that
have strutted their stuff there, and after that there were those
seven hundred dilettantes that several times made their music
there, but ordinarily what's done there is train the nags to learn
to dance too.

The ebullient, gay de La Garde also discussed the beauties
of the city at length and in loving detail:

For the visitor this easygoing life, filled as it was with never-
ending fetes, was a life of joy indeed. Vienna, to do honor to
this memorable meeting, was out to surpass the pleasures it ordinarily offers. Centrally situated in the southern part of Germany, this city seems an oasis of insouciance and peace in the
midst of the sobersided scientific and philosophical activities of
its neighboring lands. Entirely given to a life of sensuousness, its
essential being lies in fetes, banquets, dances, and, above all, in
music. And with it all, the excellent Hungarian wine that adds a
fillup to the fun and that serves to make the easy life the order
of the day.

The visitor is well cared for in Vienna: privately, he is
treated with heartfelt hospitality; publicly, the officials handle
him with outspoken cordiality. In return he is asked for only
one thing: not to agitate against the government.

Under these rules the welcome will be unvaryingly polite.
But woe to the foreigner who sins against these rules of common

sense: in a short time he will get a little note, asking him politely to appear at police headquarters the next day. Here he will be told in the softest of voices that something is the matter with his papers and that his business is at an end. In vain is his protest, his claim of loyalty to every government, his assurance that he seeks only a life of pleasure. All, all in vain. Go he must.

Schönbrunn also interested de La Garde:

The imperial palace of Schönbrunn, begun under the Hapsburg princes, became the apple of Maria Theresa's eye. The building was completed in her reign and her impatience was so great she had the work carried on at night by torchlight. The palace is charmingly located on the right bank of the Vienna River.[16] The overall architectonic impression is one of majesty. Its gardens are laid out in nobly graceful patterns, artistically subdivided by water courses. Trees of massy foliage, the most beautiful bronzes, and priceless marble statuary enhance the general splendor. The park exhibits many sprightly groups of goats, deer, and stags, which are the peaceful denizens of the woody areas and which seem to enjoy the presence of visitors. The promenades and gardens are open to the public at all hours, every day; carriages and equestrians crisscross them. The park is surrounded by amusement centers that, during the clement season, offer sport and entertainment of all sorts. This joyful abandonment seems to be quite audible at the imperial living quarters and, in the expressiveness of its happiness, serves even to add to the charm of this noble residence.

The rooms and halls of the palace are of liberal dimensions and tastefully furnished. Several rooms are still kept in black decor, mindful of the time Maria Theresa lost her spouse. A small study is decorated with sketches done by various archduchesses. It is here Napoleon usually retreated for work during his stay at Schönbrunn, and it was here he first saw a likeness of Marie Louise and the idea of the union, that was to greatly influence his fate, occurred to him.

From this room a flight of stairs leads into the garden. A

[16] A tiny (20 m.) river near Vienna.—Transl.

charming pavilion, built by Maria Theresa and called Glorietta, arises on a nearby woody knoll. This elegant edifice, with its arcades, colonnades, and trophies, lends a happy finishing touch to the whole; it is a palace and a triumphal arch at once. A dual set of stairs leads to the top. The view from the main *salon* beggars description—limitless vistas of greenery, the city in the distance, the Danube's course, and, framing this glorious landscape, the towering mountains. It would be difficult to imagine a richer panorama.

Schönbrunn's greenhouses are probably the best in Europe, containing as they do the vegetational wealth of the world. Emperor Franz, himself an enthusiastic botanist, here cultivates his rare plants.

Nearby is the zoological park. Here every animal species has its own habitat, which in all respects duplicates the conditions of free nature. Though essentially prisoners, these animals nonetheless enjoy a certain freedom. Near the palace a small, carefully tended section is maintained as a private garden for Napoleon's son. This young prince takes pleasure in cultivating flowers from which he will bind a nosegay for his mother and his governess every morning.

The Prater, also, comes in for de La Garde's attention:

The Prater park is on a Danube island on the outskirts of Vienna. Broad avenues traverse it; the shade of century-old trees keeps the grass verdantly green. As in Schönbrunn and in most German parks, deer and stags freely roam the Prater's hilly slopes and meadows, thus lending a touch of life and movement to this magnificent solitude. All around, a pristine naturalness, bedecked with the objects that art and culture supply. Coming from the city, one sees on the left a wide grassy expanse where fireworks may be set off. On the right a circus is located that seats several thousand. Straight ahead runs a broad, chestnut-lined boulevard, on both sides of which are countless shops, cafés, and social centers where the Viennese may freely indulge their love of music.

For the Viennese the Prater has a special charm, the charm of remembrance. To him, it is a book of life: here he has played as a child, dreamt his first dreams of love and youth, in later years spent his carefree evening hours after the business of a tiresome day.

A look into one of the establishments reveals a crowd of men and women, dancing the minuet with an earnestness as though their joy were thrust on them. Frequently the crush of onlookers separates the dancing partners, who immediately reunite and continue the interrupted figures of the dance as if the dance were a wrestling match with their conscience. But on the heels of this simple music comes the more lively strain of the waltz. The coiled spring of gaiety has been released, and the same pair that a minute ago seemed coolly detached now sways gracefully for fully an hour to the tunes of this semipassionate dance. On the sedate merry-go-round the city child soon learns the trick of snatching the ring without losing its balance in the saddle. Over yonder, entire families of merchants and artisans sit around tables laden with succulent food and quietly sip their Hungarian wine. Everywhere the wandering minstrels with their alfresco performances remind of an everlasting fair.

An outstanding feature of the Viennese is his look of contentment and prosperity. The money he has to spend, his quiet happiness bespeak his diligence and the paternal government whose subject he is. No ugly altercations disturb this crowd, which takes its joy seriously, with a seriousness, however, not born of melancholy but rooted in a firm feeling of contentment.

Watching the beautiful chestnut-lined boulevard, with its countless magnificent coaches and the many equestrians who handle their prancing, multiracial steeds with perfect Hungarian skill, one would fancy to see here assembled all the luxury of the Austrian lands. The Emperor himself, like any ordinary burgher, rides in a plain coach that any common fiacre, hired for the hour and unafraid of competition, feels free to cut off, only soon himself to be overtaken by a Bohemian magnate or a Polish palatine, driving his own coach-and-four. Light gigs appear, drawn by speedy horses with flying manes and containing ladies in red and white, like flowers in a basket. This kaleidoscope of changing patterns, the jostling pedestrians, the general tumult, magnified by the influx of foreigners but softened somewhat by German gravity—all this presents the most vivid spectacle: a Teniers scene in a Ruysdael landscape.

One thing struck me in particular right from the start: the number of coaches of the same type and color, all drawn by either two or four horses. This was a thoughtfulness of the Emperor who had frowned on the sovereigns or members of their retinue using conveyances differing from his own. He therefore had had three hundred identical carriages built, which at all hours of day and night were at the disposal of his exalted and illustrious guests. In a few minutes' time this living tableau had shown me all that Vienna at that moment contained of greatness.

But this surveyor of the Congress scenes well knew the stakes in the balance. With his friend, the well-known English doctor and writer Julius Griffith, he strolled through Vienna's inner city:

We met Princess Helena Suvorova, General Tettenborn, and Alexander Ypsilanti on the Danube Bridge. Going in our direction, they said they were on their way to visit the imperial family crypt in the Kapuzinerkirche. At this suggestion we accompanied them.

As we arrived at the burial chapel, a monk with a huge torch preceded us into the crypt, in which repose the ashes of nine emperors, thirteen empresses, and, all in all, some eighty members of the imperial family.

"In this underground vault," the monk informed us, "Maria Theresa for thirty years attended daily mass in front of the sepulcher she had had prepared for herself next to that of her spouse."

"This trait of Maria Theresa," said Tettenborn, "reminds me of one of Joseph II's wise remarks. When he opened the Augarten to the public, a lady of the court complained to him of being deprived of promenading there with her own kind. 'If everyone,' was the emperor's rejoinder, 'were limited to have social contact with only his own kind, I should be reduced, in order to get some fresh air, to visit the Kapuziner crypt.' "

After spending several minutes in front of these memorials of marble and bronze, we reascended the stairs in solemn mood.

Then the reflection of several other torches announced more visitors. We recognized Princess Bagration, the princes Koslovski, Galitzin, and Sheremechev, as well as several persons of rank. For some time now it had become the custom of foreigners to tour Vienna's sights, which first the turmoil of arrival and then the bitter cold of winter had curbed initially. February's warm sun, though, filled churches, palaces, and galleries with throngs of visitors. Our guide mentioned that nearly every one of Vienna's guests, the sovereigns included, had visited the crypts several times. Thus did the century's lucky ones, moved by an understandable urge, descend from the scenes of loud festivities above into these somber vaults below, there to meditate. At all times poesy has fancied the juxtaposition of life's glitter with death's somberness. But fate also is a fearful poet and all too often has joined the two.

It was Julius Griffith who most loudly sang Vienna's praise. De La Garde reports:

"Really," Griffith commented, "where in Vienna does one meet a beggar? The poorhouses are administered well and without stint. Public charity, in particular, seems to be guided by the greatest liberality. Since the people as a whole are ahead of the rest of Germany in industry and commerce, there is much evidence of prosperity. Without doubt, none of Europe's capitals measures up to the charm of Vienna's surroundings nor its quiet, carefree life. If Mme. de Staël called Germany the land of thought, Vienna might be called the home of happiness."

Other foreigners were less prone to such high praise for the Viennese. Concerning their separation into classes, Carl Bertuch confided to his diary:

Three classes are found here:

The upper nobility has little use for German culture, science, or art. This is a cohesive caste, wedging itself between ruler and people. For its younger members, nothing but horses, girls, gambling, insipid playboys, half centaurs.

The civil servant class, which actually also includes the literary coterie. But the latter cannot live by writing alone, cannot therefore quit the service. Yet as civil servants they can produce little if any in the nature of literature, lest their superiors suspect them of dereliction of duty.

The merchant class boasts of no real culture; it merely acquires certain objects and lionizes people for snobbish reasons. In this manner true culture makes slow progress.

About the "people on holiday and in the street" Bertuch wrote under date of February 26:

Over the escarpment, onto the ramparts, which are so thronged that traffic moves at a snail's pace. The ladies perspiring in their furs, many in stoles, white satin hats bedecked with flowers and large bows, medium-sized crowns, tall feathers, also black and yellow straw hats are much in evidence. English fashions are gaining no toehold at all. The spectators form a kind of defile. Dined at G.'s with Reichenbach, Conradi, and Peukert. At half past three walked with them through the Alser suburb to Hernals, not far from the Hernalser district line.[17] Really only a large village, Hernals has the appearance of a small town because of its 150 or so elegant residential houses and several factories. The name derives from the Als or Alsen brook that flows through the township, which, in the Middle Age, belonged to the Knights Templars, known as the "gentlemen of the Als," hence the name Hernals. . . .[18] Even today the Viennese make pilgrimages to the Holy Sepulcher and to Mount Calvary, which a Vienna burgher had had erected in 1714 at a cost of 80,000 gulden. . . . Countless pedestrians clog the roads to the site, where a tiny marketplace does a thriving business in knickknacks. The people are gleefully happy and chatter away until evening.

But Bertuch quickly discovered which of the arts and sciences was dearest to the heart of the Viennese:

From here to Sperl's, a fancy eatery with parquet dance floor, surrounded by private dining rooms. With great bonhomie, de-

[17] One of Vienna's twenty-one administrative districts.—Transl.
[18] The derivation makes sense only in the German original, through contraction of *Herren von der Als.*—Transl.

cent bourgeois women commingle with whores. The theaters stage all-night performances of comedies, ballets, and farces. All the world is in a frenzy, the servants receive liberal tips to go and have fun too, which usually is the theater, so passionately beloved by the Viennese.

Often the Congress was almost looked upon as a veritable school, serving to supply adult education to the Viennese of whatever class:

Overheard at the Pufendorfs' yesterday: "Vienna's people are getting highly educated now. Every artisan, every day laborer, every fruiteress is familiar with the stock market. Everybody knows exactly what the Congress is doing, when things are bogged down, when they progress. The Congress is a great medium of profit-taking due to price fluctuation of stocks."

But there were other voices, less lighthearted. Duke Karl August of Saxe-Weimar, Goethe's friend and now attending the Congress, improved the occasion by taking a keen interest in Vienna's cultural treasures. He wrote Goethe:

It is unbelievable how much treasure has been accumulated here from all branches of the arts and sciences and how many important people one meets here who are deadly serious about these matters. The archdukes head this group, but what is missing is a catalyst and the means for a more effective publicity.

In like manner, with emphasis on the "missing catalyst," a university official expressed his views to a confidant toward the end of the Congress:

A few days ago I happened to look up something in the university library. While there, I discoursed with the librarian, a churchman, who told me: "Both students and faculty members are dispirited because of the rise in the cost of living and the currency depreciation. The subsidies are of no avail and the professors are taking extra jobs to support wife and children in some decency. The students study less and with inattention. No one can make ends meet with the job he holds at the salary plus sub-sidy he gets. All the great works and the periodic publications, which should be procured but must be paid for in cold cash, are not bought, are not continued. The currency market does not permit it."

This report was of June, 1815. At this time the rate of ex-change, 290 in February, had jumped to 432. Here the course of the Congress seemed to have had a worsening effect. It was an entirely different mood in which Countess Lou Thürheim was lost in spring, 1815.

Summer was arriving. Everybody not tied to the city fled to the country, there amid nature to pray God to let our troops be victorious. We decided to spend the summer in a charming Swiss chalet near Baden which my sister Goëss had rented. As soon as our aunt Thürheim had left us to spend the summer with a friend, Countess Bonquoy, Constantina and Josephina, together with the good old Mèretout from whom we never separated, hur-ried to take possession of the house, where Isabella and I were to join them in a few days, following a visit to the Mniszeks. Our stay there this time was anything but gay, the timid Count Mniszek all but dying of fright over the war events. Serious and silent, foreseeing nothing but misfortune night and day, he took next to no food until the entry of Austrian troops in Naples and Murat's flight renewed his appetite and good spirits.

May 13, 1815: At last we four sisters are reunited in our charming country house. There is nothing more cheerful than our *salons*, nothing more comfortable than our bedrooms, noth-ing more lovely than the views from our windows and from the garden, the *Helenental* with its old ruins and pretty houses set in green meadows on the one side, on the other, over the top of trees growing at the bottom of our knoll, a sweeping view over the hamlets on the plains, the tilled fields and vineyards, in the distance the mountain range that separates Lower Austria from Styria. The balmy spring air, the verdant green, the scent of flowers, topped by the pleasure of our being together, the happy mood of our servants, the peace around us, the fine dinners, the wonderful walks, and, finally, my comfortable chaise—all this entrances us and promises us a glorious stay.

It was probably all a matter of applying Bertuch's views on Vienna's class system, for the "longing lingering look" that Countess Thürheim cast behind on society as it existed at the time of the Congress was most assuredly limited to the "upper nobility":

When I see today's irregular small faces, the expressionless, tired, or shriveled features of many ladies that are considered pretty in Vienna, or the gentlemen with their sickly colors, their burnt-out eyes and arrogant behavior, who try to fake manly energy by means of a martial moustache—when I consider that these ladies and gentlemen are supposed to be the offspring of that beautiful, vigorous generation I once knew, I ask myself the cause of this drastic change. Perhaps it is the prolonged peace that enfeebles the men and robs the women of their enthusiasm. Thus, perhaps, have impure desires marred the noble stamp of beauty.

It was this "upper nobility," also, that was the target of complaints heard often at the beginning of the Congress from foreigners, even those belonging to the nobility:

Count Rechberg, Baron Spän, Count Rossi, Princess Isenburg, as well as not a few of the lesser envoys to the Congress and a number of petitioners, complain about the lack of civility of Vienna's great houses, of which only a very few spent a penny on them, or opened their doors to them. Following their example, Metternich invites only the upper crust and the fashion fools.

On the opposite end of the class scale was found the "rabble," frequently referred to also as the Lumpenproletariat. *In his book* Traditionen zur Charakteristik Österreichs, *Friedrich Anton von Schönholz, probably the natural son of Court Councillor von Saar, enlarged on this:*

This is the secret of Austria's rulers: they know the forces they are dealing with, always act considerably, and in this they serve to set the example for the rich and the wellborn. For this reason the rabble always receive the leftovers of the fetes: the painted canvas used for backdrops, the scaffolding, the soiled draperies, the gilded decorations, and the like. On the eves of great court balls, the court confectioners put out huge bowls containing the remainders of lemons, oranges, pineapples, and shredded almonds for the poor to come and get. The imperial kitchens daily supply the needy with their surpluses. An old and admirable custom binds every court apothecary as well as kitchen chef to furnish medication and food to every really needy or ill person. . . .

The Vienna rabble is a decent sort of mob. While it is not given to be overly polite, neither has it any liking for the proletarian philosophy. It is innocent of envious malice against property owners, nor is it possessed of the impertinence that is so hateful to the educated. But one thing it feels entitled to: that the rich and wellborn "open up" a bit, let themselves "be seen," permit some "keyhole gazing," and do not destroy or "parsimoniously sit on" anything that he, the plebeian, might still need or find a better use for. Bread and circuses! During the monarchs' stay in London the comment is said to have been made that many families were reduced to poverty because of time-wasting gawking. This could not easily happen in Vienna, where the lives of the poor and social intercourse have long since become attuned to each other.

Schönholz also described the overall relationship of Vienna's populace toward the problems of the Congress. He spoke of the "opening chords of the Congress":

Few were the trades that did not find opportunity for a highly remunerative exploitation of the decorative frame into which this great historic tableau was to be set. The very first families elbowed each other for positions as ladies-in-waiting, chamberlains, or pages. Those able to sit a horse applied as equerries. Well-off people offered to don servants' garb only to be close to the wondrous events to come. Or else it was the golden snuff boxes and the monstrous tips that acted as incentives. . . .

An embroidered dress, a feathered hat; the taking part, preferably in a showy manner, in the festivities; a diplomat as lodger; a courtier as friend; and for every major event a ringside seat—this, and let Europe look after its own affairs as best it might.

The insatiable Viennese curiosity especially came into its own in the sequel. Schönholz:

In direct relation to the preparations also grew the milling crowd, the gawkers. As the imperial cooking facilities became enlarged, so did the crowd surrounding them. There a new saddlecloth was seen: hundreds pleaded for a view of only a corner. In the royal stables; in the Prater; in front of the palaces of princes, envoys, and magnates; before governmental offices and in the courtyards of the Imperial Palace: wherever a scaffold went up, equipment was carried in and out, a glass carriage washed, a rug beaten, the pushing crowd was sure to gather. Every tailor or paperhanger carrying a green roll under his arm swept a veritable avalanche of sightseers along with him.

The "alien tribal elements" haunt the Congress. Foremost, there are the Prussians, the cousins, the champions of national war. Göhausen, one of the more trustworthy of agents, had this to say about them:

The Prussian mission is not only the most numerous here, but, by simply observing Prince Hardenberg, undoubtedly the most active. Whereas Baron Frank and others are only casually drawn on by Metternich, Prussia strains every mental fiber to achieve first place. Then there is the whole Prussian retinue, eager here as everywhere to raise themselves, their mission, their king, their government above all others, to strive for comparisons with others so they may gloat over being considered first in wisdom, courage, and orderliness. They talk of nothing but their king, praising his special wisdom that enabled him to choose the right ministers who were able in such short period of peace to reorganize his badly battered lands. They comment on how the civil servants and the pensioners, who had been put on half-pay, were again receiving full pay, as several recent pay periods actually bear out. . . . One is surprised that the Prussian paper money, worse off than the Austrian in credit, had now recovered to the point where it nearly equaled the convention money.[19] By contrast, in Austria, a state ten times more powerful than Prussia, conditions were far worse, money being worthless and inflation getting worse each day.

Juxtaposed was mighty Russia, given short shrift:

The Russians couldn't possibly talk more impertinently if they were Napoleon at his best and were already masters of the world. Again they incite the Greeks by arousing in them hopes of a rebirth, just as they did in the case of Poland.

About the financially strong ally, England, the Geneva envoy Jean Gabriel Eynard, a banker, wrote in his diary:

It is passing strange how a nation that tolerates neither foreign fashions nor foreign manners at home so little adapts to the customs of the peoples whose hospitality they enjoy. This conceit is all the more out of place as it makes the British look foolish. It is a great pity to find this fault in a nation that in many other ways deserves respect.

And Eynard went on:

Everybody complains about the ingenuousness of the English. There is no incivility, no *faux pas* they do not commit which is less the result of intentional insult than of inexperience. These people, cut off from the Continent for twenty-five years, have become asocial, and their national pride prevents adaptation to others. Caught in a *faux pas,* they claim this to be the custom at home. On leave, they spend the day sightseeing in the city and its environs. In the evening they visit the few families that will receive them. Then they talk with ladies of easy virtue and get drunk on Hungarian wine. Gagern once played host to several British ministers in Layenburg and Baden.[20] They dined in

[19] Coined money whose precious metal content had been agreed on between several European states in 1753.—Transl.

[20] Two towns near Vienna.—Transl.

Baden. Several Englishmen were too drunk to walk to the carriage. All were in high good spirits.

It was quite natural that the interminable conversations, balls, and other fetes throw every good and bad trait into sharp relief. Yet it would be wrong to imagine the entertainment of the time as wild bacchanalias or great good fun. In the opinion of Count Nostitz:

The dancing is boring and completely changes Vienna. Before, everyone merrily floated along in a waltz, resting up only in the quadrille and the *écossaise*. Now it's almost all polonaise, danced by old ladies and their great gentlemen throughout the suites of rooms.

The representatives of academe or majesty had little to say in praise of the entertainment and the mania for entertainment. Said Wilhelm von Humboldt:

I am deadly tired of all this partying. There are more important things to do now.

And Emperor Franz:

If this goes on, I shall abdicate. I can't stand this life much longer.

The off-duty activities of certain highborn gentlemen in no uncertain manner aroused the ire of the police. On February 28, 1815, Baron Hager submitted this report to His Majesty the Emperor:

There is no hideaway in the city where they [meaning the Grand Duke of Baden, the Crown Prince of Hesse-Darmstadt, the Princes August of Prussia and Karl of Bavaria, and Prince Eugène de Beauharnais] do not hole up at all hours of day and night with the lowest of trollops. . . . A whole slew of gallant ladies, little or not at all heard of before, now are established in sumptuous apartments, earning much money and seducing other girls to the same trade for the ease of earning a good living. It is well known that in this type of entertainment our local cavaliers are not far behind the foreigners, setting the example for the lesser fry.

The following "Vienna General Survey" report separated the sheep from the goats:

Whereas the other princely personages, such as the Dukes of Coburg, of Weimar, and of Nassau, the Crown Princes of Bavaria and Württemberg, and the Hohenzollern princes are much respected for their probity, it is no secret that others, such as the Grand Duke of Baden, the Crown Prince of Darmstadt, August of Prussia, Karl of Bavaria, and Prince Eugène, are past masters of boisterousness. These gentlemen are in many ways compared to our imperial princes, much to the latter's advantage. It is said that among the archdukes there is none who does not at all times observe the most meticulous behavior, none who demeans the public order in any way, none who does not devote himself to some learned science, is not publicly honored and esteemed. This is the differentiation one hears made most often in public places and at parties where the other gentlemen often throw dignity to the winds.

Countess Lou Thürheim supplied some additional information:

The princes had selected a kind of temporary lodging where they would rest up during the few days of no festivities. Czar Alexander, the ardent admirer of the beautiful Gabriele Auersperg, visited at the house of his uncle, Prince Schwarzenberg, brother of the Field Marshal, spending every free evening there. Prussia's king normally concluded his day at the Finanz Hotel, where he also met his ladylove, Countess Julie Zichy, daughter-in-law of the Secretary of State. The Danish king had simpler tastes. With a face like his, he had to buy his love.

On the same subject Baroness Montet wrote in her memoirs:

His [the Danish king's] mistress was a blonde, pretty working girl for whom he rented a sumptuous apartment in the palace of Princess Paar. Arriving at the palace, the girl announced herself as the "Queen of Denmark." This so angered Princess Paar she denied the mistress entry to the apartment.

Further from the pen of Countess Thürheim:

The same was true of the Bavarian king. I never did find out where the King of Württemberg dragged his monstrous paunch, which was so enormous that a semicircular piece had to be cut from the dining table to permit the poor king to sit down to eat. The Crown Prince of Württemberg, much more agile than his father, pranced about in several salons, including that of my sister Goëss. He had asked to be introduced, following a masked ball at which I had long teased him from behind my domino. Despite his flirtatious ways, despite his proposed marriage to the Grand Duchess Catherine, he in the end regularly appeared in the *salon* of Princess Bagration, where he was a most welcome guest. The other princely young playboys also kept their own circle but routinely would gather once a week for supper at the home of Countess Molly Zichy-Ferraris, only daughter and heir of Count Ferraris, who not only had supplied her husband with a goodly fortune, but also with the second half of his name. Her house was a meeting place of the most important men and of such ladies as were in vogue at the moment. To be king alone was not enough to gain entrance to her salon, there had to be elegance as well. This forever excluded the fat King of Württemberg and the ugly King of the Danes. Countess Molly, blessed by nature with a minimum of brains but also with one of the longest noses, labored under the illusion of being a witty, elegant, influential, and piquant woman. It must be admitted, though, that despite her foolishness, her unimportance, despite her hips being where her waist should have been, hers was a talent born of exclusiveness that made her invitations the ones most eagerly sought after. This in time gave her the position of *doyenne* of Viennese society, a place she maintained for several years until, worn out, her son-in-law, Chancellor Metternich, one fine day gently removed her from the scene and put her out to well-earned pasture. Today, poor Molly, old, nearly blind, forgotten, exists on the alms of her children. She suffers her loneliness and misfortune in stoic silence, thereby proving her soul to be of greater capacity than her mind. . . . Her husband, the one they called "Mollo" and who died a captain in the Hungarian Guards, resembled his wife only in the matter of brains. The spouse of the most mundane, most affected woman in Vienna had the figure and manners of a porter. Mollo loyally assisted his wife in squandering their considerable fortune, if at other places and under different circumstances. To his many children, all of whom fortunately married money, he bequeathed only debts.

This, in an inflationary period, was even then the best means of maintaining status. Everybody, depending only on the degree of cleverness and lack of scruples, in one way or the other felt the effects of the rise in prices:

Already in June, 1814, the living cost had begun to spiral, caused in particular by the butchers who for no apparent reason increased their prices. Count Beroldingen, the Württemberg envoy, wrote home June 18 that veal had risen to 33 kreuzer a pound, a cord of good firewood to 50 gulden not including cartage, sawing, and splitting, a small three-room apartment in the city on the fourth or fifth floor at least 300 gulden annually. The Swiss Baron Müller, in an official report of June 8, calls the price rise artificially induced. Forstner, an official at the Ministry of Justice, verifies this in a letter to his brother of June 3, pointing out that the members of the butcher trade live a life of great luxury and opulence, have raised their prices arbitrarily, and are veritable leeches.

Eipeldauer also had something to contribute here:

And now everybody is speculating again with this Congress. Our dear shopkeepers are selling us kerchiefs and such so dear as if we all of us were deputies to the Congress, and because Congress is going to have a heap of washing to wash, soap's already gone up and so has the price of candles because of the more enlightenment that's now coming. . . . Well, well surely all this here is a mighty good prospectus and perhaps it'll all end up by the creditors having a Congress themselves if this goes on.

Real estate was the first to feel the price pinch. The "Vienna General Survey" of February 28, 1815, reported:

The month of September, 1814, was remarkable not only historically, but for Vienna's inhabitants as well. Each day brought new rumors and speculation about the impending arrival of the allied sovereigns and of the many important foreigners. Everything was at fever pitch: the curiosity, the love for all things foreign, the speculative spirit of the masses, the number of gawkers. People, who only just now had complained of being cramped, all at once found room to accommodate one or two foreigners for up to 300 gulden and more a month. This reached the point where yard-long lists of empty rooms and flats were being published because everybody, even the well-to-do, found the thought attractive to earn a whole year's interest and a bit more by letting a room for a few months. This led to the curious fact that, while the new arrivals initially moaned over the high rent (the innkeepers having set the pace by asking a daily rental of up to seven gulden for the poorest room), there was a surfeit rather than dearth of accommodations.

This, according to Eipeldauer, also hit the subtenants:

The ones that own sublets are just as patriotic as house-owners because they throw out their regular tenants to make way for foreigners—there's cases where a whole family will crawl into a cubbyhole so as the rest of the rooms can be used by the allies and they don't hold up the peace works nohow—there they often sit on top of one another like chickens on a roost . . . and the rent they ask for two or three rooms is a measly five—six hundred gulden or a thousand a month depending how close it is to the Imperial Palace—and all this they do for sheer love of the good cause.

This in no way depresses the appetite of either natives or visitors. On the contrary: it often seems as if gluttony is inversely proportional to the availability of food or the ease of its procurement:

Because now, hallelujah and God be praised, the massacring with people has been stopped for the nonce, now has begun a great war with the geese, ducklings, capons, pheasants, oxen, calves, lambs, wild pigs, stags, deer, and snipe, and there's been published a terrible conscription in the animal kingdom, and all that's flying, crawling, and swimming must walk the plank for peace—so that this here Congress that'll be for us people in Europe such great blessing and all, for all the dear livestock it's a great curse because often in any one battle thousands and thousands of the animals' homeguard must be killed. But the sellers of meat, of fowl, and of game get a much higher price for an animal carcass than for a human body, which in all of these wars never came to much more than six to seven kreuzers, when a capon or turkey comes to three to five gulden. Imagine what a stag or wild boar's life will fetch!

The winegrowers and wineshop keepers, swept along by the general feeling of joy and patriotism over the Congress, are beginning to knight their wines, which of course don't make them any less the poison they are, no more than a common man can deny his background no matter how high he goes up.

The bakers too have joined the parade and have come out with a Congress roll that costs a whole kreuzer, and now I always wear my glasses when I buy a sandwich so as the meat looks a bit bigger than they put in them.

But, Sir Cousin, what's the grandest of sights is the imperial kitchens. Just by looking in from outside it looks like you look into hell, the fire's so big. An ox could be roasted all at once and spits there are that have twenty-four geese or ducks on them and others with a dozen hares or twice times twelve capons or pheasants and so forth. . . . And then there are other kitchens where there's nothing but cutting and cleaning. Here you see a half-dozen boars' heads, there a score or two of leg of veal, or saddles of venison being larded or a fish six feet long cleaned, and altogether the cooks treat the poor animals like the devil treats the soul of the damned.

Like the benediction of a benevolent spirit, Archduke Johann's diary entry hovered over all these happenings:

Oh, if I might imbue everyone with my own feelings, then there would be peace in Europe for many years to come. Now is the time to forget, to forego greed and ambition. Humanity has cruelly suffered. It is time to heal its wounds. Mine is but a weak voice, but, as God is my witness, I shall speak wherever possible in a conciliatory vein. Not all ears are deaf to justice, nobility, and conscience.

The Gayer Side of the Congress

None of the visiting dignitaries needed to worry where to find pleasure. Vienna's joie de vivre, curiosity, and vanity provide a fertile soil not only for every kind of entertainment, but for those political plans that were to speed the work of the Congress as well. The Rhinelander Metternich had found in Vienna a suitable setting, in the city's enormous capacity for entertainment, the perfect arena for his statesman-cum-cavalier talents.

Court and people share in equal parts in the entertainment. Leopold I, great-great-grandfather of the current emperor, had been an excellent composer. His son, Charles VI, was an adept of the gigantic baroque opera. Emperor Franz used the court's entertainment functions to enhance his credit standing. The nobility was out to flaunt its wealth. The two imperial theaters, managed by a Count Pálffy-Erdöd, were court subsidized to the tune of 24,000 gulden annually. Roles were still assigned interchangeably: Nestroy, who later was to gain great fame as an actor and writer of farces, began by singing the role of Sarastro for years. The main competition for the state theaters came from the amateur playhouses, which no self-respecting noble family was likely to be without. In this, also, the imperial court led the way: Empress Maria Ludovica of the d'Este dynasty had followed in the footsteps of the Hapsburg ancestors. But those from abroad most often went for the popular type of amusement. Rahel

Varnhagen thought little of the acting talents at the imperial theaters. Like her, the gentlemen from north of the Main River, the Prussian king at their head, much preferred the suburban theaters, above all the one located in the Leopoldstadt. There your true Viennese felt at home; there your truly popular progeny of the Punch-and-Judy stripe could be seen; there everyone enjoyed the newly created "Staberl" [21] played by Ignaz Schuster, formerly a singer with the imperial orchestra. This was something new—Kotzebue's countless comedies could be admired just as well at home.

In the field of music the Vienna of the Congress was at once superior and more original. The novelty of a Beethoven symphony very often transcended the listeners' understanding even though it must be remembered that only the intervention of certain circles of the upper aristocracy, led by the Russian ambassador Razumovsky, who assured him of regular stipends, had made it possible for Beethoven to remain in Vienna.

But the Congress was principally entertained by those events that permitted spectator participation—in sharp contrast to our own times when the audience prefers to remain passive. In those days no effort was spared in order to take an active part. There was ballroom dancing, and the stately polonaise, lasting hours, would wind its mile-long way through the flights of suites of the hugest of palaces. There was acting out of tableaux vivants, or one tried one's skill at the tournament. Intrigues as well as gossipping and flirtation absorbed a certain amount of energy. And the people, being wined and dined, and dining and wining at their own feasts, performed prodigious masticatory and digestive feats.

Even the most malicious of mockers could not deny that there was always "something going on," that Congress was indeed in motion—so much in fact that all too soon a reaction set in and there was no end to complaints over the epidemic of festivities. Here, too, tiredness soon found its alibi in morality, and when even the specter of a revenant Napoleon loomed on the

[21] Central figure of the local Vienna farce, representing a petit bourgeois whose native mother wit conquers all situations.—Transl.

horizon, the voices multiplied that saw in the balls and the coach parades of the great not only frivolity but also political recklessness. Thus, when the Congress came to an end, so also did its pleasures. They had lasted long enough to assure this assemblage of the great ones of power and mind a unique place in the annals of history.

FETES AND FESTIVITIES

The festivities began even before the Congress opened. Emperor Franz I had returned to Vienna from the wars on June 16, 1814, following the signing of the Treaty of Paris. Friedrich von Schönholz wrote:

Tickets for a seat on the tiny reviewing platform—this part of the inevitable triumphal arch for the returning hero had turned out rather liliputian—were soon scalped at enormous prices. Those lucky enough, who through most excellent connections got hold of this priceless bit of paper, were fortunate indeed. The street decorations, of which the lighting alone came to nearly two million gulden; the paths strewn with flowers and fresh-cut grass; the hundred thousand strollers, all dressed to the nines; the Guards in their spanking new gala uniforms; everywhere freshness and ornaments and the trappings of amusement. As the vanguard swept past and Papa Franz on his chestnut charger, surrounded by an immense, glittering suite, approached the triumphal arch, his other, depressing return of 1809 in a lone carriage seemed but a bad dream. The contrast was heightened by the Emperor's appearance, for his swarthy color and his form-fitting, fashionably padded, Paris-made uniform lent an unaccustomed fullness and elegance to his figure, but otherwise he seemed much the same and acted quite his usual self: the same geniality, the same constrained joyfulness, the same admixture of dignity and modesty mirrored in his face.

Eipeldauer whetted his mockingbird beak on a minor aspect of the triumphal parade:

So I see kittycorner between the two customs houses a mighty tallish framework and I ask what's that big thing there for? So I hear they're building a triumphal gateway for the Emperor to go through . . . but it's placed in such a crazy way, is put so lopsided, that the monarch to go through it has to sidle like a crab so that his entrance into Vienna is really like a side-trance. . . . But then I did get a good look at my Emperor, in the midst of a whole squadron of officers galloping around him, throwing up the dust, and there he was sitting in his coach, the people's magnet, surrounded by his new Bohemian guard of nobles that's had the good luck never to leave his side all through the war to protect his holy person—now they really open the bellows and let go with a hip-hip-hurray for their good master and the windows of the palace like to have shattered.

But the grace, the friendliness, and the kindly smile with which he kept nodding and bowing to us, this, Sir Cousin, I cannot describe.

From the very opening day of the Congress the Viennese proved that amidst all the fanfare they have not lost their skill in fault-finding and criticizing. Herr Rosenbaum, Prince Ester-házy's agent and later the husband of Therese Marie Gassmann, the coloratura singer, kept a diary (to date unpublished) during the days of the Congress in which he minced no words:

September 23: performance at the Imperial Theater next to the Royal Palace. Everything brightly lit, the imperial box enlarged and draped in red velvet and gold, the entire court present. First the Dane, applause,—then the Swabian,[22] little clapping. At last, the imperial pair, great noise. She is in mourning, looks pale. Being close, I watch them carefully. They look bored. September 29: fete in the Prater. Entrance fee one gulden. Main thoroughfare, the monarchs' suite with German and Hungarian Guards, sixty coaches, most of them drawn by six horses. The bleachers for the fireworks enlarged by two sections. Cannon booms announce the arrival of the monarchs. Troop formation mediocre. . . . Deep mire makes walking difficult. The outdoor

[22] Meant is the fat King of Württemberg.—Transl.

illumination is rather poor because of the great variance in building heights. Only a few of the more prominent city landmarks
could be made out. . . . After supper we resumed our stroll.

*Initially, the Congress—and the festivities—had been planned
for the months of October and November only. Thus, the entertainment program is started with a rapid succession of a nearly
unbroken chain of imperial concerts, theater performances,
masked balls, royal hunts, military parades, court and private
balls, tournaments, carriage excursions, and coach parades . . . all
of it recorded by the office of the lord chamberlain. As early as
October 9, 1814, Talleyrand had reported to his king in Paris:*

Two whole days went by without a single conference: on one
there was a fete, on the other, a hunt.

*And Archduke Johann, on September 29, 1814, confided to
his diary:*

Nothing but visits and return visits. Eating, fireworks, public
illuminations. For eight or ten days I haven't been able to work
at all. What a life!

*Yes, what a life! Nobody is tightfisted. A masked ball at the
Imperial Palace on October 2 opened the round of fetes in thun-
dering full accord. Friedrich von Schönholz described it:*

The grand imperial masked ball attended by 12,000 guests
impressed me mostly by the colossal size of the rooms and the
huge crowds. Some 8,000 candles lit the two tremendous halls.
Every dais is draped in velvet, with red and gold the colors here,
silver and blue beyond.

A third, smaller, hall has been converted into an orange
grove. There are canopies for the rulers and the mighty. Everywhere there are floating buffets with the most delicious refreshments, but everywhere, too, the most murderous crush, for your
clever ticket collectors at the doors have resold these selfsame
tickets immediately after, and at a handsome profit, too. Rumor
has it that fully a quarter of the ten thousand silver tea spoons,
bearing the imperial crest, disappeared among the crowd.

*About the public entertainment in the Augarten four days
later we hear from de La Garde:*

Public festivals are Vienna's most glittering celebrations.
This particular one was the object of much general interest. I had
eagerly accepted an invitation of my illustrious guide, Prince de
Ligne and was at the door of his small house even before noon.
Soon after we were on our way to the Augarten, where the celebrations were to be held. The park is on the same Danube island as the Prater, which forms its northern boundary. It contains splendid shrubberies and trees, and broad avenues crisscross
it. Its palace, of simple elegance, was built under Joseph II who,
as an inscription proclaims, being the kind and wise ruler he was,
presented the edifice to the enjoyment of all the world.

A huge crowd milled around the beautiful place. The weather
was superb. The grandstands erected for the sovereigns and celebrities were filled with spectators of both sexes in glittering regalia.
Prince de Ligne preferred to mingle with the people.

Austrian war veterans, four hundred strong, had been invited to the show. Under the strains of a military band, they
passed in review before the grandstand of the rulers, then sat
under huge tents pitched for them. The rest of the day was spent
in playing all sorts of games. To start with, there were foot races,
followed by horse races, performed on small Oriental horses, similar to the Barbary horses that fiercely competed for the speed
record on the Corso's track in Rome. In the alfresco circus the
equestrian troup de Bach, rivals of Franconi and Astley of London, performed several numbers on foot and on horseback. In
the jousting court, young men attracted the visitor's eye through
gymnastics. On the lawn to the left of the palace a 100-foot mast
had been erected, at the top of which a huge bird spread its wings.
This provided the target for a group of Tyrol sharpshooters, who
exhibited their remarkable marksmanship with the crossbow.
The prize was a dainty vase of goldplated silver. The competition
for it was keen until at last the prize fell to a son of the famous
Andreas Hofer.[23]

[23] Austrian patriot from the Tyrol who was betrayed to and
executed by the French when he continued to fight Napoleon after the
Treaty of Schönbrunn, ceding the Tyrol to Italy.—Transl.

The final event was the releasing of a huge balloon, manned by an aeronaut who called himself Kraskowitz. Soon he was floating majestically over the heads of the crowd, waving flags of every nation. Higher and higher he rose until he could no longer distinguish individual features, only an amorphous mass, a nameless chaos. If our aeronaut high on his airy perch had felt moved to discourse on ascending and the dangers of falling, do you think he would have remembered Antony, Pompey, Napoleon, or the many other fallen stars? Hardly. In all likelihood he would have recalled the more natural fall of his colleague Pilâtre de Rozier that cost the latter his life.—An hour later our pilot made a very soft touchdown on the island of Lobau.

Now the games came to an end. Sixteen large tables were placed in a wide meadow around which the four hundred veterans sat down to eat an ample meal. The band, bedecked with warlike trophies and flags, regaled the company with martial music. In another section of the park four elegant tents had been put up in which Bohemians, Hungarians, Austrians, and Tyrolese performed national dances in the picturesque costumes of their countries.

The sovereigns meanwhile mingled, without a bodyguard, with the crowd, looked at everything, and condescendingly talked to the scarred soldiers. There was something very patriarchal in this, their mingling with the people who crowded around them.

As evening came, a hundred thousand lanterns lit the park in daytime brilliance. In front of the palace a most marvelous fireworks display took place, its main features being effigies of monuments standing in Milan, Berlin, and St. Petersburg. A tremendous crowd milled in the avenues of the park, but never was there any sign of disorder. There was a calmness, a sedateness, pervading the show of jollity as can be achieved only by the German character.

After the fireworks the monarchs strolled through the city streets, being greeted everywhere with unanimous acclamation. Then the court in a body went to the Kärntnertor theater, there to attend a performance of the *Zephyr and Flora* ballet. Every palace, hotel, and private dwelling was brilliantly illuminated, with many an edifying saying spelled out in light. The dances and the waltzes played by the orchestras never stopped throughout the night. The spectacle of happiness and splendor never broke off. Joy supreme possessed the masses, less a result of the festival than the hope of a lasting peace, bought with the incessant sacrifices of so many years.

The sharper pen of Herr von Schönholz described the somewhat smaller fancy-dress ball:

Four thousand guests were invited. But the actual attendance was half as much again because the tickets of admission, initially issued free of charge, soon fetched astronomical prices. The cost of attending was high to begin with, because those not in costume were required to appear in full dress: the ladies in white, light blue, or pink dresses, the gentlemen in blue or black tailcoats with white or blue breeches, silk stockings, dancing boots, and plumed hats, outfits that caused many an amusing contretemps with the doorkeepers. Opera hats had become so rare that their procurement was a problem. This is why up to the very beginning of the fete many valets and maids could be seen rushing around with plumed cocked hats and the hat shops were mobbed like bakeries in a famine. But the costume justified every expense, for it conferred the unique distinction of being one of the ocelli in the peacock train of the courtly assemblage. . . . Toward midnight the number of guests crowding the buffets had increased, as it had at the larger fete. Those in the rear grabbed for the food and drink over the bent backs of those in front, and behind both the broad and noisy phalanx of the waiters pushed forward to replenish their trays. A man in black court-dress, girt in dress sword, his powdered coiffure caught up in a dignified hairnet, hat under arm, betokened a ruler, thankful if only for a glass of water.

The anniversary of Leipzig's Battle-of-the-Nations was celebrated in a gigantic public festival, or rather a festival for the soldiery. Scene of the grandiose spectacle was the Prater. De La Garde gave an account of it:

At the appointed hour Tettenborn, with the punctuality of an Austrian cavalry officer, was at my door. It was a bright and mild October morn, this October 18, 1814. Soon we were galloping along the ramparts, recruiting several acquaintances on the way who, like us, were consumed by curiosity. Tettenborn wore his resplendent general's uniform, chest bedecked with numerous medals. Down at the Prater he had to leave us to join Czar Alexander's suite. Surrounded by my friends, I found a good spot from which to observe all details of this wonderful, majestically impressive fete. The war, this bloody struggle whose duration and bitterness had held the world in fear, was now ended. The "famed Colossus" had not been conquered but smothered by sheer numbers, and the delirium, the enthusiasm of success bespoke the very power of the antagonist, the unexpectedness of the triumph.

A number of infantry battalions and several cavalry regiments, among them Schwarzenberg's Lancers and the Cuirassiers of Grand Duke Constantine, were drawn up in a gigantic meadow in resplendent parade formation. The sovereigns arrived on horseback. The troops lined up in a double square, at the center of which a tent, or rather a temple, had been erected in honor of peace. Its columns were decorated with war trophies and standards that billowed in the breeze. The ground all around was strewn with flowers. An altar had been placed at the center of the tent, bedecked with rich draperies and filled with all the gold and silver pomp that the Catholic cult affords. Countless candles spread their light, dimmed by a brilliant sun's still brighter rays. Red damask carpets covered the altar steps.

Soon the state coach-and-four brought the empresses, queens, and archduchesses, who took their seats in velvet-covered armchairs. Then, when the entire illustrious assemblage, the military dignitaries, the courtiers, equerries, and pages, had taken their appointed place, Vienna's venerable archbishop, surrounded by his clergy, celebrated high mass. All of Vienna and its environs had come to witness this solemn spectacle.

At the moment of consecration an artillery salvo hailed the presence of the God of warriors. And as if on command all these princes, kings, generals, and soldiers knelt before Him who holds victory or defeat in the palm of his hand. A like feeling overcame the watching multitudes, which, to a man, uncovered and knelt in the dust. The cannons fell silent, and a solemn quiet followed their mighty roar. At last the servant of the Lord gave the sign of redemption and turned to the army for a general benediction. The service was over: the bowed figures straightened up again and the noise of weaponry filled the air once more. Then a choir started singing the "Peace Hymn" in the German language, accompanied by a large brass band. Soon, the whole army and all onlookers joined in the singing. No, never has human ear heard anything more awe-inspiring than these thousands of voices raised in joint praise of peace and the greater glory of the Almighty.

This magnificent hymn of thanks rose aloft amid the clouds of incense, under the cannons' roar, and the tolling of every churchbell. The sovereigns, surrounded by their resplendent staffs; this plethora of uniforms; this show of weapons, cuirasses, brazen cannons all aglitter in the sunlit air; the hoary-headed priests blessing the masses from the altar steps: this admixture of war and religion presented a rare tableau, such as the eye shall perhaps never again behold nor brush ever paint, a scene so poetic that it beggars all description.

Following the religious ceremony, the sovereigns and princesses moved to a knoll near the summer palace, there to take the review of the troops on parade. Grand Duke Constantine and other princes marched at the head of their regiments. There was cheering on all sides and fervent wishes for peace, a concern uppermost in the minds of all peoples. This festival had a very special character, furnishing, as it did, the keynote for all other festivities. The Austrian court did itself proud indeed in treating its illustrious guests to the most remarkable luxuries of its capital. Memory fails in recounting every brilliant detail, and the mind is incapable of describing the unheard-of pomp displayed.

The frugal Frenchman started right away to tote up the cost of the Congress:

To get an idea of the expenses incurred by the Viennese court, suffice it to state that the imperial table came to 50,000

gulden daily. There is royal dining indeed! Small wonder, therefore, that the overall cost of the five months of Congress festivities came to forty million francs. But how was the solemn task
facing this grand assembly, how was the seriousness of the situation to be compared to this carefree splurging on the heels of a
war that seemingly had drained dry all sources of wealth and of
joy?

If in addition to the expenses of the imperial court those of
the more than seven hundred delegates are added, an idea may
be formed of Vienna's tremendous requirements and the amount
of money and promissory notes in circulation. The influx of visitors was so great that everything, in particular firewood, became
unbelievably expensive. This forced the Austrian government to
grant its employees pay raises and other compensations.

*At the end of October the three monarchs traveled to
Ofen,*[24] *there to accept Hungary's homage. A confidential agent's
report described the entertainment program:*

21st: Emperor Franz arrives incognito and stays at the castle. 22nd: Czar Alexander with the Grand Duchess of Oldenburg and the King of Prussia arrive from Babolna in the afternoon. In the evening, a performance at the grand theater in
Pest. Both cities illuminated. 23rd: Big church parade in Pest's
new market square, get-together at the palace, in the evening
a full-dress ball at the Guild halls. 24th: In the morning military
maneuver near Pest, followed by grape picking on the Magareten-
insel and dinner. Ball at the royal palace in the evening. 25th:
Touring of the two cities,[25] grand concert, ball at Count Sándor's. 26th: Memorial service at the grave of the Archduchess
Alexandra Pavlovna, dinner in Bekescsaba, concert in the evening.
27th: Return trip, followed by a hunt.

*Further details were provided by the special confidant for
Hungary, Count Majláth:*

[24] The Buda part of the modern Budapest.—Transl.
[25] That is, Buda and Pest on opposite sides of the Danube.—
Transl.

Great satisfaction over the monarchs' wearing of Hungarian costumes. Everybody intoxicated with joy. . . . The Greeks, asked why they paid such scant honor to their (the Russian) emperor, replied he was no more their emperor than the King of Prussia was king of all Protestants. . . . The public's adoration of the Czar rose even higher when he danced with a commoner at the costume ball. Report has it that His Majesty, the Czar of all the Russias, immediately left Count Sándor's ball to dance all night with the daughter of an apothecary. As to how far the Czar has made headway with the Countess Orczy is indicated by this comment I overheard him whisper to her: "I am sorry not to have an opportunity for being conscience-struck but I hope to see you again in Vienna."

The upper aristocracy made every effort to keep up with the imperial court, though its members proceeded with caution and only after Metternich had set the example with a grand fete:

In the evening at nine, full-dress ball at Metternich's in his palace on Landstrasse. The entrance was done up charmingly, a tent formed the vestibule, the grand ballroom, impressive masks, everything contributed to a most enchanting fete. In attendance were the mighty of the Congress. The English ladies in Russian dress, Lady Castlereagh wearing her husband's Order of the Garter. Stewart, brother of Castlereagh. Prince Eugène in civilian attire. . . . Supper at two, a plentiful buffet spread.

Book publisher Bertuch described in his diary the masked ball at the Riding School of two days later:

Masked ball at Riding School in evening. Some 8,000 people. Following an admirable custom, the rulers for an hour and a half walked through the figures of the polonaise in the huge Riding hall. Not a leaf could drop to the ground, and to move was nearly as impossible as it was to get to the refreshments, even though huge amounts of lemonade, sweet almond juice, and ices had been supplied, only to be gobbled up by the ill-mannered lesser fry. Prince Eugène, in marshal's uniform (wearing the Order of the Golden Fleece, which attracted much attention), did not take part in the polonaise. The old Württemberger [26] as is normal, stayed only an hour. The English ladies noticeable for their coarse, hippy walk. Stewart, Castlereagh's brother, in the uniform of a Hussar. He is not well liked, has the reputation of a sot.

But now the time for the greatest spectacle of all, the so-called "carrousel," [27] was fast approaching:

Two events of vastly differing import kept the minds busy at the time: one was the fate of the kingdom of Saxony, the other the staging of a carrousel, a tournament that had been in the wind since the beginning of the Congress and which was to be held in the Imperial Riding School. Some perfunctory comments were exchanged over Saxony and the proposal to award it to Prussia as a matter of indemnity, but preparations for the tournament were discussed in the minutest detail. It was to be one of the most splendiferous fetes to be given by the imperial court. Every available detail of the carrousels under Louis XIV was studied in the full determination to surpass them in splendor.

Countess Edmond de Périgord, one of the twenty-four ladies on the planning committee, assured us the dresses to be chosen for this event would outstrip in elegance and luxury anything the Sun King's court ladies had ever heard about. "I do indeed believe," she said, "we shall wear every pearl and diamond to be found in Hungary, Bohemia, and Austria. There is not a relative or lady-friend of us twenty-four ladies whose jewelry box will not be looted and many an old family heirloom, not seen for a century, shall decorate dress or brow of one of us."

"As to the knights," young Count Woyna said, "their steeds' caparisons shall take the place of dress. They will execute their *pas* and minuets to put your most agile court cavalier to shame." There were endless talks about the colors of the several quadrilles and the probable skill of the individual champions. Mottoes were quoted whose meanings the ladies were at pains to decipher. The most excellent King of Saxony was completely forgotten.

[26] Meant is, of course, the fat King of Württemberg.—Transl.
[27] A tournament.—Transl.

At last the great day dawned—November 23, 1814:

The old romantic spirit came alive again. Today one is no longer the knight of the beautiful damsel, no longer forfends, lance in hand, the claims of her superior charms, no longer risks one's life for one of her self-embroidered scarfs. Love nowadays shuns all attention, has taken to the sidelines, is concerned mainly in wrapping itself in a shroud of mystery. . . . Prince de Ligne was kind enough to let me have a ticket that the Grand Marshal von Trauttmansdorff had sent him. At seven we proceeded to the Imperial Palace, where a number of officials, under orders of the Lord Chamberlain Count von Wurmbrand, directed the guests to their reserved seats. Curiosity had reached a point where fake admission tickets had been sold at very high prices and the Vienna police has been put to exert most detailed control.

The Imperial Riding School, built by Charles VI and later known as Carrousel Hall, had been readied for the occasion. This edifice, the nave of which approached in size that of an average church, is shaped like an elongated rectangle. A gallery, connecting with the Palace suites, runs the length and breadth of the hall. Seats in a sloping orchestra pit accommodate some 1,000 to 1,200 people. The gallery was broken up by twenty-four Corinthian columns that featured the shields, weapons, and mottoes of the twenty-four knights. Grandstands, richly bedraped, had been erected at both ends of the building. One was to accommodate the monarchs, empresses, queens, and ruling princes, the one opposing it, the ladies of the twenty-four paladins who were to prove them fairest among the fair. The band was placed above these grandstands and contained every musician of note in Vienna. . . .

Beneath the imperial box a ring game was in progress. Going at full tilt, the knights had to garner suspended rings with the lance. Roundabout the hall at set intervals were placed in effigy the turbaned heads of Turks and Moors on pikes, serving the knights, as it were, for target practice. There is no doubt that in this manner the German warrior's hate against his rapacious,

implacable enemies, the Turks, was once kept alive. To min-
imize the chances of accident, the arena was filled with fine sand
to a depth of six inches. A barrier at the admission gate marks
the entrance to the arena. Here are placed the heralds of arms
in their resplendent habiliments and bearing trumpets. Numerous candles in the chandeliers illuminate the hall to nearly daytime brilliance.

We sat between Field Marshal Wallmoden and Prince
Philipp of Hesse-Homburg. Near us stood Prince Nicolaus Esterházy in the uniform of a Hungarian Hussar, of which the rich
decoration alone is of the greatest interest and said to be valued
at one million pounds sterling. The front row of our galleries
was filled with the prettiest and choicest ladies of Viennese society: the Princesses Marie Esterházy, Waldstein, Lichtenstein,
Starhemberg, Colloredo, Metternich, and Schwarzenberg; the
Countesses Batthyány, Thürheim, and others. The galleries opposite gleamed with foreign ladies, the rearmost row containing
dignitaries and diplomatic excellencies from all countries, the
whole thing set in a frame of gold and diamonds, of uniforms
and court apparel bedecked with embroideries and medals. The
sparkling sameness was somewhat broken up by Cardinal Consalvi's red habiliment, as well as by the turban of the Pasha of
Vidin, the caftan of Maurojeni, and the calpac of Prince Manug,
Bey of Mirza, all of which served to lend variety to the incomparable pomp.

At eight on the dot the fanfare of the heralds of arms announced the arrival of the twenty-four ladies, who were escorted
by their gallant champions to their seats in the front row of their
special grandstand. Their gracefulness and beauty entitled each
and every one of them to the "Queens-of-Love" appellation conferred on them. They included the Princesses Paul Esterházy and
Marie Metternich and the Countesses de Périgord, Rzevuska,
Mariássy, and Sophie Zichy. It is impossible to imagine a more
enchanting, resplendent spectacle. The ladies were divided into
four quadrilles, set apart by the color of their dresses: smarag-
dine, carmoisin, blue, and black. Every dress was made of velvet,
trimmed with exquisite lace, and behung with precious stones.

The entire ensemble of their costumes had been meticulously copied from the sixteenth and seventeenth centuries. The quadrille that had chosen the green color wore the Hungarian national dress. This consisted of a long open tunic, held together from waist to knee by diamond brooches and revealing a white satin petticoat in the interstices between the brooches. The white satin and the diamonds stood in marvelous contrast to the dark green velvet. In the same manner was the upper part of the dress from waist to shoulder held together by similar clasps. The bodice was wide in front and covered with the most precious jewels. A broad sleevelike stole gracefully covered shoulder and upper arm. Beneath the stole there was another, puffed sleeve, like the bodice of white satin but embroidered in gold and studded with colorful gems. A small velvet toque, bestrewn with precious stones, served as headdress. A flowing, diaphanous, gold-brooched veil, fastened to their hair-do, fell to their feet and completely enveloped the ladies. The other quadrilles featured the Polish, Austrian, and French dress of the Louis XIII period. Pattern and form differed, but pomp and splendor were alike. One would imagine every treasure of the Austrian monarchy assembled here. The jewelry displayed was estimated at nearly thirty million francs. This included that of Princess Esterházy, née Thurn und Taxis, it alone being estimated at six million francs.

As soon as these "Queens-of-Love" with their angelic faces took their places, every eye fastened on them as they sat there immoveable in their long veils, awaiting their triumphal moment. Another fanfare announced the sovereigns' arrival. Everyone rose: the twenty-four ladies threw back their veils and stood revealed in their regal splendor. An ocean of applause commingled with the shouts of joy that had greeted the monarchs' entry.

The Austrian emperor took his seat center stage, at his sides the empresses, the sovereigns, and the ruling princes in their order of precedence. The gilded velvet-covered armchairs were refulgent in their embroidery. The Czar had been prevented by illness from attending. A few days later another tournament, a precise replica of the present one, was held in his honor.

As sovereigns and spectators resumed their seats, the strains of martial music swelled up and the twenty-four paladins entered the lists, representing the very flower of nobility. Most of them had earned their spurs in the late wars on other fields of battle. But though all of them could claim renown by deeds of valor or family lineage, they were no less remarkable for their pleasing appearance. It was said there had been veritable scenes of jealousy over the honor of participating in these old-fashioned jousts. The selection, tantamount to a diploma in grace and elegance, had at last fallen to the youngest and fairest. Among them were the Princes Anton Radziwill and Leopold of Saxe-Coburg, the Counts Vincent Esterházy and Fritz Woyna, Baron von Wargemont, the young Trauttmansdorff, son of the lord grand master of the horse, and the Princes Karl von Liechtenstein, Ludwig Széchenyi, and Louis Schönfeld. The knights' accouterments were exact copies of those of the Francis I period, when knighthood exploded once more into a resplendence never again to reappear. Like their ladies, they also had formed into four quadrilles of matching colors. The suit consisted of a velvet tunic, close-fitted at the waist, with wide sleeves and satin-trimmed color. The breastpiece was decorated with buttons and frogs; the trousers tight fitting; the half-length riding boots yellow, with gilded spurs; the gauntlets of like color, gold-embroidered; the broad-brimmed hat, wide-peaked in front with diamond brooch; the dress swords in diamond-studded scabbards. Each beautiful damsel had presented her knight with a wide, silken, gold-embroidered sash, which tied into a bow on the side opposite to the dress sword.

The paladins bestrode the most handsome Hungarian horses, noted for nimbleness and discipline. Beneath their rich caparisons the ebony skins of the steeds could scarce be seen. Each knight held a long lance, braced at the knee. Twenty-four grooms carried their banners before; thirty-six equerries in Spanish habiliments followed them, carrying their shields, emblems, and mottoes.

The pages and equerries lined both sides of the lists. The twenty-four paladins thereupon in teams of two rose in their stirrups and turned toward the monarchs, dipping their lances before the queens and empresses in token of respect and obedience. These acknowledged the homage with a graceful nod. Whereupon the knights turned in a body and rode to the other grandstand, there to honor their ladies with like signs of submission and reverence. The ladies rose to return the salutation and only now were the beauty of their mien, their graceful shape, the richness of their costumes fully exposed to everyone's admiring gaze. After two turns of the arena the paladins retired to await new signals.

Now the heralds blared forth an ear-splitting fanfare, answered by the orchestra in full chorus. The path was clear and the diverse games began that were to test the skills and the might of the contestants. Six knights, followed by their pages and equerries, appeared. The first joust began, the horses were put to the gallop, and each knight at full tilt speared the rings suspended before the imperial boxes. Three times each quadrille performed the pass until nearly all rings were gone and the knights' skill was reasonably proven.

Following these first games, the lances, decorated with the rings garnered, were turned over to the equerries and the second joust began. Each contestant armed himself with a short javelin, which he propelled with singular skill at the heads of the Saracens. The javelins were then retrieved at full gallop with barbed spears. Soon after, the combatants drew their sabers, leaned over their steed's neck, rushed at their immobile adversaries, took aim, and slashed at them in an attempt to sever the head at one blow. Finally, at full gallop, scimitar in hand, they cut a ribbon from which an apple was suspended, which, falling, must be split in midair. Prince Trauttmansdorff earned special plaudits in this event.

All the jousts performed by each quadrille were accompanied by martial music. The enthusiastic interest of the Queens-of-Love rewarded the paladins for their efforts and skills. Soon the scene changed, and a real skirmish was simulated. The knights wheeled in teams of four, horses at gallop, opposing sides trying to lift each other from the saddle, exactly as in the jousts of yore. Strict rules governed defense and attack, and as soon as a contestant put too much earnestness into play, the heralds of arms would intervene, break off the bout, with new knights entering the lists.

A near-fatal accident temporarily caused consternation among the royal assemblage: Prince von Liechtenstein had been thrown from his horse and, still unconscious, was carried from the arena. The fall might even have gone unnoticed in the general melee had not several ladies in the grandstand screamed in fright.

Following the last game, the entire cavalcade divided into two groups that, now commingled, now separate, now in lines of twelve, now in fronts of six or four, wheeled and pirouetted in movements as graceful as they were nimble of execution. For a finale the horses were put through a kind of dance to the rhythm of the music. Thunderous applause broke loose on all sides.

Again the paladins saluted the monarchs and their own ladies, once more with horses at walk circled the arena and retired in the same order of their appearance.

In the main hall a table with golden service had been set on a raised platform. This had been prepared for the royal guests of the Congress. To the left similar pomp reigned at another table for the princes, archdukes, heads of ruling houses, and the envoys of the major powers. A third table to the right accommodated the competing knights and their ladies. Other tables were set in the remainder of the hall and adjoining rooms, where the rest of the invited people were seated regardless of rank. The scent of flowers; the luxury of dress, whose glittering diamonds harmonized with the flowers' gentler color tones; the bright candlelight, reflected in the thousands of the chandeliers' prisms, inducing around them an iridescent halo; the golden fruit baskets passed around: a magnificent picture of pomp and circumstance. During the meal minstrels appeared, playing the harp and singing the praise of Lais in honor of beauty or Sirvente in praise of valor.

At the royal table the Austrian empress sat flanked by the kings of Prussia and Denmark. Emperor Franz' neighbors were Empress Elizabeth and the Grand Duchess of Oldenburg. A few chairs away sat the charming Duchess Maria of Weimar next to Prince William of Prussia. The ventricose King of Württemberg looked worried as usual; a large half-moon had been cut from the table to accommodate his fabulous paunch. It indeed appeared as if this ruler was out to put the human skin's stretchability to the test, whereas the Danish king served as an example of its shrinkability. But the latter's keen mind, his good humor, and his tact, all these excellent traits that would stamp even an ordinary man a remarkable person, added to the veneration in which this king was held. The open face of the admirable Maximilian of Bavaria reflected contentment and kindness.

Following the banquet, the guests proceeded to the ballroom, where more than three thousand persons were invited. All that held rank and name were assembled here. Though there was talk here and there of the fate of Naples, Sweden, or Poland, the dance strains of the waltz broke up the chill worries over politics. The quadrilles had been organized beforehand: in the center of the main ballroom was seen that of the twenty-four Queens-of-Love and their knights. The fete ended only at the break of dawn. A happy, unfettered confusion everywhere. This illustrious assemblage had been singularly privileged in having had joy as its guest, where so often boredom takes its seat next to etiquette and pomp.

A confidential agent's report had this to say about the jewelry worn at the tournament:

The foreigners are much astounded over yesterday's tournament, especially over the fortune in jewelries displayed by the ladies. The Prussians tell me: "My God, three campaigns could be fought with that." A Florentine banker said he knew something about jewelry, having seen much of it in Europe's larger cities. But, he added, he would be unable to come close in estimating this exhibition of pomp in Vienna! Even the Archduchess Catherine had been struck by the jewelry of the Austrian ladies. She commented to an English lady that she had not seen as many diamonds in London as in Vienna. Whereupon the lady answered, "That, dear lady, is because your riches come from our subsidies."

It was probably around this time that the amiably malicious Viennese society coined a new bon mot that served to mock the social whirl:

They say, "Prince Schwarzenberg now gives a tea dance twice a week. . . . The whole week is again crowded with fetes!" This indefinitely prolonged stay in Vienna of the foreign rulers leaves a bad impression in Vienna and in all of Germany. They say, "This is a new way to wage war: eat your enemy." Count Bernstorff and Count Rechberg are betting that the Congress will not adjourn until end of March.

But even the dignitaries from abroad, down to subordinate representatives of foreign powers, stood treat. The former English admiral, Sir Sidney Smith, once victor at Saint-Jean d'Acre, now champion of the anti-slavery movement, was noted for the singular originality of his parties:

Yesterday, as every Wednesday, Sidney Smith gave again an aftertheater party, at which appeared twice as many people as his two-room lodgings could hold. Following London custom, part of the guests use the servants' quarters or sit on the stairs.

But Sir Sidney by no means confined himself to these modest gatherings. His plans flew higher, but, since he himself lacked the necessary means, he organized a picnic in the Augarten park for charity's sake:

Sir Sidney Smith's negotiations about a picnic met with few difficulties. It was easier at a Viennese gathering, whose motto appeared to be to rob the have-nots for the benefit of the haves, to arrange for any kind of entertainment than to regain a throne. The purpose of this general invitation was a subscription, the proceeds of which, as stated in the invitation, would serve to purchase a huge silver candelabra for the Holy Sepulchre in Jerusalem. The admiral's own name headed the list. But it soon leaked out that Sidney Smith intended to use the sums he hoped to collect for ransoming Christian slaves from the Barbary coast. He already had submitted to the Congress a proposal to outfit a naval squadron for the purpose of eradicating the piratical states from the earth, to put a stop to their cruelties, and to destroy forever the abominable white slave traffic in Africa. Of course, none other than he himself would lead this anti-pirate force. But there were other matters to consider besides organizing a crusade, and this latter-day Peter-the-Hermit was forced to employ simpler means for ransoming the slaves. Hence the public entertainment that was to provide the money. Transplanting an Albionic custom to Vienna, he had seen in a dinner dance the road that was to lead him to his humanitarian goal.

Quite a number of tickets had been sold and a day chosen, with the Augarten park the locale of the fete. Herr Jann, the restaurateur, took over all the culinary details for this humanitarian feast. The price for the dinner was set at three Dutch ducats, that for the subsequent ball at ten gulden. Dinner was to be served at five, in the beautiful dining hall where once the courtiers of Maria Theresa and Joseph II had thronged.

The monarchs had accepted Smith's invitation and had, as a matter of fact, in great eagerness affixed their signatures. The upper ranks of the Congress, the ministers, generals, and envoys, likewise had opened their purses. Among the 150 guests were as many rulers as demi-sovereigns, warriors, and famous men. At close intervals horsemen were posted who announced each arrival of a monarch with trumpet blasts.

Jann had excelled himself. True, even though Bohemia, Hungary, and the Emperor's Austrian provinces had freely supplied their most choice products, one would have undoubtedly dined even better at the imperial court. But here was a feast such as to be had only at an inn and to be paid for by each guest himself, a novelty of such great charm that not one of the crowned, or yet to be crowned, heads would miss it. It was indeed a new and rare spectacle. Quite unbidden, memories came of some of those fetes where not long ago the kings had thronged around a victorious Napoleon. A few of those present mentioned this, though sotto voce.

During the first half of the banquet the orchestra had played the various national anthems. For the second half, the admiral, always mindful of British habits and customs, spared neither toasts nor speeches. The latter concerned the purpose of the gathering, of course. And, despite some longwindedness, no good Samaritan could possibly have preached deliverance of the slaves more unctuously than he. The fete's success must have flattered him greatly, several thousand ducats having been collected. The emperors each had subscribed a thousand, the rest according to their purse or humanitarian inclination.

Sidney Smith had finished his sermon; the plates were empty; the wines of Hungary, Rhine, and Italy had been tasted and praised according to their merits; the guests got ready to leave the table. But there, as right as rain, was Jann's waiter presenting, between two Haydn symphonies, on a golden salver to each guest the bill of three Dutch ducats as the price set for banquet, music, and illumination, to a total of 5,400 francs. . . . Jann's waiter had begun his collection, having already received his money from the Russian czar and the Danish king. Now it was the turn of His Bavarian Majesty, the most excellent and generally venerated King Maximilian Joseph, to whom the dauntless emissary of mine host presented his request by flashing the six ducats already received under his nose. Maximilian reached into one of his vest pockets, then into the other, then into those of his coat; he sought in vain. All pockets were as empty as in the days, of happy memory, when the then Prince Max found them ever empty and the Paris usurers refused to fill them. To make it short, without doubt the King, this paragon of kings, had already given his purse to some supplicant hand as he was wont to do in his native Munich, where no beggar ever pleaded in vain. A second pocket inspection followed the first, no less unsuccessful. All in vain His Majesty stretched his fingers, delving into the remotest recesses of his pockets; there was no evading it, he was without money. Put out completely, like a schoolboy caught in the act, the king sent a searching glance down the length of the table where, way down at the bottom, he espied his chamberlain, Count Karl von Rechberg. Sure of having found his rescuer, he was able to overcome his panic. But Rechberg, there at the King's cost and behest, was engaged in lively conversation with von Humboldt. Eager as any author, he was discussing his recently published great work on Russia, which assures him a prominent place among the literati. He did not notice his monarch's desperation and left all the latter's anxious looks and beckonings unanswered. In the meantime the flinty waiter stayed put and, advancing his plate, repeated his request for three ducats. Frantically, the king's eye traveled from the collector to Rechberg, from Rechberg to the collector. His torture reached the point where, with Richard III, he would have liked to shout: "Three ducats! Three ducats! A kingdom for three ducats!"

This comical scene, like an electric impulse, set off loud, irrepressible laughter around the table. God knows how His Bavarian Majesty would have solved the problem had not his neighbors finally felt obliged to end his misery. Prince Eugène had already risen to placate the waiter, whose loyal attempt to carry out his assigned task proved him a better collector than courtier. But Czar Alexander beat him to it: he beckoned the waiter, on whose plate he empties his purse, not without a loud and hearty laugh. Those present were nothing loath to follow his example. Meanwhile, good old Maximilian, still flushed with shame, conquered his embarrassment and laughed louder than anyone at an episode that may well have reminded him of his youth.

The meal concluded and paid for, the subscription list signed, too, everyone moved to the ballroom. Here, confusion reigned supreme, not, to be sure, as lively as at the fancy-dress ball and not as formal as at a court ball, but for this very reason perhaps the more pleasant to the casual observer. Few ladies of ranking families were found here, for these were already swamped with fetes. Instead, there were a great many simple middle-class ladies who hoped to dance the minuet or waltz with at least a "highness" or an ambassador. Unfortunately, nearly all had spoiled their normally fresh and sweet looks with tasteless hairdos. The elaborate coiffures they featured favored their lovely little faces not nearly as much as the classical gold-studded Phrygian cap would have done.

Hardly having entered the ballroom, the sovereigns retired

again, soon to be followed by most of the more illustrious guests. In vain the pretty bourgeoises waited for the highborn hand to lead them into the swirling waltz. Willy-nilly, they must needs relinquish their arms as usual to the newcomers. Nevertheless, they all strove to get their ten gulden's worth of admission fee, and even at daybreak few thought of leaving. The overall cost of the affair, dinner included, is said to have been only 15,000 gulden.

How short the distance from sophistication to ingenuousness and back again:

As we parted we promised each other to meet again at Princess Maria Esterházy's, who was to give a children's ball sometime soon. After the number of glittering affairs with which the sovereigns had entertained, such a fete, if only for its novelty, was sure to meet with lively and general interest. Thus it came about that the most charming *tableaux vivants* were to be seen in the Princess' salons. All young scions of the upper nobility had been asked. The crowned heads in Vienna, this time in the role of spectators, as well as the political and military celebrities, had shown up in numbers. As they amusedly watched the groups of children disport themselves in lively, ingenuous amusement, they seemed to unbend in complete relaxation. The arrangements were such that every suite of rooms in the palace offered a new surprise to the young guests. Sleight-of-hand artists there were, as well as magic lanterns and shadow plays and other amusements. As though they were her own children, Princess Maria was especially concerned over the entertainment of the very young. When the last drop of fun had been milked from the frolicsome pastimes, everyone proceeded to the great hall reserved for the ball. There the dances began, which, if lacking in routine, were nonetheless full of grace and poise. He who has ever witnessed a children's ball where the young dancers of both sexes parade in colorful costumes will have some idea of the utter charm of these quadrilles. The costumes, on whose splendor, as may be easily imagined, no effort had been spared— Turks, knights, Albanians, Neapolitans, figures from the Middle

Ages, from the era of Louis XIV, Russians, Poles, etc.—were worn by these lilliputian highnesses with a comical air of importance.

Yet it was easily noticeable that even amidst this host of little angels the demon of haughtiness had not failed to plant his tricky snares. One of the tiny female highnesses threw a tantrum over a playmate of lower station than herself. The altercation reached a point where it cast a shadow over the ball.

The arrival of some Tyrolese singers, then the rage in Vienna, interrupted the dancing. There were seven of them, five men and two women. All wore the picturesque dress of their mountain regions. They were engaged by the theater directors, the highest social circles had them at their dinner parties, and everywhere they met with unanimous praise. They had just completed a tour of part of Europe and had returned for the duration of the Congress to the scene of their former triumph.

Next, the children were led into another large room, hitherto kept locked. Here stood a large tree with golden branches, hung with all kinds of playthings and presents. These charming trinkets were raffled off in a lottery, setting off new squeals of delight.

Before retiring, the little ones danced one more waltz. The sovereigns and the whole court appeared to take the keenest part in these childlike amusements, in the face of so much innocent happiness perhaps forgetting for a moment the turmoil of their daily lives. Only Elizabeth, Empress of Russia, visibly was in a melancholy mood. It was obvious that the sight of so many children had renewed the sorrow over her own childlessness. The love she bore the Czar was so great that she smothered the daughter he had with Mme. Narishkin with kisses and caresses, even as if in this way she thought to dissemble the dual pain of wife and mother.

The ball came to an end, to live for a long time to come in the memories of these children, who would thankfully look back on this epoch of pomp and splendor. But the young mothers will recall it as an evening of triumph and happiness.

Once more the moment of fatigue was at hand:

Overheard at the Zichys': "Nothing has been decided about anything. Everything has to be started anew. On sleigh rides and at the interminable court and private parties I hear, amidst shoulder shrugging, the Italian drinking song: *Sempre è giorno di gala/ Si mangia, si beve, si balla. . . .*[28]

Time passed, winter was at hand. The air turned cold, snow fell, and a new type of entertainment began—sleigh riding:

The sleigh-ride party that the Austrian court wanted to hold had had to be postponed several times because of a series of untoward accidents. Several dates had been set, only to be changed when the weather turned unfavorable. Whenever a cold spell seemed to promise the hard, smooth surface required by this entertainment, a recurring thaw would soften the ground again. At last a heavy snowfall was followed by a biting frost. Once more, the imperial sleigh ride was announced with great fanfare. Already in the early morning hours of January 22, 1815, a great crowd milled in the Josephsplatz, where the sleighs were lined up. Nearly all were new, and those that were to carry the emperors and monarchs had the shape of light carriages, decorated with everything in the nature of splendor that taste could imagine and money buy. They sparkled in lively colors, with gold heightening the effect. The fringes and borders of the emerald velvet upholstery were set in gold as well. The harness, bearing the imperial crest, was behung with silver sleigh bells.

The accouterments of the other sleighs were no less elaborate. Silk, velvet, gold everywhere. All sleighs were pulled by thoroughbreds, caparisoned in tiger skins and rich furs and having ribbons and bows braided into their manes. Their fieriness, further inflamed by the tintinnabulation of the bells, could scarce be contained, so impatiently did they await the moment for dashing away into the distance with their light vehicles.

[28] Every day is a holiday/ One eats, one drinks, one dances. . . . —Transl.

Meantime, the invited guests had assembled at the castle, and at two o'clock the starting signal was given.

The illustrious gathering came forward and chose their seats. Each cavalier received a lady that fate had determined to be his companion for the ride. To the trumpets' fanfare the sleigh train started moving. In the vanguard rode a detachment of cavalry whose point consisted of the sergeants and the members of the billeting party. This was followed by a leviathan of a sled, pulled by six horses and containing a corps of trumpeters and drummers. Lord master-of-the-horse Trauttmansdorff with his horseman was next, to be immediately followed by the sleighs of the monarchs. The first contained the Austrian emperor, who escorted the pleasant Elizabeth, the Russian czarina. In the second sat Czar Alexander with Princess Gabriele de Auersperg, followed by the Danish king with the Grand Duchess of Saxe-Weimar, the King of Prussia with Countess Julie Zichy, and the Grand Duke of Baden with Countess Lazansky, chief lady-in-waiting. Twenty-four young pages in medieval dress and a squadron of the Hungarian Imperial Guard escorted the sleighs of the monarchs.

The Czarina was wrapped in a wide fur coat, trimmed in ermine and green silk. Her headdress was a cap of the same color, topped by a plume, set in diamonds such as was commonly worn by Catherine the Great. The other ladies were likewise protected against the cold by velvet-lined, richly colored fur coats. The one worn by the Grand Duchess of Weimar was rose-colored and also trimmed throughout in ermine, a fur that may be worn in Austria only by persons of imperial blood. After that came the rest of the sleighs, some thirty in number, containing the court notables and the most highborn of guests. In the city the horses were kept at a walk, giving the attentive crowd a chance to recognize and salute the highnesses as they passed by, before they flew off at a fast pace. The Archduke Palatine is escorting the Grand Duchess of Oldenburg, who is ensconced in a blue coat whose delicate hue favors her lovely face so well. He is followed by the Crown Prince of Württemberg, riding with Princess von Liechtenstein. Despite the beauty of his companion, his eyes were riveted on the sleigh that carried his heart's desire. He seemed to rail at a fate that teased him with half favors. Chance would have it that our "Queen," Countess Fuchs, should have been matched with Prince William of Prussia, Countess Mnisek-Lubomirska with Prince Leopold of Sicily, Countess Apponyi with Prince Eugène, Countess Sophia Zichy with the Crown Prince of Bavaria, Countess Esterházy with Archduke Charles, Countess Batthyány with Prince August of Prussia, Lady Castlereagh with Count Franz Zichy, Countess Vallutsev with Count Wrbna, and the beautiful Rosalie Rzewuska with the Duke of Saxe-Coburg. The toilets of all these ladies gleamed in their opulent elegance; the gentlemen to a man wore Polish long coats trimmed with expensive furs.

Next followed a squadron of horsemen wearing the imperial uniform. At the tail end of the train were several spare sleighs as well as another huge six-horse sled containing an orchestra in Turkish dress, offering martial airs. After the train had slowly wound its way through the streets of Vienna, the sleighs were put two abreast. The impatient horses, with reins shot, now dashed full tilt along the road to Schönbrunn.

Moments later the resplendent assemblage reached the meeting place. But since several of the delicate vehicles suffered damage, another halt was called at the monument of King John Sobieski,[29] dedicated to him in memory of Austria's liberation. The memorial consists of a tri-cornered pyramid, erected at the precise site where, during the siege of Vienna, had stood the tent of the Grand Vizier, Kara Mustafa. As the glittering train swept on again, a shout of admiration over such a rare sight of beauty went up.

The Austrian empress, the King and Queen of Bavaria, as well as several princesses in delicate health and fearful of the cold, had gone to Schönbrunn by coach. There, a grand fete, for which many invitations were issued, had been organized. The return journey was to be at night by torchlight. After the banquet for the sleigh riders, the imperial opera troupe was to put on the

[29] John III, King of Poland.—Transl.

beloved opera *Cinderella,* along with a specially written ballet. Prince Koslovski, Count von Witt, and I had gone to Schönbrunn betimes.

Skaters in elegant Nordic costumes pirouetted on the mirror-smooth ice of the Schönbrunn castle moat. Some, propelling themselves with a will, put their bodies through all kinds of contortions. Others drew make-believe sleighs representing swans with silver wings or light gondolas and containing beautiful women. Here and there gossamer tents appeared, resplendent in a variety of color. Groups of itinerant merchants, gliding over the ice as at a Dutch kermis, offered fortifying refreshment to the breathless participants. The ever-shifting scenery intensified life a hundredfold, the whole show looking like an original, kaleidoscopic painting. The sleighs of the highborn were drawn up into a circle; a multitude of servants, on foot and on horseback; the whole security force, barely able to keep back the curious mob that had come from the neighborhood and from Vienna to gawk. A young employee of the British embassy, Sir Edward W., member of London's Skaters Club and accustomed to charming Hyde Park strollers on the Serpentine, performed whirls, loops, and figure-eights with astonishing agility. An offspring of the knight who had etched Marie Antoinette's name in ice on the basin at Versailles, Sir Edward W. drew with his blades the letters of the queens and the other highborn ladies, who had left their sleighs to watch and applaud his skilled performance. Others, presumably less adept, cut their own bizarre figures: the zephyr leap, the chinoise, the garland, and the waltz. The latter was executed by two Dutch girls, dressed in the picturesque costume of a Zaandam milkmaid and earning loud and uniform praise for their presentation.

As for the banquet hall, it suffices to say that it looked its usual splendid best. But the splendors unfolded in the various salons were entrancing indeed. There were the rarest of plants from the imperial greenhouses. Myrtles and orange trees in blossom covered the stairs, arcades, and ballrooms. The charm of the decoration was further enhanced by its contrast with the intense cold outside. After the *Cinderella* performance, to which had been added several graceful ballets, the crowd pressed into the ballrooms, where the scent and variety of flowers reminded us of the halcyon days of summer. Later, several polonaises were danced.

The new year, 1815, started with a fifty percent raise in income tax. This caused no mean excitement among the onlookers of the sleigh-ride party:

At a private party that included some high-ranking foreigners it was stated for a fact that neither Alexander nor the Prussian king had approved of the sleigh ride. The King is said to have commented to Hardenberg: "In Berlin you too would not have believed that Metternich really had us come to Vienna to serve us up as public exhibits to the Viennese. . . ." While the élite personages were sightseeing in the city, I stopped in here and there and was not a little astonished repeatedly to hear the loud comment: "These they ride with our fifty percent and we must pay more each day!" The King of Prussia looked very unfriendly throughout the trip, hardly looking up once. The Duke of Weimar, alone of the sovereigns, availed himself of the sleigh-ride rights to a kiss from his lady; the others were too modest to demand like payment.

January was also the month of Metternich's grand fete. Countess Lou Thürheim wrote about it:

A few days later Metternich entertained court and city at his palace with a feast of peace, in contrast to the feast of victory. According to a set program, all ladies, beginning with the Empress, were to come in blue, with only a single floral garland of olive or oak leaves in their hair. The ballrooms and stairwells had been bedecked with the same symbols. Nothing more refreshing and pleasing could be imagined than this decorative motif, which was also in good taste, allegorically.

The Metternichs gave another ball, at which everyone appeared in the dress of the various crown lands. My sisters and I, as well as several lady friends, had selected to wear Upper Austrian peasant costumes, with dark bonnets and the colorful neckerchiefs over the black bodices. Admittedly, the costume had been a bit—idealized. At the quadrille we formed pairs together and our young, fresh faces looked pleasing enough under the bonnets. We were often pointed out, and Emperor Franz, noting the dress of one of his beloved provinces, smilingly said to us: "Ah, if here we haven't my stile hoppers!"—an allusion to the nickname for the Upper Austrian peasant women, especially those from the Salzkammergut,[30] who got the name because the many footpaths are lined by hedgerows and fences which here and there are crossed by means of small stiles.

The costume worn by Lady Castlereagh was much laughed at. Having invented her own Austrian national dress, she wore the costume of a vestal virgin, with her husband's Order of the Garter and its motto *Honi soit qui mal y pense* tied around her forehead.

De La Garde wrote about the first Metternich ball:

Despite the unusually severe cold, numerous guests had come, including, as usual, all of Europe's most prominent celebrities and the most exquisitely beautiful ladies. The Prince and Princess vied in doing the honors, exhibiting a certain coquettish grace that is rapidly wearing thin, for they thought they had gone the limit by opening the doors of the salons to the guests. And indeed, he who observed the attentive care the Prince bestowed on his guests must needs remember the enchanting manners with which he had only recently, at the beginning of his career, scintillated in Paris. If his star has risen greatly since, this has had no adverse effect on that urbanity which, to a favorite, is ever an excellent means of gilding the lily of good fortune.

On the grounds of the palace a grand dance pavilion had been erected, decorated with the same sumptuousness found everywhere. . . . Next morning there was sad news in the city: most of this dance pavillion had been destroyed by fire during the night.

But even the longest carnival must come to an end. Countess Thürheim on this subject:

[30] Famous Upper Austrian resort area that also contains ancient salt mines.—Transl.

Since the beginning of Lent one meets others, with the exception of the grand court galas, only in small coteries. Besides appearing at Molly Zichy's, the sovereigns also go to the house of Count Zichy, the Minister of Finance, whose four or five daughters are expert at receiving the illustrious guests with the most charmingly graceful manners. There's flirting, there's kissing, there's no standing on ceremony among the guests. In a word: the purest Arcadia, the prettiest shepherd's idyl. Recently, the Czar made a bet with Countess Flora Wrbna-Kageneck as to who could fastest change his dress from top to toe. Both contestants arrived in the most informal attire, and each party withdrew to a dressing room after solemnly promising not to cheat and to change completely down to underclothes. After ten and a half minutes the Countess reappeared in grand court attire, a minute later the Czar in gala uniform with orders and decorations. Later, it was said the Emperor had gallantly permitted his beautiful partner to be first so he could present her with an exquisite cashmere scarf, which he did. Others had the Czar win and were silent about the state of his partner's dress when he went to collect his bet.

THEATER AND CONCERTS

Even though visits to the theater did not by any means play the great role at the Congress that did balls and sleigh rides, the first public appearance of the monarchs, newly arrived in Vienna, occurred at the Imperial Theater (née opera) near the Kärntnertor on September 25, 1814. Umlauff's opera The Grenadier *was performed, also the* Zephyr *and* Flora *ballet by Duport, featuring the beauteous Bigottini. Though Eipeldauer says nothing about this performance, he does have something to say about the next day's doings at the Imperial Court Theater near the palace:*

Rightaway the day after when the two gentlemen kings have come, the monarch he takes them to his national court theater, where the court lodge was made bigger by three boxes and really fixed up properly with red velvet and gold borders and all. The whole triatrium was lit up brillingly with candles stuck in wall

holders and then they play a right funny little comedy titled
Which is the Bride?, because since these great gentlemen all day
long hear enough serious and often only too sad but anyway an-
noying stuff, they sure want to take their minds off things in the
theater and enjoy themselves and not hear all this aching and
groaning for a spell.

*Vienna at the time was more than ever the music capital
of the world. Not only was there a plethora of musical talent,
but there were more, and more generous, patrons there than elsewhere in Europe. Only the intervention of Archduke Rudolph,
the music-loving Hapsburg in clerical garb, of Prince Lobkowitz,
and the Russian Ambassador had prevented Beethoven, for financial reasons, from seeking employment at the court of King
Jerome in Kassel. Beethoven at the time was a highly contro-
versial figure—too loud, too forceful, too many-sided. Mozart,
also, did not by any means enjoy the fame that was to be his
later. Haydn was the uncontested ruler of the musical world.
Next to him, Salieri, Syrowetz, Czerny, and Wenzel Müller
were held in high esteem. In keeping with the grand scale of the
Congress, every effort was made to stage grandiose musical events.
No detailed records exist of the frightful "Evening of the Hundred Pianos," but about Handel's oratorio* Samson, *performed
October 16, 1814, there was a short entry in Archduke Johann's
diary:*

In the evening Handel's grand oratorio *Samson.* What noble
simplicity, what power yet melodiousness is there in this music!
Only Gluck and Mozart can follow in these footsteps.

The Austrian author Caroline Pichler wrote of this Samson *in
her* Memoirs of My Life:

The hall was nearly full and the string orchestra in their seats
as the mixed choir in stately ranks came down the gallery stairs,
all women in white, all men in black. The sopranos and altos
were first. They marched side by side, and, reaching the benches
assigned to them, the sopranos turned right and the altos left,
both taking their seats. They were followed by the black-garbed

men who similarly were divided into tenors and basses. This, we were later told, made a very fine picture. The court arrived shortly after everyone had been seated. The colorful procession of the many ruling heads arrived at the richly decorated boxes, the orchestra arose, and three times a storm of applause burst forth, reverberating throughout the hall, which was crammed with people; again a most moving moment. But it did the oratorio in. Since the court had been greeted with applause, this sign of approval could not afterward be accorded anyone or anything. Thus the most noble arias went unapplauded and, it seemed, unappreciated. This seeming slight cast a chilling pall over the artists. Enthusiasm and eagerness oozed away, and even I, who was only a member of the choir and certainly not entitled to any personal applause, felt with the rest the disheartening apparent apathy of the audience. This brought home to me the tremendous importance that the public's applause has for the performers whose very quality of performance is dependent on it. It is also true, however, that text and theme of the oratorio—Samson's death—despite the excellence of the entire composition and the profound expressiveness of the individual parts, did not quite suit the festive occasion.

A few weeks later, on November 29, the great Beethoven concert was held. Bertuch, the Weimar book dealer, wrote:

At twelve o'clock noon Beethoven's twice-postponed concert was held. First, a new symphony (seventh), noteworthy as much for its richness as for clarity and a most wonderful enrichment of the symphonic field. Second, a cantata whose text is very mediocre (*The Glorious Moment*). The music first class. . . . Third, *Wellington's Victory*, a daring musical character study, beginning with drummers' approach, the fanfares, *Rule Britannia*, the battle itself, battlefield firing that finally dies down to a single cannon shot. *God Save the King*. . . . Beethoven is excelling himself. The known world is too small for him; he strives for new horizons in his work. Both high and low are putty in his hands. The highest dignitaries are present: Czar Alexander, the

Czarina, both grand duchesses, the King of Prussia (who left after Part I), and the Prince of Sicily. The hall crowded.

As mentioned before, the keenest competitors of the public stages were the many amateur performances, of which those at court were the most carefully planned and also the most demanding. The first evening of the so-called tableaux vivants *occurred in December and, in variations, is repeated several times. As usual, Count de La Garde was present:*

A symphony, featuring horn and harp, preceded curtain time. All candles were extinguished to underscore the effect of the stage illumination. The first tableau depicted a scene, painted by a young Viennese artist: Louis XIV at the feet of La Vallière. The actors were young Count Trauttmansdorff, son of the lord master of the horse, and the charming Countess Zichy. Both were so handsome, the face of the Count reflected such tender love, that of the lovely Countess such bashfulness, surprise, and innocence, the illusion was perfect. The second tableau: Hippolytus defending himself before Theseus against Phaedra's accusation, after a beautiful composition by Guérin. Princess Yablonovska took the part of Minos' daughter, young Count Voyna that of Hippolytus. There was fiery passion at war with conscience in eyes and mien of the one; while the other's calm, antique demeanor, his reverent sorrow, seemed to call forth in his defense the very purity of his heart. Never, though stripped of the beautiful poetry of his verse, had Racine's meaning found more eloquent interpretation. The tableaux as portrayed by the most prominent people at court, the iridescently rich costumes, the excellent illumination, the entire artistic composition called forth the enthusiastic admiration of the audience. Unless one has seen it, it is impossible to visualize the charm of such a performance. The frozen positions of the actors heightened the effect, though several were so fatiguing they could be held for only a few minutes.

Next, the theater was readied for the romances that were to be acted out. Meanwhile, an orchestra, containing Europe's most famous virtuosos, played symphonies by Haydn and Mozart. The first romance was: "Parting for Syria," for which Hortense, Queen of Holland and sister of Eugène de Beauharnais, had composed the music, then popular in all Europe. Demoiselle Houbault, a young Belgian who combined a pretty face with a pleasant voice, sang the lyrics, while the Princess of Hesse-Philippsthal and young Count von Schönfeld acted out the theme. . . . I was not close enough to overhear what Alexander said to Prince Eugène, who sat near him next to the Bavarian king, his father-in-law. But it was obvious from the happy and appreciative look on Eugène's face that the Czar's praise for the musical composition had been accompanied by flattering and kind comments for his sister. The second romance was Coupigny's "A Young Troubadour Who Sings and Wages War," executed by Count Schönborn and Countess Mariássy. The third was again by Queen Hortense: "I Do What I Must, Come What May." The ballad was as beautifully sung as it was acted out by the beauteous Countess Zamoiska, daughter of Marshal Czartoryski, and young Prince Radziwill, again earning praise for the composer. . . .

The curtain had been lowered to set the stage for the final tableau, which was to put the crowning touch on the spectacle. This was no less than a picture of Mount Olympus with all its mythological godheads. No effort had been spared to make the execution measure up to the grandness of the conception, yet very nearly the whole idea came a cropper. Only suave diplomacy and intervention in high places assured the presence of all gods. Every role on Mount Olympus had been assigned. Prince Leopold of Saxe-Coburg, very handsome, drew Jupiter; Count Zichy, Mars. Only Apollo was missing. Count Wrbna was the only one in the group of troubadours who could have done justice to the role. It had been offered to him, and he had accepted. Yet, as excellently well as the count was suited for the role, he possessed something that ill fitted into the program: his upper lip sported a pretty moustache which he fancied greatly, as one fancies things that favor one. Now no one, neither on Olympus, nor in his

sun chariot, nor as a simple shepherd, has ever seen the god
of light wearing the distinctive hallmark of a hussar. The person
in charge of organizing the tableau called himself Omer, which
led to all kinds of witticisms. Omer was duly dispatched to open
negotiations with the young count concerning removal of the
ill-suited ornament. Despite his poetic name, Omer was scarce
listened to. Reasoning, flattering, cajoling, pleading: successively
they were all tried with the handsome young man, but in vain.
He was told that without him the announced tableau could not
be staged—useless. Inexorable like Achilles, who withdrew to
his tent, he seemed to have vowed to part with his moustache
only at the cost of his life. The rumor of this strange stubbornness
spread with the speed of bad news. There was much running
hither and yon, there is great unrest, there are councils, all other
festivities are forgotten, and the very Congress would have been
forgotten had anyone given any thought to a Congress being
held in the first place. The moustache dominated all conversation
and it spread general gloom.

In this hour of travail the very last straw was grabbed at:
the Empress was consulted. She joined the conspiracy with a
will and that very evening lured the recalcitrant young man into
her presence so that, conquered, or rather seduced, he disappeared
a moment, only to come back with an upper lip as white and
smooth as any girl's. The sacrifice had been consummated and
there was doubt no longer that Omer would successfully conclude
his Olympian task. At last the curtain rose: the godly congregation
stood revealed to the impatient eyes. The queen of the gods is
portrayed by the daughter of the admiral Sir Sidney; Venus by
Fräulein von Wilhelm, maid of honor of Princess Thurn und
Taxis; and Minerva by the beautiful Countess Rosalie Rzewuska.
But the enraptured eye soon left the iridescent beauty of the
whole to feast solely on Apollo, who exhibited himself in all his
splendor and who was well rewarded by a sweet smile from
high-born lips.

While the tableau was being shown, a young Frenchman,
Baron Thierry, attaché at the Portuguese legation, played a
harp solo. This young man had been educated in England, where

he had followed his parents into emigration. There he had mastered the instrument to a rare degree of virtuosity. Well-educated and interesting of face, he at the time was one of the most sought after foreigners in Vienna. His harp solo, master-fully executed, was an unmitigated success. Both royal and fair hands applauded. Even Mount Olympus was moved. At last the curtain was lowered amid loud bravos. The sovereigns arose and everyone moved to the neighboring hall, which was gaily bedecked for the ball.

CULT AND CULTURE

In Austria, Catholic domain that it was, music, social life, and religion existed in close proximity. Entertainment was accompa-nied by organ music, the militia stood at parade rest, and the Congress genuflected to the sound of music. Carl Bertuch described the Easter Eve procession:

At six to St. Stephan's from whose main portal the procession started; around the church paraded the magistrate, the archbishop, his top officials, and members of the militia. The dusk, the torches, the venerable old cathedral, the pealing of the bells—everything most solemn. There, the court; here, popular church ceremony. The entire court present in a body. In the evening recitation and music at the Kärntnertor. No theater as yet. The religious ceremonies serve the role of spectacle. The imperial coachman and the escort in Spanish dress, behind them the ranking courtiers on horseback. The horse of Trauttmansdorff covered with gold. The ministers riding in ordinary shoes. Every-thing solemnly beautiful. Alexander observed the scene from Wrede's balcony, where also had come Prince Eugène and the Dane. Ney's defection was confirmed. It is obvious that the nation was behind Napoleon.—Went to see Bach at noon; both of us drove to the Prater in the afternoon.

But everything that today is lumped under the generic terms of "culture" and "intellectualism" got short shrift at the Congress. Carl Bertuch, together with the famous book dealer Cotta

of Leipzig, raised the question. The Viennese newspaper Allgemeine Zeitung *of October 3, 1814, had this to say about the subject:*

Peace! Once again the merchant may entrust his wares to
ocean shipping without fear of piracy. Why is it then that solely
in the German-speaking countries war may still be waged with
impunity against authors and publishers by the pirates in the
book trade, who not only print what they please but enjoy the
law's protection to boot? According to Article Five of the Treaty
of Paris, the beneficent Congress assembled in Vienna is to
facilitate intercourse among nations. This end is not gained
solely by lifting the customs barriers on Europe's navigable
streams, but also by protecting all property rights of people living
in peace and harmony with one another. Now, experience has
clearly shown that writers are the salt of the earth. Pen has
vied jointly with sword to lift the tyrant's yoke from Germany.
The poet's patriotic songs and his battle hymns have inspired
the soldier to unheard-of feats of greatness. Now or never have
the writers earned the right to be protected against the gang of
robbers known as literary pirates. The German book dealers, more
than any other people, were treated most harshly by the usurper,
who hoped to subjugate all Europe under his iron-clad control.
Palm was executed; Perthes ostracized; Backer, publisher as well
as writer, thrown into jail for seventeen months.

*The two spokesmen of the German publishing trade ad-
dressed a petition to the Congress in which they stated:*

The undersigned authorized agents, D. H. Cotta and Carl
Bertuch, commissioned by Germany's most prominent book
dealers to assist the Congress in any way possible, now that
Germany is happily liberated, in injecting new life and better
organization into the all-important book trade, hereby respectfully
submit the following for consideration.

If the most urgent business at hand is Germany's internal
unity and its closing of ranks against all foreign nations, it is of
the utmost importance that the only means that enables the

various governments to learn of the true state of affairs in the safest and fastest manner possible, namely a free press, must be legally constituted and safeguarded. Freedom of the press, of paramount benefit to the nation, would additionally serve as a powerful incentive, by freely communicating all products of the mind to the public, to stimulate the mental processes thus set free. If, furthermore, the results of mental effort were safeguarded to the author through copyright laws, if the wise decree of His Royal Highness, the sovereign ruler of the United Netherlands, of September 22, 1814, could also be made to apply to book publishing and trading in Germany, then the German constitution would insure all benefits that a free press affords without fear of harmful consequences.

Culture? Protection for the fruits of the mind?—Monuments?

Yesterday, at court, Herr von Dalberg said: "It is a crying shame that Vienna has not yet erected a monument to Haydn; Paris would have done so a long time ago."

EXHIBITIONS AND SHOWS

At the outer fringe of this circle of entertainment were the firework shows, the merry-go-rounds and clowns, the gossips and market women, the cheap dance halls and brawls: Vienna on exhibition and exhibiting itself. The worthy Bertuch commented with the ingenuousness of an essentially serious-minded person:

At the Kärtner gate a new stand has been put up, where a man from Trieste exhibits a shark caught near that town, a monkey, and an owl.

But does not really everyone, the princes and the kings, the chancellors and the ladies, the dukes and the dandies play a "role" —in more than one sense? Society as theater, life a play—always watched, observed, observing oneself? The actors come onstage, they exit, the grand scene is over; even the Congress, as all things must, comes to an end. Farewell is forever partly dying. Here it is a scene from a play of cosmic scope:

The Prussian king has tipped Count Zichy's servants to the tune of two thousand gulden, Viennese currency. Leaving Karl Zichy, the King cried like a child. From the Czar, Zichy's servants got nothing. About the King, the following anecdote bears repeating: He met Countess Julie Zichy as the latter left church, prayerbook in hand. "You possess a beautiful book, beautful Countess," said the King. "It is yours, Your Majesty," answered the Countess. The King took the book home, where, leafing through it, he discovered it to be a present to the Countess by one of her lady friends and bearing the inscription: "I love you for all eternity. Love me likewise. N. N." To this, the King added a postscript: "I do as she did. I plead as she pled. Frederick William" and returned the book to its donor.

The Sorrows of the Congress

The very nature of an event as diverse and many-layered as was the Congress did not admit of sorrow—or at least refused to take notice of it. The sorrows of a being of a higher order were collective sorrows, were removed to a general sphere, where they reappeared under other names, supermundane, as uneasiness and misunderstanding, as unsureness and suspicions. Napoleon's return had been the worst of psychic shocks. But even this the Congress, as we have seen, took in its stride. Personal sorrows either occurred at the fringes or took on such spectacular coloration they seemed to belong to a different world. Accidents of all kinds happened as a matter of course, though, even if in the badly over-crowded Vienna of the time they were much less frequent or severe than those of today because of differing traffic conditions. Even the unregulated Danube, whose ice floes normally presented a danger, behaved like a lady that winter. The only catastrophes that kept recurring were the frequent fires of the day. Most prominent of all conflagrations was that which burned down the palace of the Russian Ambassador, Count, later Prince, Andreas Razumovsky, during the night of December 30–31, 1814. Friedrich von Schönholz vividly described the event:

Equally as famous as de Ligne, celebrated for his cosmopolitanism and wit, was Count Razumovsky, former Russian

Ambassador at the Austrian Imperial Court, who had bought his way into the favor of the Viennese. A piece of wasteland in the Landstrasse suburb had been converted at the command of his tremendous wealth into an Eden of a princely residence. Here, three palaces, each with elaborate servants' quarters, a riding school, court chapel, and horse stables, had been set in a gorgeous park that featured a tree-lined boulevard and a bridge across the Danube, open to the public. . . . No sooner had this Croesus put the finishing touches to the crowning glory of it all, to the "new Winterpalace," ready now to play host to the Congress in this setting of the rarest beauty, when all the beauty that years of effort and vast amounts of money had assembled went up in smoke on the eve of the grand opening. . . .

The hot-air heating system, newly imported from France, proved the undoing. One of the ducts concealed in the walls had become overheated by the huge fires maintained round the clock by the confectioners in preparation for the impending feast. This over-heated duct had first charred, then set fire to, a wooden beam. Thus, in all likelihood, the firebug had been busily gnawing away for several days in the victim's innards, even as the paperhangers were merrily bedecking the rooms with gilded tapestry and garlands. When, during the night of the fire, smoke began to seep into the center room, an attempt was made to hush up the fire, find its source, and put it out. And now, everything that must in such cases be at all cost avoided, happened; nothing that should have been speeded was done. No sooner did the draft hit the seat of fire, when the rich wainscoting, well soaked in oil, wax, and resin, burst into brilliant flames. Tapestries and draperies now became the fuses that carried the fire with lightning speed to the remotest corners of the palace. The valet was barely able to rescue the Count, already suffering from debilitation and kept alive mainly by means of stimulating spices.

Soon the flames leapt from the windows at several points, Vienna's watchtowers gave the alarm, fire-fighting equipment galloped to the scene, the military was alerted, messengers on horseback raced about, an affrighted citizenry converged from all sides on the site of conflagration, there to see a spectacle of truly heroic size. A whole army was already in action, the costly park enclosure had been partly demolished, and an engineer company was busily engaged in cutting down the rare shrubberies to permit access to the fire department from the garden side. At another point, mounted police pushed back the pressing crowd, cutting off small groups, driving these toward the pumps lined up before the palace's main entrance. Meanwhile, the crowd was swelled by ever new arrivals, more fire equipment kept reporting, more pumps, fresh troops, generals, friends of the Count, guests of the Congress on horseback, at last the princes, too—even the Czar came. Park and surrounding streets were awash with uniforms and plumed hats, helmets, bayonets, among which the gushing firehoses would discharge their contents skyward. Soon, there was not a window in the new palace that did not emit smoke or flames, the copper roof glowed a fiery red. This most valuable part of the Count's residence, with its priceless collections, its exclusive library, and all the other treasures, was hopelessly lost and now every effort was bent toward limiting the holocaust to this section of the palace.

An overeager corps of servants stubbornly remained in some of the rooms already afire, trying to save as much as possible. A valet was determined to save the Count's wardrobe, throwing dozens of vests, trousers, and coats, one after the other, from a second-story window into the park below, where they promptly disappeared in the deep mire created by the water and the milling crowd of horses and men. From other windows appeared expensively bound books, chandeliers, marble tabletops, alabaster vases, silverware, bric-a-brac, paintings, even clocks, wall mirrors, and an organ, all of which, as may be imagined, broke into a thousand pieces and were either carted away by the mob or sank into the muddy puddles. The fire raged with such ferocity that at eight in the morning the whole central portion of the main palace was an ocean of flames and all fire-fighting equipment could be completely withdrawn, to be assigned the task of preventing the spread of the conflagration. So abrupt had been the change wrought that at this time one found it difficult to recall how all had looked only yesterday. And but for the efficiency of Vienna's fire department, but for the thousands of skilled hands and the work of the well-trained and fearless engineers, this entire Samarkand would have fallen victim to the fire. It seemed unbelievable that this huge holocaust had been brought under control by nine o'clock. In the meantime, the Czar had inspected the scene of disaster, had received a report on actions taken, and had enjoined the city officials and heads of the military to employ the greatest of care. Then, having looked at the gruesome spectacle once more, he dismounted and asked to be taken to the unfortunate Count. He found him in a slightly elevated part of the park, sitting in a sable coat and velvet cap under a defoliated plane tree. His head was bent down and he was weeping bitterly over the terrible swiftness with which his creation had been erased. The bowed figure visibly moved the Czar, who touched his shoulder consolingly, only to withdraw his hand quickly when the Count, unable to rise, sought to kiss it. Here, also, the soil had become miry from water and the deep-cutting wheels of the fire apparatus. Some of the onlookers had the grace to make a duckwalk for the Czar from some boards supplied by the ruins of a nearby pavilion. Repeatedly, Alexander murmured his thanks and with an "Enough, enough" refused further solicitations. Thus walking to and fro on the boards, he observed the progress of the fire, commented on the turns it might take, and continuously consoled the Job on the bench: "This is truly a great misfortune, but we are all in God's hands.—This may happen to my knights' hall, also hot-air heated!—That's what we get for aping the French!" Then suddenly a cry of astonishment went up from the crowd, for on the dizzying heights of the red-hot roof two chimney sweeps, wrapped in steaming blankets, appeared. Some of the Count's officials had missed important papers and had offered a reward for their recovery. This had caused the two daredevils to shinny up an unobstructed chimney in order to descend another, already burning, but nearer the chancery. From where the Czar stood no one could explain the situation, and Alexander immediately dispatched an officer to stop the senseless undertaking. But before this minion had reached the palace, or the sweeps their other chimney, the copper sheeting of the roof tore asunder with a thunderous roar—curling ridgeward and allowing the flames to shoot skyward—plunging the two sweeps like moths to their fiery deaths. This catastrophe inaugurated the final act of the drama. With the lid blown off, the fire was free now to do its worst and, in doing so, consume itself. For eight days smoke rose from the ruins, and eight days were needed to cart away the ruined treasures, which now became sad relics in the basement and garret hovels of the "poor devils." To Count Razumovsky, drained now to the very core of his soul, came a token of his master's sympathy in the form of a princely title.

The train was long that moved these representatives of the world from feudalism into the modern age: emperors; kings and princes; statesmen and politicians; preachers, romantics, and dreamers; generals and field marshals; inventors, swindlers, beautiful women; great ladies and courtesans. Each of them lay arrogant claim to perfection. Nor did this prideful boast stop at that most irrevocable of all losses—death itself. As if a great theatrical producer had taken it upon himself to choose the most convincing of all symbolic figures for this role, the dying Prince de Ligne moved center stage. Field Marshal de Ligne, servant of Empress Catherine and three emperors, nearly eighty, tall of figure and unbowed, a cosmopolitan, a martial man and an epicure, waster of an enormous fortune and now reduced to two small establishments, pushed aside by the official heads of the Congress, yet sorely missed once gone, coiner of all the best bon mots about the Congress except the one that said: "Let me show these kings how a field marshal dies." No, this prince, often jolting to Schönbrunn in a shabby, mid-eighteenth-century coach, on both doors of which was the family crest with Egmont's helmet—a coach drawn by two equally shabby white horses, the coachman a hoary, huge Turk, who was the present of Prince Potemkin,—this object of annoyance and of absurdity, revered and mocked like Don Quixote, this man loved life and love, loved the Congress, and could still be found on the windy

*parapet with windy ladies in blustery December. He loved life
but hated death, whom he called Old Buttonnose. And it was on
this parapet, attending his last amorous rendezvous, that he caught
his mortal illness. His protégé, Count de La Garde, reports on
this:*

At his bedside I found Dr. Malfatti, who scolded the prince
for his carelessness during the past two nights, a carelessness
that might have dire consequences. Since morning an acute
erysipelas had set in and the patient had weakened greatly. His
daughter, Countess Pálffy, entered to bring him his medicine. We
left him. . . . Next morning at eight I saw him again, together
with Griffith. We found him depressed. The premonition of
impending death made him melancholy. "I know it," he told us,
"it is nature's way. We must leave our appointed place in the
world to make room for others . . . only, leaving all those one
loves, oh, this is what makes dying so painful." All day there
were inquiries about his condition. The rumor of his illness
had spread among all classes, there was general anxiety, a crowd
took up a steady vigil outside his house. . . . During the second
to the third night his condition worsened rapidly. His family stood
by his bedside in despair. Around eleven Malfatti entered. "I do
not mean," the patient told him, "to make much ado in dying,
for, indeed, the uncertainty and shortness of our days are not
worth the wait." And he made an effort to smile, but suddenly
he sank back in a way that frightened us. When he had recovered
a little he said: "Oh, I feel it, the soul has worn out its outer
garment. I no longer have the strength to live. . . . But I still
have strength to love you." With these words all his children
sank down on his bed, kissing his hands and covering them with
tears.

The doctor urged him to take a draft that was to give him
several hours of peaceful sleep. When he awoke he was his old
happy self again. The thought of death seemed to have receded
completely. He even began to joke. "Malfatti, Old Buttonnose's
messenger," he said to us, "has announced that she [31] may well

[31] Referring to Old Buttonnose, which is feminine in German.—
Transl.

come visit me tonight. But, if you please, none of your gallantry now. I, who seldom missed a rendezvous, aim to avoid this one all the same. . . . Like Hadrian, I shall yet wait awhile to write those verses to my soul, poised for flight." A taper burned on a stand near the window. "My friend," he told his valet, "do not put out this light. They might see it on the ramparts promenade, take it for a beacon, and assume that I am dead." Turning back to us, he said, "As I mentioned before, the faculty of perception has its application. For the time being the idlers on the parapet need not yet concern themselves with my death. But just to keep the ball bouncing before the real game begins, they prate that the Czarina is pregnant." [32] He continued to talk to us in like vein and mentioned the trips he planned to take in the spring and the labors he meant yet to complete. But, alas, we did not share this confidence in the least. The inroads of the illness were all too obvious, there was no hope, and Malfatti, in leaving, had said: "There is grave danger."

Around midnight the doctor's fears proved only too real. A relapse was followed by complete exhaustion. Then the sick man raised himself up in the position of a person ready to give battle, his wide-open eyes shone with a strange luminosity, and in a wildly excited state he began to scream: "Lock the door . . . out with you . . . there she comes! Throw her out, the Buttonnose . . . the vile thing. . . ." Next, he seemed with all his remaining strength to struggle against death, to repel its embrace, uttering the while broken words and calling on us for help. Petrified in pain and sorrow, we only answered with sighs. This last effort drained him completely: he sank back in a coma. An hour later his soul was in flight. It was Tuesday, December 13, 1814, past ten in the morning.

Rosenbaum, Esterházy's agent, reported on a scene occurring shortly after de Ligne's demise:

I was able to get in and view the body. It lay on the third floor, in the second room to the right. . . . Then I was shown

---

[32] Who, it will be recalled, desperately wanted children but never had any.—Transl.

the room de Ligne died in. Everything poorly appointed and mindful of a Don Ranudo di Colibrados. The room, like most, is hung with spotted light-blue silk drapery, full of etchings, mostly unframed portraits fastened with pins to the walls, but also a great many addresses, books, his bed, a kind of divan, the mattress torn and bloody. Yet, the overall impression interesting and bearing the imprint of genius. . . . In the small antechamber a number of hangers-on, officers, and castle guards who mourn him deeply. He was laid out in a white coffin which was put into an oaken casket, sealed twice and then, according to his own instructions, taken to the Kahlenberg. The solemn burial took place at twelve midnight, December 15. Twenty-four cannons, surrounded by prominent citizens, lined the way. Grenadiers of his regiment were the pallbearers, others carried torches and his decorations. Buried at imperial expense. All field marshals, Schwarzenberg, Württemberg, also Marshal Wrede, Lord Stewart heading the procession, which lasted a full hour.

CULT OF THE DEAD

About a month later, to commemorate someone long since dead, the French chief delegate, Prince Talleyrand, moved that a requiem mass be held for Louis XVI, guillotined January 21, 1793. Emperor Franz did not only readily acquiesce in the proposal to so honor his uncle by marriage, he even offered to defray all expenses from his own pocket. Already on January 4, Talleyrand had reported to his current master, Louis XVIII, brother of the departed, about the matter:

On January 21, anniversary of a day of terror and eternal sorrow, there will be a service of atonement held in one of Vienna's first churches. I am issuing the necessary instructions. In doing so, I not only follow my own heart's desire, but am of the opinion that Your Majesty's ambassadors, as living symbols, must do all to exhibit France's sorrow on foreign soil and before the eyes of an assembled Europe. Everything about this solemn ceremony must reflect the grandeur of the occasion

and of that of the French crown, as well as that of the participants. . . . All of the noblest personages of both sexes presently
in Vienna will deem it a duty to attend. I do not as yet know
the cost, but it is a necessary expense.

*Fourteen days later, Talleyrand, the reformed regicide, again
wrote his master:*

Preparations for the ceremony of January 21 are nearly
completed. The eagerness to attend is such that it will be difficult
to accommodate all, and St. Stephan's, largest of Vienna's
churches, is not big enough to admit everybody wanting to
come. . . . Each woman will wear a veil, sign of deepest
mourning.

De La Garde described the ceremony:

Isabey and Moreau were charged with devising and executing
the overall design. In line with the Emperor's wishes, they spared
none of the pomp and circumstance of a royal funeral. In the
center of the old cathedral, to a height of sixty feet, arose a
huge canopy that bore the attributes of kingship. Four gigantic
statues, one at each corner of the cenotaph, symbolized a weeping
France; a commiserating Europe; Hope, leading the virtuous
monarch's soul into the mansion of immortality; and Religion,
bearing in hand Louis' last will, noble example of love and forgiveness. The entire nave was hung with immense folds of black
drapery, richly embroidered with silver. Each pillar bore the
Bourbon crest. Countless candles and tapers brilliantly illuminated
this somber vault that is sealed off from all daylight. A dais had
been erected for the monarchs, lined with velvet, the black of
which set off the silver tassels to even greater advantage. The
nave and choir were reserved for the specially invited, the rest
was open to the public.

Long before the ceremonious rites began, the Gothic
cathedral was thronged with people. All Frenchmen of whatever rank who were present in Vienna had been asked to attend;
all without exception had come. The Knights of the Golden
Fleece and the envoys in their official regalia sat up front in
the choir. Behind them crowded the notables, the renowned

guests, and Viennese city officials. A detachment, composed of the guards regiments and the Hungarian Guard of Nobles, as at imperial funerals, was stationed around the catafalque. Emperor Franz had thus wanted to underscore his sympathy. In the nave were assembled quite a number of ladies, all dressed in black and wearing flowing veils, to which the customary flowers, diamonds, and glittering jewelry had had temporarily to yield first place.

At eleven the tolling of bells announced the arrival of Emperor Franz, the Czar, the kings of Prussia, Bavaria, and Denmark, of the queens, and of the Czarina. Only the Austrian empress had not come, her health being poor. Prince Leopold of Sicily, sole member of the Bourbon family, and M. de la Tour du Pin, French Ambassador, received the monarchs in the outer courtyard and conducted them to the imperial dais. The service began immediately after, held, despite his eighty-four years, by the venerable Archbishop of Vienna, Prince von Hohenwarth. M. Zaignelins, French by birth and priest at the St. Anna church in Vienna, gave a spirited sermon in French, which, some claimed, Talleyrand had helped compose. Its theme was: "The earth shall learn to hold the Lord's name in awe." First, he called attention to the power and glory of the fourteen-hundred-year-old French monarchy. Next, he described the sudden dramatic turning point of the Revolution, which, in three years' time, had totally destroyed the ancient edifice. In this terrible misadventure he professed to see the finger of God, "who erects and tears down the thrones." After exhorting all present to pious prayer for Louis XVI and Marie Antoinette of Austria, he spoke at length on the more noble passages of that Last Will which has been so aptly called the most heroic law book of love. All were in tears when M. Zaignalins descended the pulpit. After this, a choir of 250 voices sang a requiem composed by Neukomm, student of Haydn. Another choir, composed of art lovers and conducted by the imperial choir leader Salieri, supported the first to great effect. Listened to in deeply meditative mood, this hymn of sorrow seemed less a prayer for the unfortunate victim than a joining in those noble words of forgiveness just heard.

The costs of these obsequies came to about a hundred thousand gulden and were entirely defrayed by the Imperial Court. By explicit orders of the Emperor there was no entertainment on this day. In the evening Talleyrand's salons were thronged by an unusually large crowd.

The newspapers of the day were servile. In a report of a fatal accident it was not the victim, but a highly placed person connected with it, who got prime space. The wars which are now to be ended have gobbled up whole regiments. The first civil accident took one single person's life. In June, 1815, a few days before news of the final victory at Waterloo arrived, we read in the Österreichischer Beobachter:

A sad event occurred in Baden [33] on Thursday, the fifteenth of this month. After much trouble, a steel bridge, spanning the often perilously swollen Schwechat brook in Baden, had just been completed with the financial aid of a group of frequenters of the spa. There was to be a ceremonious opening on the fifteenth. Everyone was in solemn mood as His Royal Highness, Archduke Anton, patron saint of the spa, arrived at a tent erected near the bridge. Here he was welcomed, together with several others, and conducted across the still barricaded bridge by the assembled high dignitaries to a waiting coach on the far side. A crowd of people streamed after the Duke and his entourage, awaiting on the bridge the crossing of the Duke's coach, which quite accidentally was held up for a few moments. When some three hundred persons had crowded onto it, the bridge collapsed with a roar into the river bed below. The scene of horror that ensued is easy to imagine! Those who went down with the structure suffered multiple injuries. Only one person died, more of fright than from injuries received. Twenty-two were severely wounded, the number of those sustaining lighter hurts stands at forty-two at the present count. Prime cause of the accident is the fact that the bridge was not designed for such heavy loads. It may be assumed, however, that the bridge was also structurally and materially unsound.

[33] A small resort town and watering-place near Vienna.—Transl.

Herodotus: Headquarters of the Secret Police

He who would know something about the mechanism of the Congress or about those moving its levers, was forced to turn to one of the many confidants and try to lure some of his secrets from him, a far from easy task. If successful, the results were likely to be meager, which is why descriptive accounts as, for example, that of Count de La Garde deal strictly in superficialities—in gossip and conjecture and unimportant details. The reports themselves, the intercepted letters and resurrected papers, went to the Minister of Police, Franz von Hager, Baron of Altensteig, who, in his turn, would submit them daily to His Majesty, Emperor Franz. Let us cast a glance at this complicated journalistic-historical innovation.

The basis for this veritable Herodotean reporting was laid years ago. First, there was the need for information gathering. Next came surveillance. Then, close examination, interception, and digestion. Finally: evaluation. First, the observation; then, the report; then, the pouncing hand. The influx of a hundred thousand foreigners necessitated sifting and specialization, of course. In January, 1815, the persons under special police control numbered over thirty and included all Russian politicians; Stein and Hardenberg—Prussia, that is; then the Bavarian Count Rechberg and Württemberg's Baron Linden; the Swede Löwen-

hjelm, the Dane Bernstorff, and the French plenipotentiaries (Talleyrand, Dalberg, Count de la Tour du Pin, and Alexis de Noailles); Prince Beauharnais, the Spaniards, and the Italians. The police apparatus, fed by the compulsory data required of new arrivals, the postal surveillance, and the services of inn-keepers and landlords, was, in addition to Minister Hager, composed of numerous court and police officials who, under Vienna's Chief of Police, Siber, worked in the central headquarters. The legwork was done by an army of confidants, servants, coachmen, firestokers, scullions, lady's maids, messenger boys, and waiters. A level above them in repute, rank, and remuneration were the aforementioned "trusted members of the upper class." Foremost among these were these confidants:

Agent ***. He had access to Vienna's highest level of society. Nowhere in the files is his name mentioned. The Police Minister addressed him as "Your Highness" and he was called upon for advice by the authorities in the matter of Baron Wessenberg, second Austrian delegate. He was a long-time friend and confidant of Count Solms-Laubach. Every day Hager received from *** a usually detailed report on court fetes, intimate conversations, etc. Allegedly, he was a certain Count Frederick T. He demanded a good price for his services: five hundred to one thousand Austrian gulden monthly.

Others included: C - - i, the poet Abbé Giuseppi Carpani, intimate member of the circle around Beatrix, Archduchess of Modena; a Herr von L., i.e., Leurs; Count M., i.e., Majláth, who was especially active during the monarchs' visit to Ofen in October, 1814; Count K., probably Captain Káráczay, who was in Empress Marie Louise's service and who accompanied her to Aix; M. de O., i.e., Otocki, a Pole who reported on the numerous Poles in Vienna; Herr H., i.e., Hebenstreit, savant and writer, a sworn enemy of Grillparzer, with connections to the Lüzow men and other Prussian nationalists; the person who affixed the infinity sign (∞) to his reports, a Hungarian-born civil servant named Neustädter, who reported primarily on matters Hungarian.

Added to these were those "trusted members of the upper

class who do not sign any receipt" so as not to reveal their identity. But they also on occasion lifted the veil of secrecy. There was the example of Chevalier Ludovico Freddi-Battilori who spied on the Curia and was generally active in the vicinity of the southern deputies, such as Labrador and Palmella. He probably ennobled himself, was generally held in bad repute, and was considered "very restless, quarrelsome, and immoral."

In addition to the paid agents were people whose patriotic zeal lead them to submit reports, even in writing, to the government. Sometimes Hager himself scissored their signatures from the files. For their efforts they received nothing but such funds as were required to "maintain the status of their station," which sometimes amounted to quite a sum. Among them was Konrad Busch, editor of the official Wiener Zeitung *and landlord of the ambitious and always dissatisfied Russian state councillor, the Alsatian Anstett, who at times supplied him with valuable details about the Russian delegation. Then there was a Count Benzel-Sternau, an unscrupulous person who most shamelessly misused the trust placed in him by his peers. He, too, almost daily reported to Hager, having offered his services as early as July, 1814, with the remark that he thought himself capable of submitting interesting reports "through my own twenty years of intimate relations with the Bourbons and, therefore, with Louis XVIII's embassy, as well as the Bavarian and Württemberg delegations to the Congress, and several old acquaintances from Germany and Italy, expected at the Congress in Vienna."*

His Majesty's Foreign Minister Metternich also had his confidential agents. These, according to the comments of Countess Lori Fuchs, included Prince Wenzel Liechtenstein and the younger Count Schulenburg, aide-de-camp to Prince Schwarzenberg. A Prince Rohan is likewise said to have belonged. Possibly Sicily's delegate, Marquis Saint-Marsan, was also among them: there was not a single anti-Austrian comment in his diary.

Each foreign embassy, ministry, and mission had put a protective ring of defense and, not infrequently, aggressive agents around itself. Thus, the great czarist power Russia had available General de Witt; the Czar's personal physician, Doctor Jakob;

Baronet Wyllies; the strategist Jomini; and a whole army of more or less reputable cocottes, among them the famous Vienna courtesan Wolters, the beautiful Morel, and the Princess Bagration, great favorite of the Czar himself. Here also belonged Duke Acerenza-Pignatelli, married to Jeanne, second daughter of the "Courland Lady."

France was well served in the person of the Congress' "secretary," Friederich von Gentz, this "most conscientious worker of the Congress" who maintained in his own lodgings in Seilergasse an entire wing for code and post-office officials. Also working for France were Count Wilhelm von Sickingen, an adjutant of Franz II, and Prince Louis de Rohan, first husband of Wilhelmine, Duchess of Sagan, eldest of the Courlands.

Prussia, finally, frequently availed itself of the services of court councillor Heun, better known under his nom-de-plume Clauren.

There was no question of mutual mistrust since every private person and every official bureau had no illusion about being the object of espionage and therefore of being subjected to spying. To be certain, one tried as best possible to thwart the kindly interest of others, but this by no means assured invulnerability. Prince Radziwill, for example, had his drafts copied in his presence, then burned the original himself, and personally carried the letters that went abroad to Prince Hardenberg who would safely expedite them. Others again used codes and cover names in their correspondence. This was resorted to, among others, by Maria Theresa of Saxony, sister of Franz II, whose inventive genius often bore strange and comical fruit, as when she referred to Metternich as "Weedfield," to Talleyrand as "Crookedwood," and even to the Emperor as "Venus." Official beginning of this spying trend, which was fully developed by the Congress, was a resolution issued by Emperor Franz, in 1805, at the start of the third coalition campaign and still in force at the time of the Congress:

Since, as concerns the diplomatic sector of the state police, it is now more than ever necessary to supervise closely the ambassadors and other diplomatic personnel attached to my court, as well as all foreigners going to and from the city, to note all their doings, connections, and comments, and to put a surveillance on their correspondence, both within the country and abroad, it follows that to reach these important objectives more adequate funds than heretofore must be made available and no expense spared that is necessary to carry out assigned tasks. It is required, therefore, that one or several people in the pay of the police be assigned to each residence of the more important ambassadors in order to report on everyday events. As concerns the more important matters, attempts should be made to put trustworthy people from the educated classes, who have access not only to homes open to everyone, but also to the more exclusive and select circles and who are known only to the Chief of Police, on the trail of these ambassadors. For the latter group it is less a matter of paying in cold cash than of establishing a personal relationship of trust and of obtaining detailed knowledge of such special circumstances as might induce these individuals to do their best for the service.

How these explicitly stated goals are to be reached is left up to you, all the more since it would be difficult to lay down specific rules beforehand and action must often be impromptu to exploit successfully chance opportunities. But the recruiting of several people, employed in the homes of ambassadors or having free entry thereto, can no longer be delayed. Also, we must assure ourselves of the services of several informers and confidential agents among the servants of the more prominent inns and in at least those private homes that let rooms to foreigners on a monthly basis. This is necessary to develop clues whether and to what extent a closer surveillance of this or that foreigner is required. Thirdly, an adequate pool of casual labor must be established from which people under special scrutiny who seek a temporary servant can be supplied.

With the backing of this imperial resolution, Baron Hager, the Police Minister, made haste before the Congress convened to instruct his immediate subordinate, Vienna's Chief of Police Siber, appropriately:

Several deputies to the Congress having already arrived and the others due in soon, I require not only a report on each, stating date of arrival and place of stay, but I request of you to exert every effort to maintain an up-to-date file on all, including their surroundings and contacts, utilizing secret surveillance agencies for the purpose. I desire that all higher ranking police officials and confidants at once take up and vigorously pursue their special tasks. I even authorize you for the duration of the Congress to acquire capable new confidants (lower category), so that no effort may be spared in the most minute attention to duty, which the Foreign Ministry and His Majesty are fully entitled to expect from the police during this highly important period.

When the two monarchs arrived in Vienna and the Congress was unofficially opened on September 25, Baron Hager directed a letter to the Lord Chamberlain, Prince Trauttmansdorff, in which he begged the latter's intercession in a delicate matter:

Since the police have no official right of entry to the Imperial Palace grounds, and in view of the fact that the many exits and entries prohibit police surveillance from the street, I can hope to discharge my duty only if the services of those imperial household servants and grooms, assigned to the high-born guests from abroad, are enlisted. I, therefore, respectfully submit that the imperial household staff be instructed that they report daily the places which the sovereigns visit, as well as the people they see outside their own entourage.

But most of the chamberlains and doorkeepers looked down their nose at such requests. Seven-day-laborers, supplied by the police to the billeting official, were then assigned to accompany the courtiers and adjutants of the sovereigns, thus taking them away from their real tasks. The service corps of the imperial household was adept at safeguarding its privileged special position within the government machinery. Where the question was *one of jurisdiction between court and state, the former acted decently and aboveboard. In other matters such scruples were not always in evidence, not even at court, and certainly not in the circles of the upper aristocracy. Agent ***, who may well have been a nobleman himself as we have seen, wrote:*

At Prince Starhemberg's I hear much talk about espionage from court to court, embassy to embassy, and within society itself. It is said: "The courts and embassies are very busy conducting espionage operations against each other. This is quite natural and understandable. There is no doubt that when the foreign sovereigns leave Vienna, they will be thoroughly informed about our court. But the social spying among us Viennese, in society itself, is becoming disgusting. Ferdinand Pálffy works for the secret police, the Countess Esterházy-Roisin and Mlle. Chapuis are spies of the old Princess Metternich and under her influence. Prince Kaunitz, Franz Pálffy, Fritz Fürstenberg, and Ferdinand Pálffy had offered their services to the foreign sovereigns staying in Vienna but were rejected. . . . Never was there such spying in Vienna. Prince Metternich has already called me on the carpet, saying every one of my proposals is known publicly. To which I say, let Metternich put me under obligation, let him pleasure me, and I shall become his eulogist. And he really did oblige me with my lottery, and in that matter I owe him gratitude. But I don't think much of his brothers, or Paul Esterházy and his accomplices, with whom he is in league." *Dixit* Prince Starhemberg.

About himself Confidential Agent *** said:

Count Herberstein and I attend an intimate supper at Prosper Sinzendorf's every Friday. Here we compare confidential notes. Emanuel Khevenhüller, who visits Baldacci as well, is also of the party.

From another side as well the veil of secrecy was slightly raised:

Chevalier Raddi of the Sicilian Embassy relates the most astounding details about how Aldini, Campochiaro, and several other Italian deputies, M. Beausset in Schönbrunn, cavalier escort of the Duchess of Parma, several members of Talleyrand's personnel, and several members of the embassies of Baden, Bavaria, and Württemberg, have collaborated, respectively paid and received considerable sums in order to purchase and receive daily information about the secret doings of the Congress. In Raddi's own words: "Every evening Beauharnais and Campochiaro duly had their copies of every Congress note and the minutes of the day's meetings. They splurged great sums but were excellently well served. Napoleon on Elba and Murat in Naples each had as complete a Congress file as any embassy in Vienna. As little as the above-named should have been admitted to Vienna, as bad was their surveillance in Vienna. None of their dispatches to Elba or Naples was intercepted, despite the Foreign Ministry's awareness of them. Once, Murat's secret courier was waylaid, seized, and searched—before receiving the material he was to take to Naples! To this day, Bonaparte, Murat, and Beauharnais have their well-paid agents and a large following in Vienna."

Sometimes Agent *** was engaged in conversation and pumped by highly placed deputies to the Congress. This happened in November with Dalberg:

I answered: "Count Sickingen, Austrian chamberlain, as far as I know enjoys the trust and confidence of both Emperor Franz and Metternich. I have never heard it said that he is an agent of Vienna's secret police. Nor have I ever heard that Vienna's secret police maintains agents abroad. Nothing is really known about who the actual head of the secret police is. That's not in the official gazette. Ostensibly, it is Baron Hager who heads the Imperial Police and censorship office. So it reads in the official gazette. I really only know Baron Hager by sight because I run across him socially. He enjoys an excellent public reputation, is considered loyal and fair, not a man who likes and deals in espionage, etc."—"I quite understand," Dalberg retorted, "you in Vienna have not the same problems as we do in Paris. Not with your good-natured Austrians."

THE PERSONAE

THE PERSONAE

Kings, Princes, and Great Men

The monarchs were the emperors and kings quartered in the Imperial Palace: Alexander I, Czar of all the Russias; Friedrich Wilhelm III, King of Prussia; Frederick VI, King of Denmark; Maximilian Joseph, King of Bavaria; Friedrich I, King of Württemberg; and the host, Franz II, Emperor of Austria, King of Bohemia, and apostolic King of Hungary. As early as the beginning of October a leaflet was circulated in Vienna which showed the portraits of the six monarchs over these captions:

He loves for all:	Alexander
He thinks for all:	Friedrich Wilhelm
He speaks for all:	Frederick of Denmark
He drinks for all:	Maximilian Joseph of Bavaria
He feeds for all:	Friedrich of Württemberg
He pays for all:	Emperor Franz II

About these monarchs—en masse in the Imperial Palace—de La Garde wrote:

The monarchs appeared in public like any private citizens. They were visibly glad to be rid of the straitjacket of protocol. Often the Austrian emperor and the King of Prussia could be seen walking arm in arm in the streets, wearing civilian attire. The Czar would also often take walks with Prince Eugène. They visited one another and took each other by surprise like any old friends. It was, in short, a royal camaraderie. Alexander and the King of Prussia had the idea to surprise Emperor Franz on his birthday at his levee. The one presented the Emperor with a dress coat lined with sable, the other with a silver wash basin and water jug of the finest Berlin workmanship. These scenes of domestic intimacy quickly made the rounds and were endlessly talked about in the conversation of the day.

Count Nostitz expressed a similar viewpoint:

Of all people in Vienna the princes are the least noticed, their sight having become so familiar.

With the authorities there was worry, however:

The reports about the monarchs in the Imperial Palace are too sketchy because the servants of the imperial household show no interest in this kind of surveillance.

EMPEROR FRANZ II

Emperor Franz I (Franz II of the Holy Roman Empire) of Hapsburg-Lorraine, 1768–1835, succeeded his father, Leopold II, to the throne in 1792. He immediately got involved in the coalition wars against France, and in 1804, following Napoleon's self-coronation, assumed the title of Emperor of Austria. In 1806 he renounced the title of Emperor of the Holy Roman Empire and four times made war on Napoleon, resulting in Austria's loss of hegemony in Germany to the Confederation of the Rhine and in Italy, including its border territories, to Napoleon. In 1810 Franz did a political about-face by giving his daughter Marie Louise in marriage to Napoleon, only, however, to join the anti-Napoleon coalition for keeps in 1813. He played host to the Congress of Vienna where he was able, partly thanks to Metternich's wise politics, partly because of his own hard-come-by generosity, to once more raise Austria to one of the first powers in Europe. The politics of the House of Hapsburg veered now from Germany to the possessions in Upper Italy. This champion of legitimacy and the absolutist welfare state, who was under the influence of Metternich, prime shaper of Europe's politics, joined the Holy Alliance.

The emperor, with his inordinate stubbornness, which at first glance might easily be taken for steadfastness, who is diligent beyond measure but without genius or perception, forever gets lost in details, but, brooking no opposition, enforces his obstinate will on all and thereby convinces himself he is governing.

So wrote General Ludwig Knesebeck, subsequently the adjutant of Friedrich Wilhelm III and foe of the Prussian reforms, in his 1809 report to the Prussian government. Two years later Adam Müller, Catholic convert, ideologist, and theoretician of the romantic period, who was employed in the state chancery, wrote in a similar vein:

The main reason why Austria does not take a more vigorous hand in European affairs lies in the low esteem in which the imperial court is held by the people and by society. The opinion of the latter is of little moment, for the socially elect belittle the Emperor, not because he is no statesman, no warlike leader, but because he lacks elegance, is not *comme il faut*. But the Emperor's behavior and that of the princes of the blood during the late war and since, the bad faith shown against the government's creditors and in the promissory note affairs, the Emperor's visible lack of concern over the people's welfare, aggravated by his personal parsimony, . . . all this has dulled the edge of patriotism.

It was precisely against the accusation of stinginess that Franz II apparently wanted to defend himself, as much by personal behavior as by the generosity of the Imperial Court at Vienna, playing host to the Congress:

There is great astonishment and enchantment over the truly royal munificence of the Viennese Imperial Court, so staid otherwise. There is open comment that our court is completely changed. The coaches' elegance, the good taste, the excellent behavior of the people, etc., is so different from the wonted style that there's temptation to believe in a miracle since everything changed overnight. What most flatters the national self-esteem, however, is the way the foreign rulers behave towards our emperor, whom all seem to take to be their *primus inter pares* and who, on his part, exudes so much congeniality and true greatness, untainted by vanity, that he wins all hearts, even those of the foreigners whose eulogies, especially those of the Italians and Germans, I myself have often overheard.

The most famous playwright of the day, Kotzebue, to everybody's regret, including his own, was also politically active and disapproved of Emperor Franz' dynastic politics:

If Francis II [*sic*] [34] does not resume his title as Emperor of the Holy Roman Empire, an easy matter for him, his contemporaries will be sorry and posterity will pass harsh judgment on him.

That was in 1813. Two years later, the Swiss banker Jean Gabriel Eynard, representing his newly created canton in Vienna, painted an excellent likeness of Franz:

The Austrian emperor has the most unprepossessing of figures. He looks decrepit and old, is small of stature, thin, round-shouldered, knock-kneed. His gala dress is ever the same: red trousers, white coat, black boots. In conversation he is bashfully shy. It is impossible to look less the sovereign and more the petit bourgeois than he does. The ruler is much beloved by people and court, his praise is sung everywhere. His mien is indeed spiritual but shows no esprit.

One of his most often criticized traits, his tactless stubbornness, came in for special comment in a letter of his sister, Princess Maria Theresa of Saxony, to her husband, Crown Prince Anton of Saxony:

Be of good cheer: if it were possible to develop gall-bladder fever, I would long ago have had it, especially because of the

[34] The designation he had held as Emperor of the Holy Roman Empire.—Transl.

queer whim of "Venus" [35]—quite without malice—to tell the latest news at table or immediately upon getting up from it. Waiting for his interminable stories to end, one often doesn't eat for days, which leads to stomach trouble that, with me, always causes excessive sweating. I know how to keep my mouth shut and can take quite a bit. But there've been times when I couldn't stand it any more and became very angry.

Withal, the Emperor exhibited a certain careless indifference about matters that were strictly banned by authentic court etiquette. Thus, when a Russian adjutant, ensconced at the Imperial Palace with his master, smuggled the well-known Viennese courtesan, Josephine Wolters, into his billets in male attire, Franz, being informed, merely shrugged: "Don't be a prig!" The Emperor was altogether more than indulgent with his often less than considerate boarders:

Confidant D . . . O reports: The Russians quartered in the Imperial Palace behave completely immorally. Not only are they dirty, but they have girls with them all the time. Both the British and the Russian courts are said to have offered to pay for the considerable expense they cause, an offer the Emperor has refused.

His brother, Archduke Johann, often the scapegoat of the Emperor's sternness, wrote of him in glowing terms in his diary during the occupation of Paris:

About the impression Emperor Franz makes on the French: "The Austrian emperor prefers the arts, the Czar the tarts." The Emperor walks about everywhere as he does at home, everywhere he is recognized and cordially greeted. There is only one opinion about him, of which I am very glad.

Pride of family, a typical Hapsburg trait, was strong in Franz. It was even applied in the case of his son-in-law, Napoleon, and, by his order, had infected the entire police force. Agent GIYY, in 1814, was tracking down the originator of insulting

[35] The nickname the two use for Franz II.—Transl.

caricatures that showed the French emperor in a very bad light and that were disseminated in Pest. The sub-agents were instructed in line with Emperor Franz' wishes:

I feel obliged to prevent the sale of the well-known bust of Emperor Napoleon that exhibits the latter as composed of corpses. It seems ill-advised to me publicly to bandy about such garish character studies of a crowned head, an action which in my opinion not only desecrates the person, but the very highest of offices as well.

In the old and authentic aristocratic circles there was much looking down one's nose:

At Baron Thugut's there is great hilarity over our emperor accepting a regiment in Russia's service. There is much laughter also about Austrian regiments being presented to foreign sovereigns and about all the military, civilian, and court medals and decorations accepted by Emperor Franz, our ministers, etc. It was said that Maria Theresa and Emperor Joseph would have considered such frivolity beneath the dignity of the Hapsburg dynasty.

But even though the Emperor was considered a good, even exemplary, parent by his people and his family, earning him the sobriquet of "Papa Franz" even among his fellow sovereigns, his kindness and patience were stretched to the breaking point in his relations with his grandson, the son of Marie Louise and Napoleon—Napoleon II, Prince of Parma, later Duke of Reichstadt. In a letter of Zelter to Goethe a short conversation between the Emperor and the then eight-year-old Napoleon II has come down to us:

The boy   : Where is my father?
The Emperor: Your father is locked up.
The boy   : Why is he locked up?
The Emperor: Because he was naughty, and if you are naughty, you'll be locked up too.

And even ten years later, the diary of Baron Obenaus, one of the "Eaglet's" tutors, carried this entry:

Today, the Prince was spanked with the riding crop, for refractoriness.

Probably of similar import was the comment Franz made on first laying his eyes on Caroline Augusta of Bavaria, his fourth bride:

There's one who'll stand a buffet or two. At least I won't have another corpse on my hands in two week's time.

After the death of the Duke of Reichstadt on July 22, 1832, the Emperor said:

With his suffering, the death of my grandson was a blessing to him, and maybe also to my children and to the world. I shall miss him.

The usually objective historian Friedrich Luckwaldt presented this thumbnail sketch of the Emperor:

Without élan, spirit, or enthusiasm; narrow-gauge, kindless, and headstrong; an altogether subaltern nature. Yet, withal, he possessed a good deal of native wit, skill at judging fellow men, and sound judgment. Twenty-two years of governing, naturally, had taught him quite a few things, for there is a core of honest truth in the mocking bon mot "Him whom God gives an office He gives enough brains to run it." With a few pithy phrases in authentic Viennese dialect he often hit the nail on the head. His jokes bore a kindly tinge and came to be well known, making him appear more harmless and open-hearted to outsiders than he was known to be to his family and those around him.

One of the greats of the day, who at the same time was dependent on Franz, Franz Grillparzer, said about the Emperor in his Diaries:

In ordinary times he reverted to his true nature, which was not evil, not unwise, not especially weak, not low—"common" would already be too harsh a word: his nature was ordinary. There was nothing elevated, nothing awesome in him. . . . Lacking any idea of the dignity of human nature, he was suspicious of everyone. To show off was his hobby and his favorite occupation. As concerns promises, he kept those given as a private person to a fault (even as a nobleman pays his card debts); as a ruler he was not averse to breaking the most solemn ones.

CROWN PRINCE FERDINAND

Ferdinand I, 1793–1875, Emperor of Austria, eldest son of Franz II, ruled from 1835 to the revolutionary year 1848, when he abdicated in favor of his nephew, Franz Josef, and retired to Hradcany Castle in Prague. At the time of the Congress he was the crown prince and even then subject to fits of mental illness that, though never reaching the stage of total insanity as in the case of George III of England, nevertheless prevented even a pro forma *taking-part in the affairs of state. As early as January, 1815, Vienna society said about him:*

At old Count Széchenyi's there was talk of our crown prince and how little poise and self-confidence he had and how nothing was done to improve the situation.

Shortly before, in January, 1815, the problem of educating this prince, whose difficulties were well recognized, had taken an interesting, if tragic, turn. In a report labeled "Confidential! For eyes of Baron Hager only" we read:

Out of the clear blue, Baron Erberg, tutor of the Crown Prince, has had himself certified insane. . . . Though, as is claimed, the Hapsburg dynastic rules consider the Crown Prince of age at eighteen, he is even today, at age twenty-one, treated as a child. It is also said that he has been passed from the hands of one pedantic, unworldly tutor to the other; that it is impossible for the Crown Prince, who is one day to rule this vast empire, to adequately prepare himself; that he will become a petty-minded ruler where the happiness of a whole generation is at stake; that such a prince ought to have a great teacher and a small court, just as was done with the Archduchesses, who are even younger than he is; that a person so treated must needs become somber, suspicious, moody, and withdrawn, a person who will be a stranger to himself and to others. The public interprets the poor tutor's insanity a blessing for the Crown Prince, separating him as it does from a person whose ideas had been sinister and who had held the Prince in constant fear.

EMPEROR ALEXANDER I, CZAR OF ALL THE RUSSIAS

Alexander I, 1777–1825, favorite of his grandmother, Catherine the Great, ascended the throne at a young age, following the murder of his father, Paul I. There existed a deep contradiction between the romantic ideals he developed under the influence of his tutor, the liberal Swiss, La Harpe, and their application. Domestically, his political leaning was less one of liberalism than an extension of Peter the Great's idea of westernizing Russia. In his foreign policy he started out as leader in the anti-Napoleon coalition, but in the Treaty of Tilsit (1807), which followed the defeats at Austerlitz and Friedland, he was ready to share Europe with Napoleon. At the Congress of Erfurt (1808), largely influenced by the traitorous Talleyrand, he veered away again from this political line and, following Napoleon's defeat before Moscow, victoriously lead allied Europe towards peace. During his sojourns in Paris, London, and Vienna in 1814–15 he became arbiter of European politics. Under the influence of the pietistic Julie de Krüdener, he fell prey to mysticism. He was the champion (together with Prussia and Austria) of the Holy Alliance. Yet, for Russia herself, he pursued a policy of expansion that nearly led to another war with Austria and France and in the course of time netted Russia Finland (from Sweden), Bessarabia (from Turkey), and (from the Congress), Poland, where the constitution and independence promised by Alexander were soon annulled. He died mysteriously in Taganrog. Credible sources stated his death to be a ruse and his burial a fake, claiming that he became a monk and died at a hoary old age in Siberia. He was married to a daughter of the Grand Duke of Baden. Together with Metternich and Talleyrand, Alexander played one of the leading roles at the Congress of Vienna, a role he owed to his public image and his gift of showmanship. Judgment about him vacillates. Modern psychology would probably include him in the group of charming schizophrenics. The complexes that dominated his life were his complicity in his father's murder and his hate–love for Napoleon, whom he tried to replace and outperform following the latter's downfall.

Following are the comments of the Countess Thürheim, written years after the events they describe and therefore likely to be reasonably objective:

Count Capo d'Istrias, later the Russian Foreign Minister, told me about Alexander: "The Emperor was witty but lacked the so-called *coup d'oeil.* He mistrusted even his own convictions and preferred the guidance of others. But he was kind and noble withal and did not desire the best only for his own country but wanted to see it applied throughout the world. . . . In himself he personified the philosophers' dreams of human kindness, but their utopias of a happy humanity presupposed perfection in the ruled, as well as in the rulers. Since Alexander could satisfy only one half of the requirements, the poor Emperor died a victim of his noble illusions. The terrible circumstances that marred his ascension to the throne and that caused him to become guilty, even against his will, left a dark blot on his conscience that never faded. In fiery letters he read engraven in his heart the word 'PATRICIDE.' "—Alexander's features are not regular, yet on the whole he is rather handsome. His eyes are deep-set, yet display wit and liveliness. His nose is somewhat that of a Kalmuck, his mouth small and well shaped, his teeth unusually white. His stature is truly majestic, but he carries himself head slightly forward, possibly because of the high, narrow, military collar he wears. In order to appear relaxed, he ambles as he walks. His facial expression is one of natural pride, mixed with a geniality that is alien to him. His look is steely, but his smile enchanting. At first glance, when the Emperor is "on stage," the impression is that of a forceful personality. Yet, once he lets himself go, he appears distinctly mediocre, even strikes one as a "jolly good fellow," which is what he probably is at heart. He speaks French and German fluently, without the trace of an accent. His conversation is by no means especially witty. Since his arrival in Vienna he has not been heard to utter a single witty saying, whereas in Paris, where he was adored, a number of bon mots that he allegedly coined are repeated. He is voluble only where it concerns military matters and he delights in repeating the phrase: "We soldiers . . . ," hoping to annoy Metternich, who is anything but military. He is especially cordial with officers and favors the lowest lieutenants with the flattering greeting: "Friends and brothers!" Alexander is diligent beyond words. His Secretary of State Nesselrode claims there is nothing left for him to do. Of course, the Emperor's political ambitions are not complex: he wants really only one thing—Poland. Not the opposition of several cabinets, not the tricks of a Metternich, Talleyrand, or Castlereagh could change his mind in the least. If there is hope that eventually boredom or loss of temper will make him concede what he has so far stubbornly opposed, it may well be that his beleaguerers will have died of starvation first.

In an objective vein Friedrich von Schönholz wrote:

Alexander presented a typical Slavic appearance, though he did not belong to any of the Slavic tribes. He was a natural cosmopolitan, the whole world being his playground. At home everywhere, he was least at home at home. No one could characterize him better than he does himself: "I am only a lucky accident in Russia."

His great antagonist, Napoleon I, told Metternich about Alexander:

Though there is much that is prepossessing about him, there is that in his being which I cannot describe and of which I can only tell you that in everything there is a certain "something" he lacks.

De La Garde reported a rather sympathetic incident:

Riding in the Prater one day, Emperor Franz wanted to dismount but in vain looked around for a helping hand, his grooms having become separated from him by the crushing crowd. Alexander guessed his intent, quickly dismounted, and hastened to assist his friend. Thus the great Friedrich had once held the stirrup for Joseph II. The tableau caused much jubilation all around, showing how much the crowd appreciated Alexander's charming gesture.

Count Nostitz, in his memoirs, underscored the change that Alexander's public image underwent in the course of time:

Years ago everyone uniformly praised the fairness and solid virtues of the Czar, calling him "Prince Charming" and thereby seeking to conceal his lack of character. But the passing years have brought about a change in this opinion, and the Congress has entirely set the record straight. Now he is seen as a foxy simulator, and the discovery has hurt his image. He senses this and seeks consciously to confuse public opinion by a show of ingenuousness and apparent devotion and by often appearing in public arm in arm with the most unimportant people, who can boast of nothing but manners and youthful deference, but who, despite their outward charm, are known to be shallow and inexperienced. To these belong Moritz Woina, who is first among the favorites, the young Liechtenstein, and whoever else there is of young dandies.

Nostitz also mentioned Alexander's major, and well-known problem, women:

The Czar is the perfect cavalier. His penchant for women is so obvious that the Russian ladies are annoyed at times over the attention their monarch pays the Viennese beauties. But, as far as is known, his chivalry remains within socially acceptable boundaries.

The unusually large number of agents assigned to Alexander reported in entirely different terms and on entirely different subjects. Their handling of the Czar's woman problem was not as discreet or considerate as Nostitz's. Above all, they scrutinized closely the Czar's relationship with his wife:

Yesterday at court the rumor was circulated that the Czarina will go via Munich to Karlsruhe soon after February 12. Her brother, the Archduke of Baden, is to accompany her. This un-happily married lady never dines with her husband, nor with her sisters-in-law, the Grand Duchesses. Since departure of the Queen, her sister, she dines with her brother-in-law, the King of Bavaria. The consensus is the Czarina will spend the rest of her life in Karlsruhe. There will be great excitement in St. Peters-burg when the Czarina does not return, for she has a great follow-ing there. . . . At Stephan Zichy's the story was repeated that the Czar last Friday peremptorily ordered his poor wife to attend the ball given by Princess Bagration. She went against her own will. The sofa offered her was in such poor state that it collapsed under her. Last Saturday, during a family dinner attended by the Czarina's brother and sister, the Czar was extremely rude to all three. The rumor persists that the Czarina will go to her brother in Karlsruhe and not return to Russia. This from Count Seilern, allegedly based on comments of his grand duke.

The Princess Bagration, widow of the great Russian general, together with Countess Maria Antonia Narishkin, were the de-clared mistresses of Alexander in Vienna:

At Eskeles the story was told that when the Czarina arrived at the ball of la Bagration, several voices were heard proclaiming loudly: "Oh, how beautiful she is! It must be admitted, the Czarina is a real beauty, a superb woman!" The Czar, believing this to have been said for his benefit, said in a loud voice that his wife could not fail to overhear: "Upon my word, I do not find it so. That is not my opinion at all!"

The budding love affair between Alexander and the Princess Bagration, who was known as the "naked angel" because of her daring décolletés, created a tremendous stir in Viennese society, all the more since the confidants are convinced that political se-crets were exchanged during the hours of dalliance. By chance, the Princess was quartered in the same palace with the Duchess of Sagan:

Tryst between Alexander and Princess Bagration, Friday evening, September 30. All the world talks of nothing else. It is known that Alexander sent word to the Princess, informing her of his visit at six, before the court reception. He sent her his adjutant general, General Uvarov, who was detained, however, and saw her only after the reception. Alexander himself appeared at half past nine, went into her boudoir, and remained alone with her for nearly three hours. Next morning at ten, Mr. Fortbrune [36] came to the bedside of the Princess to try to learn what she and Alexander had discussed. But she had been warned against Fortbrune and told him nothing despite his flattery. She keeps her secrets to herself, but it appears all the same as if she has no real conceptions about the alleged complete agreement between Alexander and our government. I might learn more about this soon but can already report that she deeply enjoys her triumph over the lady of Ratibor,[37] her successful rival with the premier. Hers is the distinction of being the first to receive Alexander's favors.

Quite a few repartees have come down to us from the many colloquies between Alexander and those he wooed:

The following anecdote is told about Countess Széchenyi-Guilford at the ball given by Franz Pálffy. Czar Alexander, who finds the Countess most attractive, said to her: "Your husband is not present. It would be pleasant to occupy his place temporarily."—"Does Your Majesty take me for a province?" replied the lady.

It was not only politics that made enemies of Alexander and Metternich; the ladies played a role here too, above all Madame Sagan and Madame Bagration. In as much as the Duchess of Sagan was on friendly terms with Metternich, Alexander did his best to hurt her where he could:

Most of Princess (sic) Sagan's wealth is in Russia. Alexander, jealous of Metternich, made it difficult for her to get hold

[36] A British agent and one of her lovers.
[37] The Duchess of Sagan.

of it. She therefore tried to see the Emperor, without success. Her situation steadily worsened, and Alexander informed her through a third party that only a formal break with Metternich will satisfy him. Sagan took the hint and hardly looked at Metternich any more, favoring Alexander at every opportunity. Sometime later, she asked Alexander for an audience in Metternich's presence, whereupon Alexander answered: "Never mind the audience. I'll come to you tomorrow." This so infuriated Metternich that he went to upbraid Madame Sagan, who refused to see him. Only when he was told that she also had a secret affair with an Englishman, did he calm down. Now the break is official, and Alexander is happy. There is also the story of Julie Zichy whom Alexander told he knew of her affair with Metternich from Metternich himself. Whereupon the Countess dissolved in tears and will have nothing to do with the latter any more.

Archduke Johann likewise commented on the subject in his diary:

Emperor Alexander told the Duchess of Sagan concerning her relations with Metternich: "It is not fit for you to maintain relationship with a scrivener."

All this had political ramifications:

The Czar is enraged at Metternich. He accuses him of the most evil intent, namely of wanting to sow discord between Russia and Prussia. He says that someone [38] had shown him the entire secret correspondence with Metternich. Countess Aurora Marassé, Princess Bagration's obliging lady-in-waiting who often meets with the envoys, ministers, and other delegates to the Congress before she arises, has assured me that to mention Metternich and make an enemy of Alexander are one and the same. She was quite crushed when she told me this, because she takes the part of Metternich and Austria. Princess Bagration, for this reason, enjoys a kind of triumph and thinks herself properly avenged on her faithless lover. Countess Marassé tells me she

[38] Princess Bagration.

sees trouble brewing for him.[39] "But," she says, "he always finds the time to run to the Duchess of Sagan, yet he has not a minute to listen to me. This worries me greatly, for I should have very much liked to prevent all this."

Linked with the criticism of playing fast and loose with women was the accusation of juvenile wildness and lack of self-discipline. The Italian Abbé Carpani had this to say:

The kings currently in Vienna cannot conceal their jealousy of the Russian emperor who is so obviously the favorite, though he personally is nothing but a mad-brain.

From the Austrian side we hear Count Spaur:

Emperor Alexander is a madcap, there is no imagining his wildness.

The aristocratic "confidant" hewed to the same line:

There is only one opinion about Alexander among the kings and sovereigns and their cabinets and ministers currently assembled in Vienna: If only he had stayed home, his reputation would have been assured! "He will never be able to retrieve his personal standing, this madcap, this titan!" they say about him. I also hear it said: "Thank God, the Russian delegation at the Congress is second-rate at best, with Anstett the only one who is talented and knowledgeable. Nesselrode is the weakest of the lot. Even the Prussians, when amongst themselves, are prone to poke fun at the extreme ineffectuality of the Russian delegation." The members of the secret police whom the Russians brought with them to Vienna—to which I count the Duke d'Acerenza-Pignatelli and the Baron Bühler family—seem more interested in intrigue among themselves and for their own individual benefit than serving the interests of their sovereign.

The following report from the closing days of the Congress has been preserved:

The Countess Zichy-Ferraris gave a dinner for the Russian emperor, Countess Flora Wrbna, and several others on Tuesday.

[39] Metternich.

ILLUSTRATIONS

Emperor Franz I of Austria, Czar Alexander I of Russia, and King Friedrich Wilhelm III of Prussia receive news of Leipzig victory from Prince Schwarzenberg, October 20, 1813. Engraving, after an oil by Peter Krafft.

The Congress of Vienna. Engraving by Godefrey, after a sepia drawing by Jean-Baptiste Isabey.

Upper row: Franz I (1768–1835). Oil by Sir Thomas Lawrence. Alexander I (1777–1825). Oil by George Dawe.

Bottom row: Empress Maria Ludovica of Austria (1787–1816). Miniature by Guérard. Czarina Elizabeth of Russia (1779–1835). Oil by Heinsius.

Upper row: Friedrich Wilhelm III (1770–1840). Oil by C. Begas.
Karl Reichsfreiherr vom und zum Stein (1757–1831). Engraving by
Friedrich Fleischmann.

Bottom row: Karl August Prince von Hardenberg (1750–1822).
Wilhelm Baron von Humboldt (1767–1835). Crayon drawing by
Johann Schmeller.

Prince Metternich (1773–1859). Oil by Sir Thomas Lawrence.

Prince Talleyrand (1754–1838). Oil by François Pascal Gérard.

Upper row: Friedrich I (1754–1816). Engraving by J. G. Mansfeld. Maximilian Joseph I (1756–1825). Engraving by C. Schule.

Bottom row: Friedrich August I (1750–1827). Engraving by
Rossmäsler. Frederick VI (1768–1839). Engraving by C. Schule.

Promenade in the Prater, circa 1815.

Requiem mass for Louis XVI of France in St. Stephan's Cathedral, January 21, 1815.

The "sleigh-ride" of January 22, 1815. After an engraving by Reinhold.

Upper row: Robert Stewart, Viscount Castlereagh (1769–1822). Arthur Wellesley, Duke of Wellington (1769–1852). Oil by Lucas.

Bottom row: Friedrich von Gentz (1764–1832). Watercolor by Leybold. Karl Joseph Prince de Ligne (1735–1814).

Upper row: Prince Andreas Kyrillovich Razumovsky (1752–1836). Oil by Ferdinand Waldmüller. Prince Franz Seraph Rosenberg-Orsini (1761–1832). Engraving by J. G. Mansfeld.

Bottom row: Tadeusz Kosciusko (1746–1817). Engraving by Friedrich Fleischmann, after Olescymski. Grand duke Constantine of Russia (1779–1831). Engraving by C. Schule.

The Grand Ball of November 10, 1814. Pen drawing by Hoechle.

The tournament at the Imperial Riding School, November 23, 1814.

Upper row: Countess Laura Fuchs-Gallenberg. Watercolor by Rungaldier. Catherine Bagration (1783–1856). Watercolor by Jean-Baptiste Isabey.

Bottom row: Dorothea Duchess de Talleyrand-Périgord (1792–1862). Oil by Prud'hon. Emilia Bigottini (1783–1858). Watercolor by Jean-Baptiste Isabey.

Ludovica (Lou) Countess Thürheim (1788–1864). Self-portrait.
Count Auguste de La Garde. Lithograph by Carbonnier.

It was a hilarious party, with the whole neighborhood getting drunk and sharing in the fun. They created such a stir, all surrounding villages and suburbs are talking about it.

Alexander also exhibited a certain obfuscation that might even be called hypocrisy. Said Abbé Carpani, unkindly disposed toward Alexander:

At times Alexander affects a supercilious, now French, now Russian, manner, and no one trusts his entirely forced politeness. He is considered two-faced, frivolous, vacillatory, at the same time tight-lipped and haughty.

And an anonymous police report of November 2 said about Alexander:

He is taken as a deceitful person who acts the philanthropist in front of honorable men, but who also attracts the rabble to himself so as to curry favor with all the world. He is thought to be hypocritical and without moral scruples, even though he talks about religion like a saint and meticulously observes outward appearances.

"Deceitful," "hot-headed," the reports continued in like vein:

In intimate circles the talk is: "The Russian emperor is an ambiguous, hypocritical, weak person, a poor friend, a poor enemy, a blusterer who turns tail quickly when firmly faced. He has lost all countenance in Europe. In St. Petersburg, also, they are ashamed to have a dance-crazy butterfly for emperor. The ministers, as soon as installed, are in constant conflict with whoever belongs to the Emperor's retinue at the time. In sum: the Russian emperor has many weak points and is by far not the terrible fellow he believes himself to be. . . ."

Often an evil interpretation was put on the Czar's completely harmless escapades:

The nuncio talked to me first about the scene that occurred between Alexander and Countess Wrbna. "This stupidity is unbelievable! There you see who the rulers of the world are!

The scandalmongers of the Congress will add this charming adventure to other abominable and blameworthy traits of this bedroom hero, and history will one day remind posterity that the Austrian emperor's palace served the Czar of all the Russias for a bordello."

The nuncio here referred to that wager between the Czar and the Countess as to who could most quickly change dress from top to toe. Alexander in general had the singular talent to be the center of outlandish events, something quickly seized upon by the confidants:

General Chernitchev told Countess Suvorov the following on Thursday evening at the Bühlers': "Imagine the embarrassing incident that occurred between our Gospoda [40] and Field Marshal Schwarzenberg. The Czar saw Princess Auersperg drive by and ordered his coachman to follow her. She went to Prince Schwarzenberg at the War Ministry; he after her. She met the Field Marshal . . . in great dishabille, for, it being rather warm, he had just removed his gala uniform to cool off a bit. Suddenly, the Emperor was announced, and at the same moment when the Prince said, 'That is really the limit of this pushy person!' and upbraided the servant for not having denied him, the Czar entered. Chernitchev swears to have distinctly heard the Field Marshal's last words. The Emperor is said to have been embittered and to have left again immediately." The Princess Suvorov also learned from Chernitchev that the Czar had told him, "Today I discovered by chance that Schwarzenberg, too, has turned against me."

It cannot be denied, on the other hand, that in his relations with the "common people" Alexander was quite at ease and natural. Von Schönholz told an illustrative anecdote:

Alexander possessed the invaluable gift of appealing to the national pride of whatever people he visited. In Vienna in particular he openly showed his pleasure over the Austrian way of life, even praising its lesser faults to high heaven. Here is an

[40] i.e., Alexander.

example: the amount of the most expensive food and drink that was daily removed, untasted, from the tables of the most illustrious guests, only to find its backstairs way to other sections of the palace, was quite considerable. One day a most marvelously decorated pheasant with gilded claws and beak was served at the Czar's table in the manner of the times of the late Philip of Burgundy, when princes and knights still pledged each other at table with the set formula "By the Virgin Mary, my lady, and the pheasant!" The much admired roast, like many before, remained untasted, and when the Emperor returned to his apartments in the evening, he noticed behind a curtain in the vestibule the telltale tailfeathers of the romantic meal. Looking closer, the monarch discovered a basket filled with the finest wines and delicacies, topped by the Burgundy bird, all of which he immediately removed to his own rooms. Next morning he invited Emperor Franz for breakfast, at which the pheasant was served. But Alexander asked that the collector of the delicacies suffer no further punishment except their loss, which caused much laughter and to which Franz all the more readily agreed as he believed in the principle of live-and-let-live.

About Alexander's popularity with the lower classes, agent *** had this to say:

In every home, in every circle, there is talk of Alexander. For example, that he drinks wine in the cafés "City of Vienna," "Hungarian Crown," and "Spanish Cross," and that he even went to a pub and asked for beer. They say: "In the Czar's coterie social games form the major entertainment. Like making faces, where he who puts on the strangest grimace receives a prize."

Quite remarkable was Alexander's comment about himself:

A prince as a rule is only a prince, but La Harpe has made a human being out of me, and I shall be eternally grateful to him for it.

His energy and physical stamina were great, as Gentz has already noticed during Alexander's stay in London:

The Emperor arrived at three in the morning at the Poultenay hotel in London, together with the Grand Duchess of Olden-burg. He had just returned from Oxford but changed immediately and went to the ball given by Lady Jersey, where he danced until six. At ten he was on the move again to inspect several public institutions. In the evening he dined with Lord Castlereagh, went to the Drury Lane at eleven, and after the show to the Marquess of Hertford's, where the party remained until three.

And his politics? In the end, he did get a goodly slice of Poland. In the end, the Holy Alliance was concluded under his initiative, after the Congress. His plans were much more far-reaching, though—especially in the religio-politico-ecclesiastical area:

Yesterday there was a wedding celebration at the Bühler resi-dence. Prince Koslovski [41] talked at length about Czar Alex-ander's penchant for uniting the Roman with the Greek Church. But the Prince does not deny that ulterior motives play a certain role here and that at the moment Alexander is especially out to court the Poles, using the Jesuits for this purpose.

KING FRIEDRICH WILHELM III OF PRUSSIA

Friedrich Wilhelm III, 1770–1840, ascended the throne in 1797, in the midst of Europe's revolutionary turmoil. He was burdened with the curse of being a "Judas to the German empire," the epithet his luxury-loving father had earned for himself and his heir by becoming signatory to the Basle Treaty of 1795. For years he tried to keep Prussia out of the coalition wars and was extremely cool toward the reform attempts of Humboldt and Hardenberg. When the old Prussian army and state collapsed in 1806–07, he tried a thorough revamping of the governmental machinery, and in 1812–13 jumped at the chance to become champion of the Wars of Liberation by exorcizing spirits with his proclamation "To my People," which he soon wanted to

[41] The Russian Ambassador in Turin.

shake off again but could not. At the Congress of Vienna he was totally eclipsed by his Russian friend Alexander, whose Polish claims he tried to match, unsuccessfully, with a bid for all of Saxony. He became a most zealous champion of Metternich's restoration politics; in his own land persecuted the students' movement, rid himself of Hardenberg and Humboldt, and thus cleared the way for his romantically confused son, Friedrich Wilhelm IV. His noble and beautiful consort, Queen Louise, died in 1810.

Count Nostitz described him:

The King of Prussia forever looks like a thundercloud. But appearances are very deceiving, and he is really rather susceptible and exhibits a romantic attachment for Julie Zichy that might also be called habituation. That woman now knows all about Potsdam [42] parades and how the former and the current Prussian is dressed, etc., and on her part entertains His Wooing Majesty with sublimity and religion. The talks often last all evening, in intimate, albeit seemingly gloomy, tête-à-têtes.

Countess Thürheim was even more malicious, especially where the King's mooning love affair was concerned:

In character and mind the King of Prussia is no match for Czar Alexander. Once weak and demeaningly dispirited in defeat, he is proud, harsh, implacable, and grasping now that his star has risen. Right at the start of negotiations he demanded twelve million new subjects, Saxony, that is. In vain, the injustice of such presumptuousness was pointed out to him; in vain was an attempt made to indemnify him somewhere else: the good king counts and calculates and, not finding twelve million subjects anywhere else, must needs have poor Saxony. The subservient role he plays in his relation with Alexander is more that of an adjutant than a king. He is one of those who can

[42] German royal residence, with enormous parade grounds that aided materially in making Potsdam the symbol of Prussian militarism. —Transl.

tolerate debasement but whom independence depresses. Tall, stiff, and cold—Prince de Ligne aptly called him the "armory type" —the King talks little and then in spurts. His features are not lacking a certain regularity but convey the impression of unhappiness, suspicion, and coldness. The only interest that brings him alive is his honest sorrow for his wife, for whom he sheds tears daily and to whom he would love to tell all his thoughts and deeds. Yet, despite this deep and honest sorrow, the King throughout the Congress does not tire of paying court to the beauteous Countess Zichy, née Festetics ("the Heavenly Beauty"). There is no doubt that this devotion casts no reflection on the spotless reputation of the Countess. At least it seems to me that, without detracting from the merits of either, the virtuous lady's struggle cannot have been very desperate in view of her swain's coldness and tediousness.

A letter, written from Vienna, near the end of the Congress to his twenty-year-old son, later Friedrich Wilhelm IV, affords a glimpse into the inner life of this uninteresting, average person:

I have every reason to hope and expect that you, dear Fritz, will not miss going to Easter communion, even without my reminding and encouraging you. Still, I thought it best to call your attention to the matter, for it seems certain now that I shall not yet have returned to you at that time.

Since the opportune reappearance of the nearly forgotten Napoleon on the Continent, everything unfortunately reassumes a martial look. The preparations to put everything in readiness this time are in full swing, and there is no thinking, of course, of leaving Vienna until it is clear how the matter will develop.

May heaven grant that this impending evil does not survive its birth.

Your gay and comical letters afford me great pleasure and joy. They show me that you have retained your good humor, and, on the other hand, I see with satisfaction that you are diligent and are making good progress in the educational development you need. For several days the weather has been changeable and inclement. Tomorrow, weather permitting, there is to be a coach parade, the surrogate of a sleigh ride, to the Augarten. There the premiere of *Ioconde* is to take place, which in German is called. . . . Farewell, dear Fritz, I embrace all of you with all my heart.

> Friedrich Wilhelm, Vienna, March 14.

P.S. Undoubtedly your cousin will also attend communion.

Vienna left no flattery untried to win over this difficult, un-Austrian, person:

The Prussian king is very pleased with the reception the Emperor gave in his honor. Also, he is flattered beyond measure by being assured, as was cleverly done, that he has cut a much better figure with the local populace than has the Czar.

Politically, his word isn't worth much. His top advisor, Wilhelm von Humboldt, said about him:

As concerns the business at hand, I hardly ever see the King, which is all to the good. It is bad indeed to have to argue with him when he is not of the same opinion to begin with. And in the present state of affairs, the opposite must often be the case.

MAXIMILIAN I, KING OF BAVARIA

Maximilian I, 1756–1825, of the Pfalz-Zweibrükken House, assumed the regentship also over the Bavarian mainlands in 1799, his brother Karl Theodore, Elector of Bavaria, being without heir. Following the Regensberg Diet of 1803, he joined France and through acquisition of vast territories became ruler over the largest of the German central states. In 1806 he accepted the royal title and joined the Napoleonic Confederation of the Rhine. In 1813, under the influence of his prime minister, Montgelas, he changed over to the Allies and at the Congress of Vienna stood up for a strictly anti-Napoleonic policy that even rejected the idea of a German Confederation. In 1818 he granted his country a constitution. His was a natural genius. Many of his intuitively right judgments were widely circulated at the Vienna Congress. Thus he once commented about Saxony:

We toppled Napoleon because he deprived other princes of their thrones. Are we any better when we partition Saxony?

Maximilian had a strong predilection for common expressions; that is why popular opinion promptly relegated him to the so-called "pig's corner." Count Nostitz wrote:

The Bavarian king looks like a coarse, ill-tempered Bavarian drayman but exhibits withal a touch of uprightness and honesty. He is the most bourgeois of kings.

Even though he had given his daughter in marriage to Napoleon's stepson, Eugène de Beauharnais, the King of Bavaria transferred his dislike of Napoleon to other members or in-laws of the Bonaparte family as well. Thus he hated with a passion the then King of Naples, Joachim Murat, who had married Napoleon's sister, Caroline, and who for the time being was still allied with Austria:

Day before yesterday, Prince Leopold of Sicily, youngest son of the Bourbon, Ferdinand IV, visited the Bavarian king. Talk got around to Murat and the King told the Prince the following, which the latter wrote his father: "There is no doubt, this rascal must be sent packing. But that is not enough: he should be strung up. Who deserves the gallows more than he? I, I know all his tricks. . . . He is a scoundrel such as never has existed before."

But the fact was that Maximilian was not taken very seriously at the Congress of Vienna. The King himself complained to Abbé Carpani about this:

Our life here is pleasant enough, only we have no idea what is going on or what will happen to us. The Viennese cabinet treats us in the same manner as formerly the French were wont to do. We are told nothing.

Matters were not improved by the fact that Maximilian's wife was not exactly making friends in Austria with her currency speculations. A confidant reported about her on February 7, 1815:

The Bavarian queen is likewise said to have taken several hundred thousand florins' worth of coins over the border with her. These were obtained in exchange for Austrian paper money bought in Bavaria. Because of the impending currency export embargo, the money was taken out under the immunity enjoyed by the Royal Court.

FREDERICK I, KING OF WÜRTTEMBERG

Frederick I, 1754–1816, was the oldest of the monarchs assembled at the Vienna Congress. He was the one most disliked as well, despite his liberal tips. He, like the Bavarian king, owed royal title and territorial gain to Napoleon. At the Congress he was at once the foe of Bavaria and sworn enemy of all attempts at German unification. Politically he was outspokenly reactionary, but as early as 1815 he granted his country a constitution, possibly to beat the opposition to the punch. Schönholz commented about him:

Here should be mentioned the gay appearance which the odd makeup of the king's equipages created in public. The coach itself was a conchoidal chaise, offering room for just one person large of girth. It was pulled by four bays, of which the lead pair had their tails cropped, whereas the other two wore theirs naturally long. Each pair was guided by a jockey dressed in a scarlet blazer with yellow sleeves. It cannot be denied that this rig contrasted oddly with the fashion of the day. Unfortunately, King Frederick always wore a grim expression and seldom returned a greeting. He seemed to be averse to tipping his hat, and soon the Viennese also stopped it.

The "Württemberg Monster," as the king was called, did not in general enjoy a "good press." An agent report said about him:

At court an anecdote is repeated about him that the British have caricatured him as an unshaped mass of rotundity on whose fly button is painted the kingdom of Württemberg and who cries with uplifted arms: "Oh, how unhappy am I who cannot see my country!"

His widely known homosexual tendencies likewise created public resentment. The proud young noblemen took little gaff from this monster. There was the story of a scene between him and a page boy serving at table:

King (to the page): "Will he bring me a glass of water." [43]

Page (a stripling): "Your Majesty, I am Baron Beck, and my emperor says 'you' to me."

King: "All right then, will *you* bring me a glass of water."

Whereupon the page was forthwith relieved, but without prejudice. The King's tremendous hunting passion was also taken amiss:

Much talk about yesterday's wild boar hunt. It is said the King of Württemberg alone caught thirty-two boars. Baron Linden commented: "It is this accursed hunting passion that makes my king so widely hated. Until the king is home again and can shoot his own wild pigs, there is nothing for it but twenty thousand [sic] peasants must beat the bushes night and day and not get a farthing for it."

On the opposite end of the scale was found an entirely different set of traits, as, for example, his liberality with money. Earlier than any other monarch, he left Vienna already at the end of December, 1814, and distributed largess to the imperial household staff in the amount of sixty thousand gulden in ducats, snuff boxes, and the like. He was an eccentric and had his tics. Thus, for example, each morning four chamberlains had to enter his bedroom simultaneously to waken him. One of his letters to his minister, Mandelsloh, was intercepted in Vienna:

Since I have reason to believe that the German question will soon come up for discussion, I consider it necessary, for

[43] In the German of the day inferiority of rank was indicated by address in the third person singular.—Transl.

reasons I have mentioned to you before my departure, to call for the services of legation councilor Feuerbach, who is to come to Vienna with all dispatch. I shall send you further news with the next courier.

> The clouds are gathering ominously,
> But soon the sun will scatter them.
> And then the heaven's blueness
> Will shine forth gloriously.

FREDERICK VI, KING OF DENMARK

Frederick VI, 1768–1839, after 1784 co-regent with his father, Christian VII, ascended the throne in 1808. Following the two British raids of Copenhagen (1801 and 1807), he was forced to cede his fleet to England and thereupon joined Napoleon, likewise a costly undertaking. In the Treaty of Kiel he lost the island of Heligoland to Great Britain and Norway to Sweden, receiving in compensation at the Congress of Vienna only the tiny Duchy of Lauenburg and Holstein by virtue of which he, as foreign monarch, became a member of the German Confederation. This development led to a resurgence of Danish nationalism and accounted for all subsequent conflicts with Germany. Countess Thürheim wrote about Frederick VI in her memoirs:

The King of Denmark is one of the most revolting of men but withal the best king in the world—noble, openhanded, kind, witty, and forever concerned over the welfare of his people. He was probably the most beloved and popular of the monarchs in Vienna. He was called "King of the Rag Fair," [44] in allusion to the travesty "Hamlet, Prince of the Rag Fair." He was very lean of build.

Count Nostitz judged the King solely on the basis of his exalted rank:

[44] A pun that even in the original German seems strained: *Tandelmarkt* (Ger.= rag fair) is substituted for Dänemark.—Transl.

The King of Denmark, here called "King of the Rag Fair," scampers around everywhere, is well meaning and at times sensible. Only he is too condescendingly ordinary, always lost in the crowd. They say he is witty, but the bon mot on which this is based is not known, unless it is his retort to Alexander's effusive farewell words: "You are taking every heart with you!" Said Frederick: "Yes, but not a single soul!" since Denmark, despite his efforts, was the loser at the Congress.

The Danish king, also, was surrounded by spies, something this open-minded man particularly despised:

Captain Schuhmacher of the Danish mission is complaining about the secret police. They all, including the king, are convinced that the valet Müller, supplied by the Austrian Court, is spying on them. Nor does the King's suite like General Steigentesch, furnished as escort to the King.

Friedrich von Schönholz has left a detailed description of Frederick VI:

King Frederick Christian of Denmark, of medium height and slender build, wearing a long green coat, walking through deep snow leaning on a walking stick, looked for all the world like a scholar. This impression was even heightened by an oddly shaped profile, a square forehead, and his sparse hair. Yet, his entirely unprepossessing features reflected a deep kindness and an unmistakable fund of lucid urbanity. In his own manner charitable, he left no street beggar empty-handed, no supplication unanswered. Devoting his first interest to the educational and charitable institutions of Vienna, visiting its surrounding monasteries and, strangely enough, even a nunnery, this heretofore unknown man soon enjoyed the candid admiration of the people, who held him in great respect, calling him a well-informed, enlightened, "sound and solid" gentleman.

After his return to Denmark, the King's praises were sung in correspondingly favorable terms:

There is still much talk of the Danish king, who left May 16. His gift to Baron Nathan Arnstein, a gorgeous snuffbox valued at six thousand gulden, as well as the fact that His Majesty has settled a lifetime annuity of between twelve hundred to 2,000 Viennese florins on his Vienna-born mistress, are especially discussed. This female, nicknamed the "Danish widow," is now seen strolling on the promenade every evening, followed by a cluster of people.

NAPOLEON II, KING OF ROME

Napoleon II, 1811–1832, son of the great Napoleon and Marie Louise, daughter of Emperor Franz II, was born to the purple and received his title in the cradle. With Napoleon's abdication in 1814, he was brought, together with his mother and a retinue of French tutors, to the court of the Austrian emperor at Schönbrunn. Initially titled the Prince of Parma, he was created the Duke of Reichstadt in 1818, when he received as patrimony the small holding of Reichstadt in Bohemia. Virtually an Austrian prisoner, he was kept from everything French. He died of tuberculosis. A detailed report has come down to us from de La Garde, who visited the four-year-old "Eaglet" in Schönbrunn, together with Prince de Ligne:

Soon thereafter Mme. de Montesquiou took us in. Immediately upon seeing Prince de Ligne, the young Napoleon jumped up from his chair and threw himself into the old man's arms. He was really the most beautiful child imaginable. He favored his great grandmother Maria Theresa to an astonishing degree. The angelic cut of his face, the unblemished whiteness of his skin, his sparkling eyes, and the beautiful locks of his curly blond hair, cascading down to his shoulders, would have tempted any painter's brush. He was dressed in the richly embroidered uniform of a hussar and wore the Legion of Honor star on his dolman. "A Frenchman, my Prince," the marshal said to him, pointing to me. "How do you do, monsieur," said the child to me. "I like the French people."

Remembering the words of Rousseau that no one, least of all a child, likes to be questioned, I silently bent down and embraced him.—Napoleon's son is no more. Inexorable death cut short at twenty-one a life that had begun on a throne, cut it off at a moment when his most admirable traits clearly destined the young Prince for fame and when his noble mind had won him every sympathy. He had an alert and precocious mind and astonished everyone with the preciseness of his talk. His memory and quickness of learning were wonderful to behold. He mastered German in a short time and spoke it as fluently as French. His character was sound and his decisions, the result of deep thought, unshakeable. The least movement he made was full of grace; the gestures he used to underscore a point were beautiful to see and were solemnly graceful. His love of things martial was revealed in his words and eyes.

He was keenly interested in his father's life story and his grandfather, the Austrian emperor, convinced that truth must be the basis of all education, most of all that of a prince, ordered that nothing be kept back from the boy. The child listened in rapt attention to the fable of a life that in twenty years seemed to have reached the outermost limits of the believable. His gaiety and the impatience behind his desires and moods were entirely childlike, while his eagerness for knowledge and his meditative quietness bespoke a riper age. Everything about him seemed to prove that genius is hereditary. His quickness of mind stood revealed in everything relating to his famous father. The day before our visit, the English commodore, Sir Neill Campbell, who had escorted Napoleon to Elba, was announced to him. "Does it please you, my Prince," said Mme. de Montesquiou, introducing the officer to him, "to see this gentleman? He has left your father only a few days ago."

"Yes, I am very happy," he answered, putting the finger to his lips, "but let us not talk about it." The commodore took him into his arms, saying: "Your father has charged me with embracing you." The child, at the moment holding a top in his hand, threw the toy to the floor with quick and shattering force. "Poor Papa," he exclaimed and burst into tears.

Prince de Ligne showed him the commemorative coins, struck off at his birth.

"I recognize them," he told de Ligne. "It was in the days when I was still king."

Then the young Napoleon went into a corner of the room to fetch a regiment of wooden uhlans, a present of his great-uncle, Archduke Karl. A very simple mechanism caused the horsemen, mounted on moveable ribbons, to execute all sorts of military maneuvers, such as flanking, in-column movements, and the like. "Now, my Prince," said de Ligne in stentorian tones, "to the maneuvers!"

Immediately the regiment was removed from the box and set out in battle order.

"Attention," shouted the old marshal, drawing his saber and standing like a general on parade.

Immobile and attentive, solemn as a Russian grenadier, the young Prince took his post at the left flank of his troops, hand on the lever of the mechanism. A command, followed by instantaneous execution. Another—the same obedience, the same seriousness on both sides. Indeed, looking at the child's lovely face aglow with the fervor of battle and at the battle-bitten old veteran growing excited over the child's play, one would be tempted to say that the one had inherited from the parent a lively passion for the arts of war, while the other, having sloughed off forty years, was about to relive his glorious campaigns. A most delicious contrast and a picture worthy to inspire any painter's genius. The grand maneuvers were interrupted when the Empress was announced.

From all sides political events impinged on the castle walls where the imprisoned "Eaglet" sat. An early May report read:

It is said that Italian troops stationed in Vienna are openly showing their enthusiasm for young Napoleon, crying "Long live our Napoleon" when they catch sight of him in the coach or at the window.

The Russian czar, ever eager to be on good terms also with the women around Napoleon, had once more promised more than he could carry out:

There was much laughter over the Czar's latest Don Quixotic prank, when he seriously insisted that young Bonaparte in due time was to become entailed sovereign over the Duchy of Parma because he had so promised in April. But Emperor Franz and the other allies are agreed young Napoleon shall never rule. The Duchy is to go to the infant upon the death of the Archduchess Louise.[45] This so infuriated Baron Linden, Württemberg's deputy, that he exclaimed: "How is it possible for Granddad to be so unnatural as to do his daughter's child out of what is rightfully his? This is highly misplaced highmindedness."

EUGÈNE DE BEAUHARNAIS, VICEROY OF ITALY

Eugène de Beauharnais, 1781–1824, the stepson of Napoleon I, was the son of Josephine and General Beauharnais. In 1804 Napoleon raised him to the rank of a French prince and several years later adopted him and made him heir to the throne of what was then Italy. Residing in Milan, he commanded the army of the south in 1809 in the war against Austria. He was married to the daughter of Maximilian I of Bavaria. At the Congress of Vienna he was known as one of the gayest of blades among the princely crowd and was on intimate terms of friendship with Alexander of Russia. Later his father-in-law deeded him the Landgraviate of Leuchtenberg and part of the Duchy of Eichstätt. Countess Thürheim spoke of him:

Alexander all but took the dissolute Eugène Beauharnais to his bosom as a brother. Both could be seen wandering arm in arm through the most disreputable sections of the city. Many a story was told about the adventurous pair. One of Beauharnais' personal guardsmen once met two gentlemen on the stairs of a bordello. About to throw them out as rivals, he recognized, to his horror, the Czar and his own master. The position of Beauharnais at the Congress was most peculiar. While he might pass as the Bavarian king's son-in-law, his sight automatically recalled memories of the exile at Elba. His friendship with the autocrat [46] has undoubtedly given him more than one chance to secretly

[45] Marie Louise, wife of Napoleon I and young Napoleon's mother.—Transl.
[46] Alexander of Russia.—Transl.

supply news of interest to his father-in-law. Handsome, young, and gay, the Prince liberally spread his love around, running the gamut from girls of the lowest social stratum to the feet of the cold Princess Yablonovska, who, like her husband, considered it a signal honor to be singled out by Beauharnais.

Count de La Garde arrived at a rather more favorable judgment of the Viceroy:

Seeing Prince Eugène standing by himself, I approached him. At every festivity that he was forced to attend he stood out through his quiet dignity. His gentle, normally gay, face was at the time marked by somberness. Even though he was not entirely able to hide his sorrow,[47] he nevertheless courageously sought to suppress it since duty and position required this. In a word: he was a man.

Although it would be difficult to imagine a greater antithesis than Eugène and the Archduke Johann, the latter had some kind words to say about the Prince:

I liked the fellow well enough. We spoke about the campaign, the places we had opposed each other, what had happened, and the like. He of all the French was the most upright. How he must feel now, who a few months ago stood at the head of Italy, one of the first in Europe. Now he barely ranks as a French marshal and must go begging for some small piece of land. That's the world for you.

Emperor Alexander sang Eugène's praises wherever he could. Confidant *** wrote:

Alexander loves Beauharnais dearly. The Bagration woman claims he has told her: "Prince Eugène is not only an exceptional soldier, he is also a completely decent person. If he should desire to enter my service, I would be very glad to have him. He has marvelous manners."

[47] His mother had died in 1814.—Transl.

ARCHDUKE JOHANN OF AUSTRIA

Johann, 1782–1859, sixth son of Leopold II, was, like his brother Karl, slated for a military career but flunked out, first at age eighteen in the winter campaign of Hohenlinden, and again nine years later as Austrian commander of the Army of Italy, when he arrived too late to decide the battle of Wagram. From the very beginning, he had taken the Alpine peoples to his heart, suffered after the betrayal of Andreas Hofer, got involved in a well-meant conspiracy, and was put under orders by his brother, Emperor Franz, not to leave Vienna, an order later amended to ban his setting foot on Tyrolean soil. He married the post-master's daughter, Anna Plochl, and, at an advanced age, achieved a signal honor when Baron Heinrich von Gagern, President of the Frankfurt Parliament, offered him the high office of Imperial German Administrator, not because of but despite the fact that he was a prince of the Holy Roman Empire. He accepted the honor, only to relinquish it in the winter of 1849, when all was lost again.

Publisher Bertuch of Weimar wrote:

. . . together with him to the Archduke Johann in the Johannesgasse. Am introduced to him. This most excellent prince combines profound learning with dignified simplicity. His outward appearance reflects this, and one surmises oneself in the study of a scholar. He spoke about Marcel de Serre's humbuggery. Then about Styria, the definitive history of which he has worked on for years.

Much is also revealed in a letter to the Archduke from the Hohenzollern Prince William, the later German emperor:

How happy your kind letter has made me, dear Johann! Once more do I thank you from the bottom of my heart for your affection and hospitality. Even before our meeting, I loved the Archduke Johann, his fame having been sung to me in glowing terms. And then your affectionate reception showed me right away that we should surely become great good friends. If in this

I now gave free rein to my affection for you and for my dear old princely House of Hapsburg, I was again forcefully struck by the long-cherished desire that Austria and Prussia might at long last form an everlasting firm and close union, for their own lasting security and for the preservation of their mutual German fatherland against false friends and avowed enemies. Often I felt that our own feelings for each other must needs lead to closer ties between our countries. At least we have set a good example, for nothing could cloud our understanding, though the political heavens have never lowered so threateningly. I was very happy to hear about your being posted to Italy, for I know how pleased you are and how this will surely win over the new provinces. Still, I should have preferred to have seen you in command of the army that is fighting Joachim.[48] Especially at first, when news from there was anything but good, I was annoyed not to know you, or your brother Karl, there. But Frimont and Nugent have taken the offensive and with that I am placated again. There is general admiration of the good grace with which you have accepted your assignment under Schwarzenberg, and the Archduke Karl his posting to Mainz. Surely this shows the fine traits of self-denial of our caste and should eternally serve as noble examples to emulate. The heroic decision of the Sicilian Leopold is remarkable but excellent news, because in this war there cannot be enough legitimate princes to participate in the struggle.

Berlin, April 29, 1815.

GRAND DUKE CONSTANTINE OF RUSSIA

Grand Duke Constantine, 1779–1831, was the son of Paul I and brother of Alexander I and Nicholas I. He was at the Congress because of his military rank. In Vienna he attracted attention because of his unbridled temper, inherited from his father. He caused several scandals and was at last shipped off to Poland, there as general in charge of supervising the mobilization of Poland's pro-Russian fighting forces. He renounced his claim

[48] Murat.

to the throne in favor of his younger brother Nicholas. Count Benzel-Sternau supplied a short confidential report on him:

Constantine resembles his insane father. He likes to tease the enlisted men. From a hiding place in the palace courtyard he will shout: "Present arms!" The guard will tumble out and come to present arms, but no one appears, whereupon the Grand Duke dies laughing. The white uniform of his own cavalry regiment gives him an opportunity to show off his stocky build in all details, which caused many a lady's fan to flutter, arousing many a gallant memory. . . . Almost daily the Grand Duke orders the troops to move out and himself comes galloping with drawn saber, shouting "Attention!" Then follows a series of wheeling, enfilading, and defilading movements until the horses steam in hot perspiration.

There are other stories told about this enfant terrible:

Not long ago the Grand Duke on a wet, rainy day went cantering through the palace gardens at Schönbrunn. He answered the polite remonstrances of the guards and gardeners not to destroy the beautiful walk with deep hoofprints with an annoyed, unnatural roar and continued his ride to all corners of the garden.

CROWN PRINCE WILHELM OF WÜRTTEMBERG

Crown Prince Wilhelm of Württemberg, 1781–1864, later succeeded his tyrannical father, Frederick I, as Wilhelm I. His was a democratic, enlightened regime, and he was highly popular. His first wife was Caroline, daughter of Maximilian I of Bavaria. This Napoleon-enforced union was later annulled so that Caroline could ascend the Austrian imperial throne as the fourth wife of Franz II. Wilhelm thereupon married Catherine Pavlovna, the Czar's sister, who soon died, however. He was one of the most resplendent of male figures at the Congress and a friend of the Princess Bagration. Archduke Johann, jealous of Wilhelm of Württemberg as much because Catherine Pavlovna had re-

jected his brother Karl as for his own personal reasons, talked
of the Crown Prince at some length in his diary:

Dec. 11. Well, who was it fished in troubled waters again?
I fear greatly the Crown Prince would have dearly liked to do
something, for it seems he is of the party.

Dec. 20. The Crown Prince of Württemberg plays a peculiar
role. Hoodwinked by Prussia's promises, he sides with that state,
in this even opposing his father. . . . Already in London he
declared in a hostile manner that Austria was not a German state
and should not be permitted to take a hand in German affairs
but should be thrown out.

. . . . At court in the evening. Boring conversation at the
tableaux showing. Conversation between the Crown Prince of
Württemberg and me gets chillier every day. Since the day I
openly told him my mind about Saxony we don't discuss politics
any more. Instead, he asks peculiar questions, such as if I chose
the military profession voluntarily. Whereupon he said that
waging war became an addiction in the end. I made no answer,
for this is too silly.

March 4, 1815. The Crown Prince of Württemberg seems
to distance himself from Russia. He gets nowhere with his plan
to acquire his own territory on the Rhine or to obtain the command over the imperial army or the inspection over the Reich
fortifications. He wants to play a role at all cost, even courting
now the same Austria he so loudly used to rail against. Yes, he
is looking for a post: Milan and the command against Murat
course through his mind. Achieving this, he would also have a
pretext to sever relations with the Grand Duchess Catherine,
of whom, it seems to me, he has tired. The break would otherwise be awkward, he having gone much too far already. What
good are courage, knowledge, talent, if the character is not
straightforward, sound, incorruptible?

Lulu Thürheim had some details to add:

The features of the Crown Prince of Württemberg are
noble, if not handsome. His build is stocky, yet he appears elegant.
Because of the astonishingly rapid movements of his facial muscles,

his mien changes continuously, and he appears successively somber, stern to the point of hardness, then jovial, wild, sad, and tender. His is a strong character, his power of resistance is great. At home he is very popular. It is said he will marry the Princess of Oldenburg,[49] the Czar's sister—a second empress Catherine, who will try to enlarge the kingdom of Württemberg. The Prince of Württemberg loves her not; it only flattered his ego to have taken the Grand Duchess away from his rival, who could offer her nothing, in addition to his love, but the Vice Regency of Lombardy, which they would have given him, had this marriage been consummated. She was as good as promised to the Archduke Karl, when Grand Duchess Catherine met the Prince of Württemberg in London—and fell in love with him. She then exacted her brother's promise that she might betroth herself to whomever her heart chose. In Vienna the fickleness of the Prince of Württemberg aroused Catherine's jealousy. Inconstant and vain, he wooed more than one beautiful woman.

KARL JOSEPH, PRINCE DE LIGNE

Karl Joseph, Prince de Ligne, 1735–1814, enjoyed equal fame as soldier, cosmopolitan, and witty author. He was a great European figure, without a single deed to his credit that in itself bore the sign of greatness. He was an estate owner in the then Austrian Low Countries and served in Maria Theresa's armies, but was also well known at the court of Versailles, as a paladin of Marie Antoinette's and a friend of Rousseau and Voltaire. He lost his favorite estate, Bel-Oeuil, near Brussels, partly because of politico-historical events, partly because of his own prodigality. For a time he was in the service of Catherine the Great. He was unhappily married to a Princess Liechtenstein, who nonetheless bore him seven children. He was highly decorated and, though long since poverty-stricken at the opening of the Congress of Vienna, was nonetheless the paradigm of the eighteenth century, the last flower of Walloon knighthood and, in the words of

[49] Catherine Pavlovna.

Goethe, "the gayest man of the century." In 1807 Goethe wrote in his Annals:

Here at Carlsbad I was introduced to Prince de Ligne, whose name has been familiar to me for years and whose personality has become most remarkable to me because of his connections with my friends. His presence bears out his fame. He is ever gay, witty, master of any situation, and, as a true cosmopolitan, welcome and at home everywhere.

De Ligne had always been partial to Metternich's realpolitik. When his sworn enemies continued to call Napoleon "Bonaparte" after his marriage to Marie Louise, de Ligne said:

It is news to me that the Imperial Princess Marie Louise is now called Mme. Bonaparte. The hostility toward Napoleon is without doubt a sure sign of stupidity and would have proved our nemesis had not Metternich and Schwarzenberg found in this marriage, in the alliance, and the meeting of the monarchs in Dresden the appropriate countermeasure. The whole pack of lies that arrived here from Dresden was a miserable fabrication but was believed in toto by the Viennese automatons, to whom at best I concede their hatred of Napoleon, if they please, but not their finding him ludicrous. This is not at all a laughing matter.

It was precisely about de Ligne's last days in the Vienna of the Congress that we are well informed, especially by de La Garde, whose protégé and sponsor he was:

At the time, Prince de Ligne was in his eightieth year, yet it would be no lie to say he had remained young to spite old age. He had managed to retain the genial character, the airy originality, and the charming manners that made his society so entrancing. Rightfully and unanimously he was acclaimed the "doyen of European elegance." I owed him a visit and hurried to pay him my respects the day after my arrival. "You come at the right time," he told me, "to witness great events. Europe is in Vienna. The woof of politics is completely shot through with festivities. At your age one dotes on merry get-togethers, balls, entertain-

ment in general, and I guarantee you, you'll not be idle much, because the Congress does not march, it dances. It is a truly royal
mélange. . . . Who is there to sort out this chaos, to put up
a dam against this torrent of demands? I for my part want nothing
but a new hat, having ruined mine solely in tipping it to the
sovereigns that one meets at every street corner. But the time
will come, Robinson Crusoe—I mean Napoleon—notwithstanding, when a general, lasting peace will be concluded. The peoples,
hostile for so long, have at last united, their most prominent
representatives having set the example. A most curious case,
seen here for the first time: levity is winning the peace. . . ."

The Prince had retained his old habit of dining early. At
four o'clock I went to his charming house on the ramparts. It
was only the width of one room wide on all floors, and he
jokingly referred to it as his birdcage. Others were also wont to
call it "Hotel de Ligne." Soon after I arrived, he sat down to
dinner, surrounded by his genial family. Truth to tell, the repast,
like the well-known suppers of Mme. de Maintenon when she
was still the Widow Scarron, needed all the sparkle of his conversation so as not to seem more than frugal.

*The Geneva delegate and banker Eynard also mentioned
the frugality at mealtime at the de Lignes':*

He receives his guests in his bedroom. A divan, serving as bed
at night, occupies the rear wall. His two daughters, the Princess
Clary and the Countess Pálffy, are always there, as are any number of charming friends. . . . At midnight a poor supper is
served, always the same, be it for seven, eight, or thirty guests.
After supper there is talk for one or two more hours, the departure signal being the valet coming to make up the bed. For
foreigners it is the most pleasant home in Vienna.

But the Prince was no enemy of good eating. Eynard again:

To see him eat is a joy to behold. He did let himself be
coaxed a bit before he sat down, because at three he was invited
by the King of Bavaria for dinner and it was already a quarter of
an hour before two. But His Highness dearly loves the dainties

and cannot resist the temptation to taste a universally praised dish. One course followed the other, and at each the prince would exclaim: "My, but this will kill me!" With it all he drank a whole bottle of champagne all by himself. At a quarter before three he asked the time and cried: "Isn't that the limit? I have only a quarter hour left to drive to the King of Bavaria."

Gräffer, in his Viennese Memoirs, *described de Ligne's tiny house on the wall of the Mölker ramparts:*

On the wall of Mölker ramparts, six steps from the Pasqual building, there stands a tiny house with two outjutting pillars. This small house was the grand palace of the Prince de Ligne. Its outside walls were stained the same pink as were the adjoining stables and domestics' quarters. Pink as the walls were the Prince's cheeks, and pink as his cheeks was his humor, was his talk. Pink as his talk was his stationery, pink as this was his livery: everything in pink.

Countess Thürheim made de Ligne the special object of her admiration:

The main attraction of his originality and mind lay in his witty conversation. His charming phrases, mostly uttered with eyes nearly shut, remained in the memory of those who knew and talked with him. There was nothing at all malicious about his *aperçus*, though they sparkled with wit and humor. Thus he said of a general, known more for epicureanism than bravery, that he loved laurel so much because it was needed in the kitchen. Asked once by Emperor Joseph II, who had just blessed the Low Countries with new taxes, what the Dutch were saying about him, de Ligne's answer bore a double meaning: "They say Your Majesty wants everything that is good for his subjects." In his youth de Ligne pulled off many a crazy exploit, positively squandering his wealth. Once, being financially embarrassed but desiring to go from Brussels to Vienna by stagecoach, he played his own courier and ordered six horses for Prince de Ligne. He thus made the whole trip without money, paying for everything only upon arrival in Vienna.

Gräffer wrote about his final period in Vienna when there was already bitter evidence of decay:

It was late autumn when I saw him walking down Herrengasse. He wore his field marshal's uniform with nothing in the nature of an overcoat. His tunic unbuttoned, short trousers, shoes, thin silk stockings, hat under his arm. The stiff fall breeze played with his hoary locks. The noble head itself, this volcano of wit, shook. His gait was unsteady, his steps hesitant. The whole tall, hoary figure, though erect, was striving to maintain balance, was cracking, breaking up. One saw and heard this in astonishment, in fear, and with trepidation.

PRINCE ANDREAS RAZUMOVSKY

Andreas Kyrillovich Razumovsky, 1752–1836, was the son of a low court underling of the Empress Catherine II, whom she later ennobled for personal service on her behalf. He pursued a diplomatic career, became ambassador in Vienna in 1793, was later recalled in disfavor. Under Alexander he returned to Vienna where, as a newly created prince, he again became ambassador and later married the elder sister of Countess Lou Thürheim. The fire at his palace was the sensation of the Congress and was described earlier. The background story of the palace was contained in a note of an anonymous confidant:

It is known that Razumovsky has made a present of his house in the suburbs to the Czar. What is probably not known is the dialogue that accompanied this transaction. Here is a synopsis: On the day that Alexander had dined there, Razumovsky went up to the Czar with a piece of paper in his hand, saying that since His Majesty had deigned to dine at his own home in Vienna, he Razumovsky should be permitted to put the document he held in his hand at the Czar's feet. Alexander answered: "But I have dined at *your* home." "No, sire, it is at your own home that you have dined. House and park are yours, and if you condescend to accept them, here is the gift deed. It was not just a whim that made me take a million rubles out of Russia. I felt that your

Vienna embassy rated a better site than it had and decided to give it an abode deserving its status. . . ." "But your heirs! I do not want to rob them." "My heirs will be rich as it is. My brothers and I have laid something aside, so they will be well off even without this. Be assured, we certainly have considered this." Whereupon Alexander said: "In that case I accept with thanks. In a few days you shall have a token of my esteem." It is said that Razumovsky in this matter acted like a student of Malin. The Russians, who to a man are jealous of Razumovsky and are his enemies, tremble when they hear this story and see the Count [50] anew as the ambassador in Vienna—the only post the Count really cares for.

PRINCE FRANZ SERAPH ROSENBERG-ORSINI

Prince Franz Seraph Rosenberg-Orsini, 1761–1832, was a cavalry general, Commander of the Order of Maria Theresa, and Knight of the Golden Fleece. He distinguished himself in the Coalition Wars, maintained countless mistresses, and was a great spendthrift. About him von Schönholz said:

Here I must mention the evening when the councillor von L. of the War Department of country X whispered to my companion in the delicatessen "Jean de Paris" in the Herrengasse, where at the time many that belonged to the diplomatic service, or thought they did, titillated their palate and ruined their stomachs, that tonight, at ten, one might see one of Mme. B.'s "exhibitions," consisting of tableaux similar to those shown by Quirin Müller or Regenti, only minus the plaster-of-Paris coating, the gauze, or the tights. To boot, Madame limits herself and her walkers-on (each a beauty) to female "statuary." But the entire art establishment maintains such modest silence that one may enter only through the good offices of those who have already been initiated to this Byblos and its Adonis festivals. Madame B., as high priestess of Cotys initiated in all rites of that

[50] It will be recalled that princehood came only after the fire. —Transl.

goddess, in great delicacy seated the various categories of her clients separately in a show room that was entirely decorated in black. Thus, the high-ranking were placed with those of like rank, the old with the old, so that rank and years found themselves in suitable proximity. For those who came here, came with the desire of the elders who once upon a time spied on Susanna in her bath: to see, but not to be seen. Therefore, as we younger and lesser fry waited in a side room for the art show to begin, the older and more exalted ranks were led to their boxes, since the sight of a faded, pinkish parasol would put the Prince's presence beyond doubt. This telltale parasol was all that remained as souvenir of a deceased, once dearly beloved, female friend, a souvenir that never left this gentleman's side. Be the weather ever so sunny and the barometer high, the umbrella went into the coach with him. In winter, on dry and frosty days, the umbrella rode with His Highness to the opera. But, had I been this umbrella, I should not have expected to find myself at Madame B.'s. And something did at last happen to this treasured item which the Prince in all likelihood did not expect: in the hands of a merchant, to whose wife the Prince was just "paying a visit" and who had secreted himself in the alcove, the parasol transmogrified into a cudgel.

KING FRIEDRICH AUGUST I OF SAXONY

King Friedrich August I of Saxony, 1750–1827, nicknamed "the Just," because of his loyalty to Napoleon, was the one prince of the Rhine Confederation completely hated by Prussia and Austria. Initially, he did not at all pursue the traditionally anti-Prussian policy of his forebears. It was only with the 1806 defeat that he dropped Prussia and joined the Confederation of the Rhine. Soon after, by the grace of Napoleon, he became king and turned out to be the French emperor's most faithful adherent, maintaining his alliance with France even during the Wars of Liberation. At the Battle of Leipzig he was taken prisoner and brought first to Friedrichsfelde, then, via Vienna, to Bratislava. At the Congress of Vienna it was his country, next to Poland, that proved the greatest bone of contention. Friedrich August, in the end, lost two-fifths of his territory. Countess Thürheim related a touching story about the imprisoned king:

In the midst of these glittering and gallant princes, Friedrich August I, King of Saxony, meekly and modestly stayed out of the limelight, victim of his loyalty toward Napoleon. Much of his territory gone, robbed of his generals and soldiers, he sought justice or at least consolation in prayer. Those attending mass or vespers could often see him kneeling in a corner of St. Stephan's cathedral, imploring the Lord of Hosts to give him the patience needed to suffer without rancor the intrigues of the temporal lords against him. Once, at the time of the Annunciation, the Countess Hatzfeld, a Saxon lady, visited the cathedral but found all seats taken. Her flunky, carrying the prayerbook, approached a nondescript man and offered him a piece of copper for his seat. When the man did not move, the Countess ordered her servant to proffer a piece of silver. But even this promised reward failed to budge the man. Enraged at the stubbornness of this devotee, the Countess was about to mention her name, thus claiming her seemingly just due, when words failed her: she had recognized her own king.

Even after Saxony's royal family had been transferred to Bratislava on March 4, 1815, the secret police kept an eye on it:

It is reported that the King and Queen of Saxony seldom hold court at Bratislava. There is much visiting the theater, however, for which the presence of the Saxon court is a windfall. There is little hope that Baron Zinneck and his group of actors will soon come to Baden this summer.

Statesmen, Politicians, and Lesser Lights

METTERNICH

Klemens Wenzel Lothar Nepomuk, Prince Metternich-Winneburg-Ochsenhausen, 1773–1859, leading Austrian statesman at the time of the Congress and later Europe's foremost politician, was the scion of an ancient Rhenish noble family. Like his father, he entered the Austrian imperial service in Vienna at an early age. He represented the Empire at the Rastatt Congress, was Austrian envoy in Dresden and became ambassador in Paris in 1806. There, he fell in love with Caroline, Napoleon's sister, and became acquainted with the sly politics of Talleyrand and Fouché. He engineered Austria's declaration of war on France in 1809 but, following defeat, changed to a policy of conciliation and resolutely sponsored the marriage of Marie Louise to Napoleon. In 1813 he first played a waiting game, but, after a talk with Napoleon in Dresden, he led Austria from a neutral role into the camp of the allies. Even after the Battle of Leipzig he sought a rapprochement with France, fearing an all-powerful Russia. His main effort at the Congress of Vienna was devoted to curbing the territorial appetite of his allies in Poland and Saxony. His post-1815 politics were conducted under the banner of legitimacy, conservatism, and confederacy. After 1830 the Metternich "system" slowly disintegrated, collapsing entirely in 1848, with Metternich fleeing to England. He returned to Vienna in

1851, and he was occasionally consulted by the Emperor on politi-
cal questions. He died shortly before the battle of Solferino. Met-
ternich was entirely unprincipled, tricky, and absentminded, but
incorruptible and loyal. He was very suave and, above all, highly
intelligent—shortsighted only where it concerned those under
him. At the Congress, as always and everywhere, these traits
earned him undying hatred on the one hand and unconditional
friendship on the other.

At the time, Prince Metternich could be counted for a young
man. His features were handsome and very regular, his smile
enchanting. His face expressed wisdom and kindness. He was of
medium, well-proportioned height, and there was something noble
and elegant about his gait. At the very first meeting one was
pleasantly surprised to recognize in him one of those men who
are lavishly endowed by nature with those attributes that seem
meant only for frivolous social success. But there could be no
doubting his extraordinary political genius once one had looked
into his eyes and made a careful study of his physiognomy, revealing at once great flexibility and steadfastness. Then he became completely the statesman, used to directing people and to
guiding the most momentous affairs of state.

Active for thirty years in the enormous task of reshaping
Europe, Metternich has put to ample proof the unusual agility
of his mind and that rare perceptiveness and penetrating intellect which foresees coming events and shapes them. His judgment,
the product of prolonged meditation, is unshakable and his words
decisive, as befits a statesman who is conscious of the influence
of his least pronouncement. Metternich is incidentally one of the
foremost raconteurs of our time. Politically, he has been re-
proached for being an entirely too firm believer in the laws of
inertia. Surely, a mind as developed as his must have realized that
mankind is not destined to remain forever at the same level and
that to remain stationary is tantamount to retrogression in our
century. But he doubtless also knew that convulsions are not always progressive and that men must be led with due regard to
their habits and real needs. If the moment was not yet come to

render a definitive verdict about Prince Metternich, contemporary history must content itself with putting beyond doubt the peaceful and untroubled happiness that his calm and quiet stewardship have brought to the Austrian realm. This happiness, sufficient unto itself, justifies his claim to fame and will be duly entered in the balance.

Metternich's negative political qualities were sharply limned by Talleyrand, the French chief delegate. The latter was adept at focusing the sights on the deep-rooted conflict between Metternich and Alexander I. He wrote in his memoirs:

In the morning of the day of my departure for Hungary, the Czar had a talk with Metternich in which he apparently treated the Austrian minister with such rudeness and overbearance that even the servants were shocked. When Metternich remonstrated with the Czar that if it were only a question of creating a unified Poland, Austria could also bring this about, the Czar not only called this comment improper and indecent but angrily declared Metternich to be the only Austrian who would dare to be so recalcitrant. It is said their differences reached a point where Prince Metternich declared he would ask the Emperor to appoint another minister for the Congress. After this talk, according to his intimates, he was in a state never seen in him before. The same man who only a few days ago told Count Schulenburg, Saxony's representative, that time was on his side and patience his weapon, might well lose his balance should he be exposed to another such trial. The views of the military minds and of the archdukes will hardly allow Metternich any longer to abandon Saxony. It is therefore quite likely that the Austrian emperor will harden his viewpoint considerably.

In this regard a complaint was voiced, which Abbé Carpani formulated in this manner:

Metternich treats the sovereigns a bit too offhandedly, talking to them without getting up and employing an insulting tone.

Talleyrand blamed Metternich also for the way in which he treated members of the royal family:

This person does not strike me as the Prime Minister of the Austrian dynasty, for he dethrones one member of the royal family after the other, in the end probably also his master. . . . Metternich will even lend his hand to depriving his monarch's sister of her patrimony.

Time and again the confidential agents' reports during the Hungarian visit concerned the Czar's desires to see Metternich removed from his position:

Since the day before yesterday I have heard much talk at Count Rechberg's, Alt-Pergen's, and Baron Pufendorf's about two scenes Metternich had before the Hungary journey, one with the Czar, the other with our emperor. The rumor is that the Czar wants Metternich fired and will use the trip to Hungary, when he is alone with Emperor Franz, to achieve his objective. About this, Prince Metternich's enemies are openly delighted, eloquent proof of the reciprocating influence of the Austro-Russian court intrigues and the Congress intrigues. They mock and sneer over the fact that the Congress took place in the capital and residential city of Vienna.

*Domestically, also, there was much for which to blame Metternich. Says Agent ***:*

There is no doubt that even though the proven friends of Prince Metternich proclaim him to be a truly good person who treats well even those who slander him behind his back, I think I have noticed that Prince Starhemberg, the Stadion crowd, the Schönborn-Leyens, Dalberg, Schönborn-Stadion, and Hatzfeld would gladly see a change at their Foreign Ministry. To achieve this, the Congress must break up. To break up the Congress, there's intrigue and rumor-mongering at Razumovsky's, Castlereagh's, Humboldt's, Rechberg's, Stein's, etc. Prince Starhemberg says: "It is true I never was close to Castlereagh, my English contacts being with the Grenville family, but in Vienna I assiduously cultivate Castlereagh's house in order to learn what I can and influence where I may. . . . At the state chancery all those over whose heads Count Mercy was appointed are disgruntled, and they foresee another such disregarding of seniority forthcoming in von Handel's appointment. All these people plot against Metternich and may well involve the foreign courts in their intrigues. There certainly is no solidarity at the chancery. I do not know if Prince Metternich knows how little the chancery personnel heeds the need for secrecy or how weak is its attachment to him. Baron von Limpens tells us all we want to know about the chancery."

Everything in the Vienna of the Congress was suffused with a touch of erotic intrigue, which was really also at the bottom of the antagonism between Metternich and Alexander. A lengthy confidant's report throws some light on this matter. Though the report was anonymous, it concluded with the phrase: "Submitted with reference to the author."

The Prussians, in particular the Humboldt circle, heap much ridicule on our ministry. They say: "Metternich is beside himself with love and hurt vanity. Each morning he wastes five to six hours by not arising before ten and, scarcely dressed, going to sigh in the ears of the Sagan woman. Thus, he has barely time to see three or four of the forty people who daily need to meet with him, so much so that Hudelist, Gentz, and Kruft have to cool their heels for hours. Despite this, he is completely convinced he rules the world, as four years ago in Paris he was under the delusion of having brought about eternal peace." Stadion is said to be no financial wizard but, out of love of bigotry and coquetry with women, does not even make a serious attempt at business. The laziness of Schwarzenberg is said to be such that he thinks of nothing but hunting. Ugarde [51] is totally incompetent and only concerned with whoring. Under these circumstances, Prussia has no trouble pushing through all its plans. In all Austria, it is claimed, there is no effective opposition, and it follows that the Prussians play the leading role in Germany, a role all other powers must needs support since nothing can be expected from Austria.

Princess Bagration takes revenge for Metternich's neglect by

[51] Minister of Interior.

openly revealing all she knows or has heard that might hurt
Austria. Not only does she inform Alexander, but La Harpe,
Osherovsky, her brother-in-law, Anstetten and Nesselrode as well.
She does not hesitate to tell, especially to the Austrians, every
horrible tale concerning Vienna. Metternich, for his part, is
meanwhile trying to get Duchess Sagan's abuse of him out of
his mind. He didn't see her at all last night and assiduously pays
court to Julie Zichy. This is happy news to all those who wish
the monarchy well, because there's no one more adept at intriguing than the Duchess nor anyone who has cost him more
time. There is no doubt that he had become the laughingstock
of the young people, even though he is head and shoulders above
them. Incidentally, Julie Zichy is too religious and truly virtuous
for any scandal to attach to this liaison.—Wenzel Liechtenstein, Count Schulenburg, aide-de-camp to Prince Schwarzenberg,
and Prince Louis de Rohan are, among others, three individuals
who serve Metternich's secret purposes well.

*Mention was also made of friends of Metternich who
stood by him in the cabal game:*

Vis-à-vis the many voices that debunk and mock Metternich,
there are several families, such as the Esterházys, Karl Liechtenstein, and others, who speak highly of him. They claim: "He
is only doing his duty when he seeks to frustrate Alexander's
design to become King of Poland. If the police had only sent the
Bagration woman and the other tricky one from Courland packing as early as August, this whole hurly-burly would not be with
us. It would really be something if two foreign princely whores
should succeed with their cabals in effecting ministerial changes
in Vienna."

*It is somewhat surprising to hear the far-from-puritanical
Talleyrand call Metternich frivolous:*

What is to be expected of a person who in the gravest
of situations spends most of his time in trifling and does not
hesitate to stage a dress rehearsal of *The Pasha of Suresnes* at
his house?

One of Metternich's most outspoken foes was Karl-August of Saxe-Weimar:

Every sensible Austrian, with the archdukes in the lead, is convinced that the whole miserable mess is caused by the frivolity, trickery, short-sightedness, and general ignorance of this goddamn Prince Metternich. . . . The Emperor has confidence in him, but no one else does.

Gentz, the so-called "secretary of the Congress" and Metternich's right hand man, made up his mind about the latter even before Congress opened. He confided to his diary:

The Prince always keeps a hundred balls in the air and is perhaps a touch too active for his own interest. He is talented, skillful, and intrepid, but at the same time careless, often given to trifling, and is self-centered. If his luck holds out—he believes himself to be fortune's favorite—he may well succeed in doing himself and Austria a good turn.

Metternich's incorruptibility seems beyond doubt and is corroborated by Baron Peter Mayendorff, former Russian chargé d'affaires in Vienna:

He has not abused his position to amass wealth. His income is no more than one hundred thousand gulden silver, yet he is in debt to the Rothschilds for half a million, despite the fact that during his incumbency he has received material gifts, including diamonds, from the sovereigns in excess of two million guldens' worth.

Toward the end of the Congress, Joseph de Maistre, the great philosopher of realism, wrote home from St. Petersburg, where distance may well have lent perspective:

There is no understanding Austria. From the very lowest of depths it has catapulted itself into the clouds. To deny Metternich's resourcefulness is not being very bright, for without a great deal of it there could never have been such returns for smaller stakes than the others had dared to risk.

TALLEYRAND

Charles-Maurice de Talleyrand-Périgord, 1754–1838, was born into French high nobility. Despite his profligacy, he was destined for the Church. A year after he was named Bishop of Autun, he renounced his religious vows and endorsed the civil constitution for the clergy. He went to England on a peace mission for the Convention. Unsuccessful in this, he was forced to take refuge in the United States. He returned to France in 1795 and soon became champion and a minister of Napoleon when the latter became First Consul and Emperor. As Foreign Minister he participated in all of Napoleon's adventures and failures but abandoned him in Erfurt in 1808, betraying him to the Czar. Berated by Napoleon for this, Talleyrand vowed revenge, which he carried out in 1814 by winning over the Russian emperor to the Bourbon cause and to that of legitimacy. At the Congress of Vienna his energetic stand and skillful maneuvering made him the most successful of statesmen. In his late years he was appointed French Ambassador in London and died at an advanced age two days after he had made his peace with the Pope. Talleyrand was a womanizer, but, in contrast to Metternich, he was not the servant of the ladies but their master. He was ugly, misshapen, corrupt, and imperturbable—without doubt one of the greatest, if probably the most revolting, figure in the European politics of the time.

A Countess Romer, recently from France, relates that Napoleon, talking of Talleyrand, had said: "Twice I have been in the wrong with Talleyrand: once, in not following his wise council, and the second time, in not hanging him when he failed to obey the policy I laid down to him."

Napoleon said this in 1815, after his return from Elba and after time had run out for him. Honest Bertuch, the publisher, shortly after he arrived in Vienna, wrote about Talleyrand:

Talleyrand plays a highly important role. Ostensibly it is Dalberg who is the French delegate at the Congress. In actuality it is Talleyrand who pulls the strings and who is the great brain that, because of Saxony, pulled even England over to his side to serve his interests. It is confidentially reported that Talleyrand has submitted a note in which he states that France makes no claims whatever, except for the sovereignity and integrity of every one of its allies. Should one of them (Saxony) be insulted, 220,000 French troops stand by its side.

The role of gray eminence was initially much to Talleyrand's liking. A confidant put it this way:

The difficulty of making a detailed study of Talleyrand will be apparent to everyone who takes into consideration his character and, especially, the nature of his house. The latter is a veritable fortress in which he and his intimates are ensconced. He looks like a fabulous monster, half man, half serpent (because of the way he drags his legs), or like an old, lame, drunk village schoolmaster.

Nostitz, who was also able to observe Talleyrand at close range, was apparently unable to form an independent opinion about him that is free of contradictions:

Talleyrand finds it less and less possible to prevail, as if it is now time to witness a France denuded of all glamour. One hears: "His political efforts are in vain, since they are no longer supported by four hundred thousand bayonets." He has actually achieved nothing, but by means of quite a few clever intrigues he certainly succeeds in keeping separated those parts that France does not wish to see united. "I want nothing for myself," he says. "France wants nothing. I am here only to safeguard political principles against attack." But such talk notwithstanding, he undoubtedly has specific tasks to perform, none of which he has carried out so far. Is it not logical to believe that Louis XVIII would like to see a Bourbon once more on the Neapolitan throne? Is it not natural, instinctively to recall France's deep-rooted desire to see itself surrounded only by weak sovereigns?

A few weeks later Nostitz revised his judgment:

Talleyrand is the most important of the diplomats, even though he effaces himself in view of his country's vicissitudinous past, or out of increasing indolence, or perhaps even on principle. About the sovereigns he says: "They have neither the courage to break apart nor the sense to unite." As from another, possibly hellish, world, this old curmudgeon gazes into the arena and does nothing except send notes to everyone, pointing out to the recipient the advantages to be gained by this or that action, the mere thought of which creates an atmosphere of static stubbornness against each other. Thus it happens, as it was bound to do, that because of the basic illiberality and inflexibility of all parties, there is no end in sight for the Congress, which by now resembles nothing so much as an Archimedes screw with which the gentlemen are mutually trying to outdo each other. In the course of time all nations have developed a lopsided position to each other. As to the Congress itself, it will probably terminate finally because of some outward cause that in the end always guides events if reason fails to prevail. The simplest cause would be simply the need for going home.

An entirely positive but greatly overdrawn picture of his fellow countryman was sketched by de La Garde, who was socially much indebted to Talleyrand. He described a levee of the Prince:

The Prince gave the luncheon in honor of his birthday. On this day, February 13, 1815, he entered upon his sixty-first year. Those who cherish the collecting of the most trivial peculiarities of the life and character of a famous personage have not failed to describe the worrisome care that the Prince lavished on his appearance, nor the coquetry he exhibited at his levees. And it is a fact that the latter reminded one at once of Mazarin and Madame de Pompadour. Eager to learn the details, I accompanied the messieurs Boigne de Faye and Rouen into the bedchamber of their illustrious benefactor, there to wish him happy returns of the day.

The doyen of diplomats appeared at this very moment from behind the thick folds around his bedstead. A small number of intimates of both sexes had already gathered in the room.

Wrapped in a powder cape of pleated and embroidered muslin, the Prince began his toilet. To begin with, he delivered up his luxurious hair, not, as might be expected, to two women, but to two male hairdressers, who set busily to work and finally achieved their well-known creation of a free-flowing hair-do. Then, it was the barber's turn, who finished by enveloping him in a cloud of scented powder. Following the care of head and hands, the feet came next—a less delectable detail because of the nauseating smell of the eau-de-Barèges used to lave his limping leg. Now all was done to perfection and, though not his valet, we could gaze at the hero of diplomacy in his negligee. To me, it was in this get-up, rather than in his ministerial robes, that he appeared the very epitome of those aristocratic and courtly manners that now, sad to say, are a thing of the past. Now it was the first chamberlain's turn to put on the finishing touches, complete the whole, put the last lick into place. At table M. de Talleyrand not only maintained his wonted urbanity and suavity but showed himself more congenial than in his salons, where it was evident, despite his ingenuous mien, that he was on his guard. Here no longer reigned the usual silence, said to have been perfected by him to the point of eloquent rhetoric, as he showed how to raise experience to prescience. If his talk was less profound here, it was perhaps, by the same token, more irresistible: he spoke from the heart and without restraint. Although Mme. de Périgord was present, it was the Prince alone who did the honors: he personally served from all the dishes, offered every kind of wine, and directed a few well-meant and witty words to each of his guests.

On another occasion, de La Garde was less concerned with Talleyrand's physical traits than with his political thoughts:

Vis-à-vis a man like Talleyrand one involuntarily experiences an unconquerable feeling of diffidence and awe. . . . That power which Talleyrand failed to find in his government he found in himself. There is no denying that he was the focal point of the French delegation at the Congress, however great the contribution or personal influence of the others might have been. With his miraculous perception that seemed to foresee coming events and shape their course, he soon regained for France its rightful place. In the steering committee, composed of the four major powers, he turned every opinion, every trend, upside down. "I bring you more than you presently have," he told those powers, "I bring the idea of legality." He split apart the powers that until then had been allied. He hinted at the danger that a greatly enlarged Russia would be for the rest of Europe and presented a scheme for rolling back Russia toward the north. He was able to convince Austria and England of his arguments. It was for this reason that Alexander, who six months ago under Talleyrand's influence and in his very salon had decided on the restoration of the Bourbon dynasty, in great displeasure saw his projects go awry through the efforts of the delegate of a state that owed him, Alexander, its very existence. In his uglier moods he would often state: "M. de Talleyrand plays the minister of Louis XIV here."

Talleyrand steadfastly remained champion of a just balance of all powers. In a confidential report of January 28, 1815, we read:

At Talleyrand's the talk was mainly about the progress made at the Congress. The Knights of Malta, Serra-Capriola said, remembering the terms of the Treaty of Amiens, would scarce be content if Malta were not returned to them. Talleyrand joined in: "Quite right. Everyone should leave the Congress a little discontented. Everybody must make some sacrifice. Out of these sacrifices grows the community of all: the commonweal."

About Talleyrand's pet idea, the balance of power, an intercepted letter from the Swedish delegate, Löwenhjelm, to Sweden's Foreign Minister, Engeström, had this to say:

Prince Talleyrand misses no chance on behalf of his sovereign to preach moderation and a fair balancing of power in Europe. A few days ago he said that if Russia's claims were any indication, it seemed as if war had been made on Napoleon more because of his successes than on account of his political ambitions. It would be bad indeed to topple one colossus only to raise up another.

Even Archduke Johann's verdict about Talleyrand was not unfavorable. On October 22 he wrote in his diary:

Talked to Talleyrand. What an interesting man! A worm-eaten heart but an excellent head. He speaks quite sincerely about the past and told me about Napoleon's adventure in Spain. Napoleon, Talleyrand assured me, never had had a long-range plan. The latest events always had furnished him the key to the next venture. Thus, on termination of the Russian campaign, he had Constantinople on his military timetable. An ultimate goal he did not reach.

On Talleyrand's "heart" some light was shed by reports of episodes occurring during the visit of the Allied sovereigns and their leading politicians to the King of Saxony in his exile at Bratislava. On this occasion Talleyrand met an earlier love. We read about this in his own memoirs:

The affection that Countess Brionne and her daughters, the Princesses de Carignan and Charlotte of Lorraine, called Mlle. de Lorraine, bore me compensated me for my vexatious church career. The beauty of a woman, her noble pride linked with the nimbus of a high and famous descent, lends a special charm to the feelings she arouses, be it in a friend or a foe. For this very reason I have recalled with far greater joy the time I was in disfavor at court than the much more happy episodes of my life that have left no trace in my mind or heart.

Then Talleyrand described the reunion:

Countess Brionne had for many years showed an affection for me otherwise only showered on one's children. But then she had fallen out with me over an imagined slight. When I arrived at Bratislava I hurried to throw myself at her feet. She kept me there long enough for me to have the pleasure of feeling her tears on my face. "Finally, you have come," she said to me. "I never gave up hope of seeing you again. I had reason to be angry with you, but I never ceased loving you. My feelings for you have accompanied you everywhere." Unable to speak, I wept. In her infinite kindness she tried to calm me by questioning me: "Your position is an admirable one," she said. "Oh yes, very admirable indeed." My tears choked me, and my sensitive feelings were so deeply stirred that I had to rush out to regain my composure on the banks of the nearby Danube. When I had become somewhat calmer, I returned to her. She repeated her questions, and I was able to answer more coherently. . . . Several days later, death robbed me of this friend, whom I had been so happy to meet once again.

Sentimental, cold, and imperturbable, never at a loss:

When asked once what had occupied him in the interim between the allies' crossing of the Rhine and Napoleon's abdication, Talleyrand answered: "I kept limping along."

VISCOUNT CASTLEREAGH

Robert Stewart, second Viscount Castlereagh, 1769–1822, Irish landowner, became, after the death of the Younger Pitt, the guiding spirit of the battle against Napoleon. He was the outstanding figure in Liverpool's Cabinet. Ideologically in agreement with Metternich, his secret alliance between England, France, and Austria in January, 1815, avoided imminent war among the allies. On the domestic front Castlereagh was the scourge of the Fourth Estate. It was he who in the final analysis bears responsibility for the Peterloo worker massacre. During the divorce proceedings of King George IV, his position was precarious. Suffering from a persecution complex, he finally committed suicide. In Vienna the "noble lord" was never taken quite seriously, was always seen as somewhat of a caricature. His name was nearly always linked with that of his wife. His political turnabout was the one event that the Viennese observers made much of. Archduke Johann also made mention of this in his diary:

Only yesterday I learned the confirmation of what I had heard, namely that Castlereagh, Stewart, and Münster received instructions via courier to insist on the continued existence of Poland and Saxony and to support Austria in all this. Also, it is clear now that France is adopting a moderate, legalistic position and firmly opposes the impertinent demands of Russia and Prussia, even as the other sovereigns ought to do. Now, only steadfastness and courage and not so much talk, and surely all will go well!

Count Nostitz, judging from externals only, said about the Castlereagh couple:

This extraordinary ambassador appears very unprepossessing and, for an Englishman, strange. His wife, on the other hand, runs true to type: dresses in a ludicrously theatrical manner, is colossal and heavy-footed, plump and garrulous. She is thus butt of society and resembles an alehouse wife.

Agent *** joined in the general mocking of the couple:

There is also much laughter over the fact that Lord and Lady Castlereagh always walk arm in arm, whether on the street, in the homes they visit, in the rooms, or in the shops. There is likewise comment about their demanding that everything in the shops be shown to them, without buying a single thing. They are called: "the small-town Englishmen" and about them is said: "There never have been such cheapskates of Englishmen in Vienna before." At the much-admired masked ball there was tittering over Lady Castlereagh wearing her husband's Order of the Garter ribbon around her hat.

Only banker Eynard, the Swiss delegate, had a kind word to say about the Castlereaghs:

At their house everyone is made to feel at home so that one goes there with great pleasure. Their home is comfortable and the atmosphere relaxed. Formalities are at a minimum, host and hostess self-effacing, and one gathers at the house of the Minister of Great Britain as in a Viennese café. . . . Toward eleven the servants carry two richly laden tables into the salon, whereupon

Lady Castlereagh invites two of the guests to sit next to her, and every remaining seat at her table is immediately taken by an Englishman. This leaves the second table for the guests.

BARON VOM STEIN

Karl, Reichsfreiherr [52] *vom und zum Stein, 1757–1831, born of old Rhenish nobility, joined the Prussian civil service at an early age. He caused the abolition of serfdom and of the class system in Prussia. Dismissed from the Prussian service in 1808, Stein was engaged by the Russian czar. His influence in Russia, as in Prussia, was great and included persuading Alexander I to cross Russia's western borders after Napoleon's defeat in 1812. He was the foremost champion of German unification, once victory was achieved, and opposed the Confederation of the Rhine and Metternich. He enjoyed a quiet old age at the Kappenberg Abbey in Westphalia. About him Göhausen wrote:*

In Saxon circles it is said as a matter of fact that Baron Stein is trying to persuade the Austrian emperor to resume his title and role as ruler of the Holy Roman Empire. In this he sees the only chance for German unification. This is the reason, also, why he insists on a revival of the constitutions of the imperial cities and of the imperial knighthood caste. Out of the latter he hopes to create a middle class which, solidly united, will serve as counterweight and foil against any bold action of the powerful German princes and thus become the mainstay of the Holy Roman Emperor.

At the Congress Stein was one of the most enigmatic of figures, one which baffled the confidants:

Baron Stein lacks more in form than in substance. Accustomed to combat revolutionary trends, he has gone from one extreme to the other. . . . Well-meaning in intent and the goals he seeks, his means of getting there are often harsh and have

[52] A baronial title bestowed by the sovereign of the realm and admitting of no other allegiance except to the sovereign.—Transl.

saddled him with the onus of Jacobinism, even if it is only in the outward forms that he errs.

Above all, Stein was courageous. Even his master, Alexander, got told off:

Baron Stein is said to have incurred the Czar's displeasure for openly having told him that to go back on previous declarations and to insist now that this member of the Napoleonic dynasty (Eugène Beauharnais) be indemnified with German territory would forever besmirch the Czar's great name.

PRINCE VON HARDENBERG

Karl August, Prince von Hardenberg, 1750–1822, of Hanoverian descent, became Prussian administrator of Ansbach and Bayreuth, concluded the Basel "Treaty of Shame," was appointed Prussian Foreign Minister, and soon after became Chancellor. He mediated between Stein, the radical reformer, and the King. In Vienna he was highly successful on Prussia's behalf. Greatly handicapped by deafness, he turned this adversity into a virtue and, set free from social and erotic ties, put out a prodigious amount of work. All agent reports were in agreement on this point:

He is looked upon as the most diligent statesman at the Congress. As early as April, in Paris, he worked out an all-embracing plan for a new order in Europe and came to Vienna prepared as no one else. Since then, he has worked without letup. Starting on Metternich's side in the Polish question, he was directed to switch to Russia only in November. Contrary to Humboldt, Hardenberg is conciliatory and ready to compromise. . . . The Sicilian delegate, Marsan, claims that Hardenberg received one hundred thousand ducats from Eugène Beauharnais. Marsan, acquainted with Hardenberg from his Berlin days, knew of the latter's often precarious financial straits. Yet in Vienna an entry in Marsan's diary is said to state that the Prussian chancellor spends two thousand gulden daily. But Marsan is conscientious enough to admit that on the selfsame day he himself lost 962 gulden in three rubbers of whist. . . . A low-ranking agent, assigned the mission of observing Prince Radziwill's daily pro-Prussian activities, in a report of October 25, 1814, stated that the Czar's two court Jews had carried a bag filled with money to Radziwill, who, in his turn, took it along to dinner with Hardenberg and left it there. Could this money, a present of Alexander, have been meant for Hardenberg?

WILHELM VON HUMBOLDT

Wilhelm von Humboldt, 1767–1835, began his career in the field of education, became Prussian Minister of Education, and founded that nation's humanistic high school. At the Congress of Vienna he was a much more radical element than Hardenberg, whom, as second delegate, he ably assisted and spurred on in the interest of Prussian expansionism. On terms of friendship with Goethe and Schiller, Humboldt left the Prussian service in 1819. His correspondence with his wife Caroline, née von Dachröden, affords an excellent insight into his inner being and at the same time into the workings of the Congress. Believing in a Prussian manifest destiny, he opposed Metternich, but upon Napoleon's return from Elba he energetically sponsored joint action of the two principal German powers.

Baron Humboldt was much worried about the turn of events and their results for France and, especially, for Prussia. Prussia's sole interest at the moment, he said, would be the closest collaboration with Austria, and every Prussian patriot should do his utmost in this direction. Austria need not fear Napoleon, because she only made war on him and had no part in his dethronement. An Austrian (Count Clam, in April, 1814, through an exchange of uniforms) had even saved Napoleon's life, worse luck now. Humboldt added that there was still no reasonable explanation how Napoleon's escape from Elba had been engineered and where the money had come from.

Even de La Garde, to whose flighty mind this happily married humanist must have seemed a strange bird indeed, paid attention to Humboldt. He mentioned the latter in connection with the portraits which the French painter Isabey was commissioned to paint of the more prominent Congress members:

Isabey had been assured that Humboldt would be difficult to deal with, for his aversion to being painted was well known. Even Princess Louise Radziwill, sister of Prince Ferdinand of Prussia, had drawn a refusal. Thus briefed, and somewhat intimidated anyway, Isabey bearded the diplomat. His feigned or real embarrassment put the generally good-humored baron in an expansive mood, and, transfixing his visitor with his great blue eyes, he told him: "Now look at me carefully and you'll have to admit that nature has been too unkind for you not to agree that to paint me you should not waste a single penny. Don't you agree? Nature would indeed think me a fool, should I entertain such silly vanity. No, let her realize that I am nothing daunted by the mean trick she played on me." Struck by his answer, the astonished painter studied the highly irregular features of the minister. "But I wouldn't think of letting Your Excellency pay me for this pleasant task. If you would only kindly pose a few times."—"Only that? I shall sit as often and as long as you wish. Don't be bashful. But I must insist that I pay you for my ugly face." And so the witty diplomat did indeed pose as often as the artist desired. When done, the painting was universally acclaimed as the best likeness and caused Humboldt often to remark wryly: "True, I did not pay for my portrait. But Isabey took his revenge: he made it look like me."

FRIEDRICH VON GENTZ

Friedrich von Gentz, 1764–1832, the son of a Prussian civil servant, at first joined the Prussian civil service himself. He translated Burke's Reflections on the Revolution in France, *sharing the Englishman's views. In 1802 he accepted Austrian employ and very soon became Metternich's right-hand man. In Vienna he was known chiefly as the "Secretary of the Congress," but he also served Metternich as go-between and aide in the latter's private love affairs. Psychologically, Gentz was a modern man, yet he championed Metternich's system of legitimacy in all European matters. He was epicurean, corrupt, money-hungry, interested in art, and sentimental.*

A later age, quite unjustly, has depicted Gentz as one of the most frivolous actors in this frivolous world concert, as a voluptuous old diplomat, a comic opera figure who wore make-up and who, with opera glass in palsied hand and nibbling dainties, skulked after court ballerinas. There is little truth in this picture. Gentz was in fact one of the most diligent workers at the Congress. His function, as he himself put it, was "to lend style to the events" and avoid all ambiguousness by clothing everything of moment in the most apt of all possible French or German wording.

Thus a source of that "later age." He bore the title "Secretary of the Congress" for good reasons, for it was he who formulated every important resolution and, above all, the final report of the Congress. Count Nostitz, Prussian to the core, saw Gentz quite naturally as a product of decadence:

Gentz is the harassed businessman and is like a woman in labor—*parturiuntur montes*, etc.[53] This person, once such a scatterbrain and epicure, has positively turned pharisaical. He has completely lost his *élan*, and nothing of lasting greatness will grow out of his "trip-along" wisdom. . . . Gentz is getting old and gray. His soul and body shake in an everlasting febrile chill of a moral and physical cold. While fits of youthful ardor may still move him occasionally, he keeps them well under control and rigidly stops short of complete surrender. Also, the old diplomat is cribbed by the strictures of his adoptive fatherland and now stands in fear of the very spirit that once was strong in him. That is why he is ill at ease with former friends if they do not travel along his road. But the written word will not be

[53] *Parturiunt montes, nascetur ridiculus mus* (Horace, *Ars Poetica*): No matter how the mountain strains in labor, it will bear only a silly mouse.

erased: the Gentz from Berlin is not the Vienna Gentz. Doubting Thomases should read what the former wrote in earlier days.

Foremost in the ranks of "former friends" stood Wilhelm von Humboldt who, in his relations with Gentz, held a unique position between hate, love, contempt, and admiration. His wife's attitude towards Gentz was much less equivocal: she rejected him and emphatically said so to her husband in her letters. In his replies Humboldt tried to reassure her on this score:

I seldom see Gentz any more, almost not at all. Two things have drawn me to him in the past: the profit one may derive from his well-known qualities and a certain loyalty I have always felt for him. The Prussians to a man are against him, thus bearing you out. Baron Stein recently called him a man with a dried-up brain and a moldy character. Hardenberg doesn't trust him.

In a subsequent letter Humboldt wrote his wife:

Since coming here I have looked up Gentz only when I needed him for my own purposes, now no longer necessary. Ours are disparate natures and what attracted me in him in my youth, his attempt to draw fruitful reflection from the very opposition of our natures, all that is dead in him now. He has gone dull and has very much deteriorated.

Caroline left no stone unturned to set her husband against Gentz:

Gentz is Prussia's most active opponent, always trying his best to hurt her. . . . Oh, believe me, he is another one whose better nature succumbed to loose living and physio-moral drifting. The most sacred cause of our time finds no echo in him. Because I sensed this very deeply in him, he has become revolting to me. To me his speeches are mere bombast; they no longer transport one. Don't trust him!

Gentz changed to the extent that his fanatic hatred of Napoleon turned into a more tolerant attitude. Even before the Congress opened he wrote to Count de Damas, an enthusiastic champion of the Bourbons:

Don't be so stubborn in your opinion that peace cannot be signed with Napoleon. You are in error there. All powers, even England, can come to terms with Napoleon, may do so any moment. If Napoleon signs, he remains on the throne.

Here Gentz was in error, even as his master, Prince Metternich, was in error at Châtillon. Following Austria's rapprochement with France, after the first Treaty of Paris, supported by Gentz, Talleyrand went all out to woo the secretary over to his side. Interesting here is an entry in Gentz's diary:

December 30 (1814). Dined with Talleyrand. In the name of the French king, he presented me with a munificent gift (24,000 florins).

In matters of the heart of his lord and master, Gentz identified with Metternich to the point of self-effacement. Gentz, who was extremely garrulous, talked about this in several letters and in his diary:

On May 8, 1814, the Duchess of Sagan left for Paris after having lately caused me much embarrassment by starting certain new affaires that fit in ill with those to which I was privy. I was nearly ready also to go to Paris, unasked, but dropped this half-baked idea again.

The pot began to boil even more vigorously during the summer when the Metternichs vacationed at Baden near Vienna, at the same time the Duchess of Sagan was there. Here the diary reveals:

The arrival of the Duchess of Sagan made the stay a rather stormy one. My own relations with the prince had taken a very worrisome turn, and I often had to pay dearly for the honor of being the confidant and mediator in these affaires. Yesterday, a long conversation with Metternich, sad to say not about political matters, but about his and my relations with the Duchess of Sagan.

There is no doubt that Gentz, friend and connoisseur of the ladies, had more than a passing interest in the Duchess of Sagan himself. At least he often let his concern arouse his jealousy, as for instance in the case of an old and new favorite, Princess Windischgrätz:

It is not only that this *tendresse* annoys me because I cannot stand anything that in the least detracts from other feelings which alone I want to see in complete command in her. No, I also find it revolting because the recipient is not at all worthy of it. Besides, it is not love at all, not the shadow of it, but the kind of sentiment a very common woman has for her husband. This is precisely why I am so greatly opposed to this affaire, because all else about Windischgrätz is in the grand, heroic, virile style. But when the talk is of this homunculus, she grows weak, small, and common. This grates on me, since it is in complete disharmony with everything else.

Often mishaps in his love affair with the Sagan woman did indeed interfere with Metternich's political activity. Gentz ran interference for him, as a diary entry of October 12, 1814, shows:

After dinner, between seven and eight in the evening, a very important discussion, and, in the presence of Wessenberg, I used the most forceful language yet with Metternich. This day is one of the most momentous of my public life. Perchance this was the happiest day of my whole life.

Officially Gentz was never rewarded for having rescued the leading statesman of the Congress from the thralls of love: Franz, who could not stand him, did not bestow the greatly coveted title of Privy Councillor on him. Putting salt in the wound, the many enemies of Gentz enjoyed his disappointment. Countess Lori Fuchs, one of his outspoken foes, left no doubt about this in her comments:

At one of her parties Countess Fuchs-Gallenberg said: "Why this eagerness to see Gentz! You're fine ones! I myself deeply regret I went. If I didn't like Metternich so much, I wouldn't think of setting foot in his house. Are you (this to a friend of the reporting confidant) also out to cultivate Gentz? Are you also eager to dine well, meet with the Matadores? Just go, tell it to the Neipperg fellow. I am always angry when he fusses so over Gentz! But it's enough to talk sweet, no matter what you really think, to enchant Neipperg. My, how I've palavered with him over this; it beats everything. No real patriot really ought to go see him (Gentz). The fellow will yet sell out the whole monarchy—me, I'm only glad the Emperor refused Metternich's request to make Gentz a Privy Councillor."

CHARLES WILLIAM LORD STEWART

Charles William Stewart, Third Marquess of Londonderry 1778–1854, younger brother of Lord Castlereagh, was British Ambassador in Vienna throughout the Congress. As a soldier he served with distinction in Spain and during the Wars of Liberation. He represented England also at the later congresses of Troppau and Laibach in Austria. Very handsome, hotheaded, and irresponsible, he was the butt of the more or less good-natured raillery of the Viennese. His overbearing, often haughty, demeanor even offended Count Nostitz, by no means a meek aristocrat himself:

The ambassador, Lord Stewart, also called Lord Pumpernickel, is an insolent Englishman who seems out to kick everybody in the teeth. The cabbies, healthiest of the Viennese erratics, have amply given his lordship his comeuppance. Whatever the newspapers might say about his strength and prowess, his lordliness and largess, the fact remains that the cabbies have beat and kicked the devil out of his lordliness.

Lord Stewart's adventure with the Viennese cabbies seemed to have created a mighty stir, there being nary a report about the ambassador in which the episode is not mentioned. Eynard from Geneva described the incident in some detail:

The story goes that his lordship, after drinking several bottles of Bordeaux at a luncheon, picked a quarrel with an equally drunk

222 The Congress of Vienna

fiacre cabby. It seems the noble lord tried to make his way between a line of fiacres and a wall when, being rather unsteady of
leg, his lordship, with a loud "Goddamn!" fell over one of the
horses and shook his fist at the cabby, who retaliated with his
whip. His excellency now gestured his desire for fisticuffs. But
the cabby, considering himself once again provoked, descended
from his driver's perch, belaying his adversary with the whip so
that a regular Donnybrook resulted. Since no one knew the lord,
none of the onlookers tried to save him from the coachman, with
whom he was rolling in the gutter. A policeman at last put a stop
to the fight and, all witnesses clearly putting the ambassador in
the wrong, was ready to haul him off to jail when Stewart finally
identified himself. But this only increased the abuse, he now
being thought a swindler. Because he kept up a loud barrage of
"Goddamns," he was thought to be a stable boy and taken to
the embassy. Arriving at the gate, he was saluted as "Your Excellency" by the sentry, and all doubt vanished about the identity
of the assumed servant. The completely crestfallen policeman
repeatedly asked to be forgiven.

*Yet Lord Stewart played a representative role as permanent
British Ambassador:*

The many Englishmen in Vienna hold their church service
at the home of Lord Stewart. It is said that the English are so religious that they tolerate no music on Sunday. . . .

*As ranking member of the embassy, Lord Stewart also had
social duties to perform:*

Lord Stewart, England's ambassador, gave a great ball in his
lodgings at the sumptuous Starhemberg Hotel, the occasion being
the queen's birthday. Nothing was spared to lend the requisite
dignity to this important day and to demonstrate the power milord
represented. His Excellency, who liked to be in the limelight at
all times but, being an eccentric, was not always lucky in this regard, on this occasion had whimsically put on his invitations the
polite but urgent request to come in the dress of Queen Elizabeth's day. His countrymen, of whom there were not a few in

Vienna, easily guessed his intent. However the majority of the other guests did not heed his request. But it was enough for those who had chosen the period dress to achieve a most singular effect. Milord himself wore the uniform of a colonel of the Hussars, the scarlet of which was so richly embroidered and so thickly bedecked with civil and military decorations that he looked for the world like a living coat-of-arms of every European nation. This oddity aside, the ball was a replica of every other ball: many sovereigns, princes, high-born ladies, and political notables; an expensive supper; finally, a lottery of exquisite English knick-knacks, distributed to all present by a lady dressed as Queen Elizabeth. Dancing continued until daybreak, something that was already becoming unusual in Vienna, the court balls rarely lasting beyond midnight.

There was much guessing as to how Lord Stewart came by his curious streak of eccentricity:

Tuesday, because of Lord Stewart, dinner was held up at Karl Zichy's until six o'clock. He sent his apologies, saying he had forgotten. Actually he was with his mistress, a Frenchwoman. . . . It is said that Lord Stewart had been mentally ill even in London, where he was under treatment with Dr. Willis, the known quack. He is said to have recently received another beating.

On all occasions Lord Stewart's odd behavior came to the fore:

About the ambassador, Lord Stewart, one talks of nothing but his impossible mental lapses. For example he recently said to the Viceroy, Beauharnais: "Now I have the pleasure of making your acquaintance after having faced you elsewhere. We battled each other in Spain." "Maybe you battled in Spain, but I, Beauharnais, never was in Spain. I flatter myself that had I had the honor of facing you in Spain, milord, I should also have had the honor of defeating you." Thus Lord Stewart is in such mental fog he doesn't even know who opposed him in Spain.

At times Viennese gossip was titillated by some entirely harmless prank or venture of Lord Stewart's:

Day before yesterday Lord Stewart, the British Ambassador, was much in the news again. The story has it he rode home on horseback via the ramparts wall and the Kohlmarkt. His horse's head was bedecked with lilies of the valley. He himself carried a big bunch of the same flowers in his left hand, laughing and seemingly quite drunk. Every so often he would stop, shaking with laughter. . . . There's much talk, too, of Lord Stewart's sixty thoroughbred English hunting dogs, which he had sent for from England. His lordship wants to sell them now but finds no buyer, these dogs being very expensive to buy and to keep up. Besides, they are only good for fox hunting.—Also picked up: the Messieurs Geymüller refused Talleyrand any further credit, whereupon Lord Stewart vouched for Prince Talleyrand with M. Geymüller.

All this happened when Napoleon was already back in France from Elba. Lord Stewart seemed oddly unconcerned about the entire affair:

Lord Stewart commented: "Are we Napoleon's keepers? We are not at war with him. What right do we have to keep him under guard?"

CARDINAL ERCOLE CONSALVI

Cardinal Ercole Consalvi, 1757–1824, was exiled by the French as early as 1797, the time of the conquest of the Papal States. In 1800 Pope Pius VII, who owed the papacy to him, elevated Consalvi to the cardinalship and appointed him Secretary of State. Consalvi, in 1801, concluded the Concordat with Napoleon but resigned his office in 1806, having once more incurred Napoleon's displeasure. In 1809 he was not even permitted to continue a trip to Paris, but was stopped at Rheims. At the Vienna Congress he succeeded, despite Metternich's initial opposition, in re-establishing the Papal States, whose Secretary of

State he remained until 1823. Of him the confidants, not always kindly disposed, reported:

Of Cardinal Consalvi it is said that a better mediator for looking after his sovereign's interest would be impossible to find. He is all the time with Talleyrand or Castlereagh. At the latter's, if there is a ball, he remains past midnight. He is considered an enlightened person with whom religious matters can be reasonably discussed.

He was accused of egotism, a trait considered incongruous in a prince of the Church:

Yesterday, at Talleyrand's, verbal fireworks in which Talleyrand, Noailles, Pozzo, Ruffo, and Consalvi took part. The cardinal irks everyone at the Congress because he single-mindedly pursues his own interests to the exclusion of all else. He is blamed for his egotism and for never having come out for the principles of legality and legitimacy. From him, who in Talleyrand's words was a minister of the "oldest and most legitimate of all European monarchs," as well as a minister of the Viceroy of the Lord of all Justice, from him, especially, words about these principles would be most effective. To which the cardinal replied that he had mentioned them in all his speeches. Whereupon Talleyrand claimed that, according to his own notes, he had never mentioned them. The cardinal rejoined that his actions had shown his intent, for he could have come to terms with Murat, could even do so now, and in doing so, regain the lost territories if the Pope would have only recognized Murat as King of Naples.

Toward the end of the Congress, Consalvi's stock appreciably declined:

There is much talk of Cardinal Consalvi recently. They claim he has outlived his reputation in Vienna, has stayed too long. The cardinal has been too intimate with dubious characters like Bartholdi, Marsan, Salmour, Aldini, Marescalchi, et al. There is talk of strange scenes between Ambassador Stewart and the cardinal, who often barges in on the ambassador when the latter is still in bed, and whom he does not leave again all morning. . . .

FRÉDÉRIC DE LA HARPE

Frédéric-César de La Harpe was born in 1754 in the Swiss canton Vaud. He was called by Catherine the Great to Russia as tutor for her favorite grandson, Alexander, whom he influenced in the direction of liberalism. After 1795 de La Harpe was active in Paris in an attempt to get revolutionary France to intercede in the name of liberty in domestic Swiss affairs. For two years he was a member of the directorate of the Helvetian Republic. At the Vienna Congress he used his influence with Alexander in the interest of an autonomous Switzerland and an independent Canton Vaud. Göhausen submitted an astonishingly unbiased report on La Harpe to the chief of police:

It seems Lt. Col. Klaus met La Harpe on the trip to Paris and has made the following comments about him: He is a man of great political acumen and a decided enemy of the Bonaparte family. He long ago recognized the necessity for Napoleon's removal and predicted this as certain to occur back in February, 1814, when the armies moved on Langres. Yet he seems no friend of the current regime, least of all of its ministers. He hates Prince Talleyrand, who, he says, differs from a chameleon only in that he cannot turn red any more. . . . As concerns Switzerland, he is known to belong to the newer party, for which he applies his influence with Alexander in Vienna. . . . La Harpe unfailingly speaks of our monarch and the members of his family with the highest regard. Only recently, following an audience with His Royal Highness, Archduke Johann, he declared himself deeply touched by the latter's fatherly interest in the people of Styria.

THE DUKE OF DALBERG

Emmerich Joseph, Duke of Dalberg, 1773–1833, was a nephew of the Archbishop of Germany, who was also primate of Mainz and Coblenz. He began his career as emissary of the Duchy of Baden in Paris. A close friend of Talleyrand, he mar-

ried the Marquise de Brignole, lady-in-waiting to Empress Jose-phine. Taking out French citizenship, he was made state coun-cillor and a peer of France. At the Vienna Congress he was the second delegate of the Bourbon king. Later he became ambassa-dor in Turin. His first concern at the Congress was to obtain a pension for his uncle, the archbishop, to achieve which he was not choosy in methods used. He explained to a confidant:

We happen to have in our possession an original letter in which Metternich pleads with Caulaincourt to do everything to keep Napoleon on the throne. That was in Châtillon. We are going to use this letter now in Vienna to make sure of the pension for the primate. Bavaria has given its promise.

Agent *** knew a thing or two about Dalberg's subsequent activity in Vienna:

Dalberg told me that the France-England-Austria alliance negotiations are dragging their feet. Also, that an attempt would be made to involve Austria in the imminent Turkish war, which would then of necessity ignite all Europe. . . . Dalberg also told me how glad he was to leave and not be forced to stay. "The peo-ple here, especially the nobility," he said, "make me sick." He bemoaned his bad luck at cards, saying that a few days ago he had dropped 16,000 florins at whist.

De La Garde also wrote about the Duke of Dalberg:

He was worthy of taking his place beside Talleyrand. A scion of one of Germany's oldest and most noble of families, he contrib-uted mightily to the resolutions of March 31 that put the Bour-bon dynasty back on the throne. At the same time, however, he came out for applying such constitutional measures as would serve to calm public apprehension and to reunite France.—Talley-rand, before setting out for Vienna, is said to have worked out his own instructions, to which, I am assured, he has faithfully adhered, having foreseen and foreordained with his remarkably acute mind the various turns the negotiations would take. Not gen-erally known is the fact that the French Embassy maintained two lines of communication with Paris: the one, handled by M.

Besnadière, is entirely anecdotal and went to Louis XVIII. Here, Talleyrand injected those original, piquant thoughts, those finely honed and profound commentaries, that characterize him. The other, entirely political and edited chiefly by Dalberg, went directly to the Foreign Office.

JOHANN VON ANSTETT

Johann von Anstett, 1766–1835, an Alsatian, was in Russian service since 1789. Later, he was employed in the diplomatic service and for a time was with the Russian Embassy in Vienna. It was he who negotiated the treaties of Kalisz and Reichenbach. At the Congress he was forever complaining about Alexander's and Austria's ingratitude toward him. He was an epicure and spendthrift. He tried at every turn to undermine his immediate superior, Nesselrode, with the Austrians:

Nesselrode, Anstett recently told me, had long since sold his soul to the Austrians, receiving suitable reward, of course. For services rendered in connection with divers negotiations and agreements, the Austrians are said to have presented Nesselrode five gifts in the form of snuffboxes, etc., each worth 100,000 rubles. He, Anstett, himself had concluded the agreement that was most advantageous and profitable to Austria (1813, in Prague), for which he had received an inferior snuffbox that had fetched only 350 ducats from a Vienna jeweler. . . . He is always in financial straits, lives like a sybarite, and spends more for wine and even more debased entertainment than many a large household. In the evening he is usually dead drunk.

Another confidant explored the possibility of recruiting Anstett's services for Austria:

I don't think it impossible to get to this man. Not with money, not through some specific bribe, for even though the acquisition of the Kolck estate has greatly embarrassed him financially, he is too sensitive, too proud, too much the philosopher to be bought outright. His weakest point probably is his vanity:

he craves praise and flattery. A few kind words from the Emperor, some special favors of the Minister, would not fail to achieve the desired result. He loves neither Russia nor war, not even government service. He longs for peace and enjoyment.

FRIEDRICH LUDWIG JAHN

Friedrich Ludwig Jahn, 1778–1852, a schoolteacher from Berlin, was affectionately known as Turnvater *(German: father of gymnastics) for his efforts to help rebuild Prussia by training German youth in gymnastics. In 1813 he joined Lützow's Volunteer Corps for a short time. Later he was imprisoned for his part in the Burschenschaft movement.*[54] *Until 1842 he was under police surveillance. In 1848 he was elected as delegate to the Frankfurt parliament. He was the archetype of the bearded freedom fighter of limited intelligence during the pre-revolutionary epoch in Germany. About Jahn's visit to Vienna we have a report by von Leurs:*

Jahn, the Berlin professor who arrived here several days ago, is Teutonic to the core. He's at the head of those who desire to sponsor Germanism via the linguistics society in Berlin. He is the one who has written a book on Teutonism that favors the idea of confederation. This is at the bottom of his mission here. Four or five days ago the Privy Councillors Begulin, Küster, Stägemann, and Hoffmann spoke of the probability of his success in the presence of Count Reichenbach. Hoffmann was the only one with some hope, the others merely shrugging their shoulders, saying that in Vienna one dealt with a calm, quiet, coolly judging mind in possession of fundamental facts. Here the impassioned clamor, the insulting vanity, and the ostentatiousness of the Berliners could not possibly gain a toehold. Here the high-flying, dainty phrases of a Jahn only nauseated, for here the substance of the dispute was what mattered, not the words employed. They

[54] Patriotic student organization at German universities that with the onset of reaction became suspect of being hotbeds of liberalism.—Transl.

thought Jahn was wasting his time, effort, and money, would publicly expose himself a few times and then, like Heum,[55] leave without having achieved anything.[56]

BARON VON THUGUT

Johannes, Baron von Thugut, 1736–1818, a pupil of Kaunitz, was of bourgeois background and was personally sponsored by Empress Maria Theresa. In 1793 he took charge of Austria's foreign policy. He successfully defended Austria's claims at the third partition of Poland but failed against the French when he was obliged to conclude the adverse treaty of Campo Formio. He resigned before the Treaty of Lunéville of 1801 and after that remained in the wings, a sulking and malicious observer:

Recently, when the talk was of the many imperial embassies maintained by Austria, Baron Thugut commented: "In 1801, when I resigned, I had left nearly all posts unfilled. Most of these posts serve no purpose and are only created and filled to oblige certain people and families and to buy obedient creatures. Prince Trauttmansdorff, to whom I turned over my portfolio, was most happy at the time to be able to offer positions to Count Stadion, Count Clement Metternich, Count Eltz, and Count Kaunitz. There is no doubt that since 1802 until the present luck has been with Prince Metternich. Now our only care is to see how things develop, what the imminent war will bring."

THE ARISTOCRACY

*Throughout the Congress, Austria's high nobility not only played host, but wire-puller and go-between as well. The reward was not long in coming. On April 26, 1815, Agent ***, himself known to be an aristocrat, wrote in a report:*

Yesterday Prince Trauttmansdorff exhibited six snuffboxes which the meeting of the monarchs had netted him. These six

[55] i.e., Clauren.
[56] He left in two days.

boxes had been appraised at a minimum of 40,000 gulden, hard currency. The greatest fortune is known to have gone to Prince Clary: in addition to his snuffboxes, he received 5,000 ducats in compensation for the damage sustained in Töplitz at the hands of Russian troops. . . . The requirements of the highly placed and numerous personages who were put on part-time service with the court and who also received gifts must be added, and it is no exaggeration to say these circles would dearly love another such congress to convene in Vienna soon.

Generals, Money, and Minds

Arthur Wellesley, Duke of Wellington, 1769–1852, was the last of the British generals who also played a political role. He was of Anglo-Irish descent, chose a military career, serving first in India, later as Commander-in-Chief in Portugal and Spain. In 1813 he rid Spain of the French and became England's representative at the peace conference in Vienna upon Castlereagh's recall, February 1, 1815. When Napoleon returned from Elba, Wellington took command of the allied armies. As victor of Waterloo, he was a national hero. In 1828 he formed a Tory government. He opposed military as well as parliamentary reforms but allowed the passage of the Catholic Emancipation Bill. Already quite old, he still held a Cabinet post in Peel's reformist, albeit Tory, government. Wellington was haughty, intelligent, handsome, and imbued with that democratic spirit which in those days was uniquely the hallmark of the British High Tories. His arrival in Vienna was a sensation of which Count Nostitz wrote:

Wellington's arrival is the latest interesting development of the Congress. He is to relieve Castlereagh, who goes home to open the new Parliament. This circumstance raises hopes for a speedup of affairs, since it may be assumed that the Right Honorable Lord wants to appear with some news before Parliament. I am sorry to see the Duke of Wellington as a diplomat. He who rose to such military heights must now debase himself as a politician. His role should have remained to guide the sword that cuts the evil Gordian knot. Britannia ought not so carelessly dispose of the "Victor of the World." Of course, he may be here, as I suspect, more to impress than to become actively engaged. The first public appearance of the noble lord was at his banker's, Herz, where he asked to be invited to dine the day after his arrival. Since nowadays the world's great ones gather at the homes of the moneymen, it was no surprise to find assembled there the entire top echelon of the diplomatic corps: Metternich, Talleyrand, Löwenhjelm, Castlereagh, Cathcart, Palmella, Gentz, General Koller, Chernichev, and a few "courtesy" guests, to which group I belonged. Wellington wore his top decorations, having attended a reception at Castlereagh's before supper. He is a tall man whose simple but firm bearing invites trust. He carries head and shoulders with an easy openness, his nose is decidedly aquiline, his forehead high, his eyes are clear, though not very bright or penetrating. He lets people talk and listens attentively. His answers are to the point, his objections couched in courteous terms. His whole being exudes calmness rather than pouncing forcefulness and shows a soberness that is most attractive. His eagle-eyed, dignified appearance is adversely affected when he opens his mouth, whose crooked teeth disturb the harmony of the whole. But, without searching out the details, one is struck by an overall expression of sureness and simplicity. . . . As Lord Nelson once traveled with Lady Hamilton, so Wellington also has his lady, the well-known singer Grassini, with him, a lady who has often before accompanied prominent men, as for example the Duke of York on his visit to Germany. Napoleon, too, kept her at his side in Italy and later, though clandestinely, even in Paris. She is what the French call a *belle femme*, that is, beautiful of flesh, tall of stature, dignified of mien, yet, despite this flattering appellation, she is in the neighborhood of fifty. It is in the style of a heroic past to see Fame accompanied by Art, this most exalted admixture of human excellence which, at the same time, is so naturally ennobled by the difference in sex, each in its higher state of transfiguration.

Bertuch, the publisher and book dealer, from his bourgeois point of view was also very impressed with the Iron Duke. He wrote in his diary:

Masked ball in the evening. Very crowded. Around midnight Wellington showed up, accompanied by Sir Sidney Smith and Lord Stewart, at his side a lady in black mask, Lady Castlereagh. Wherever he appeared, a great crowd would gather, flowing back and forth in his wake. Wellington in civilian attire, blue in color, round hat with red band, above average height, excellent features, a serious mien that seems to savor itself. Beaming a benign smile on the crowd, he disappeared in the gallery.

De La Garde reported on the same appearance of Wellington at the masked ball:

"Do you intend to go to the masked ball tonight?" Prince Koslovski asked me. "You'll find Wellington there and all Vienna will flock thither." It was strange indeed that Wellington's arrival in a city already playing host to every celebrity of the day should cause such excitement at court and in diplomatic circles— at court, because here was an all-too-sorely needed novelty; with the diplomatic corps, because it was said he would replace Castlereagh, whose politics were generally criticized adversely. Also, it was no trifling matter to have to deal with a new colleague. . . . Curiosity had reached its highest peak. Everyone was eager to lay eyes on the man on whom the fortunes of arms had smiled so consistently and to whose patient perseverance the Napoleonic genius had been forced to bow. The sovereigns hastened to him to pay their respects. There was no honor, no attention, that was not heaped on him. When it became known that he would attend the imperial masked ball, some seven to eight thousand spectators thronged the salons in the evening. When he entered in the company of Lord Castlereagh, arm in arm with a masked lady thought to be Lady Castlereagh, the whole mob rushed to follow him. Though undoubtedly used to such scenes, he must nonetheless have felt greatly flattered by this general show of adulation. His arrival in Vienna even caused a flurry on the stockmarket, where the profits and losses in government bonds reached several millions.

A confidant described the intrigues connected with the recall of Castlereagh and the arrival of Wellington:

Lord Auckland, Member of Parliament, who left yesterday to return to London, took lessons on the German Constitution with Baron Pufendorf. He is taking much material with him, to be used in his opposition to Castlereagh in Parliament. Baron Pufendorf and his wife recently dined with Canning, who is also taking instructions from Pufendorf on the German Constitution. . . . Wellington's impending arrival is the big sensation. The diplomats say: "Lord Castlereagh is no negotiator. He is too easily swayed by Humboldt and his cohorts, a fact of which he is himself aware. Talleyrand has put London wise to this. France, England, and Austria must not let themselves be isolated and dominated by Russia and Prussia. Humboldt has gone too far. Castlereagh did not impress anybody but took everything. Wellington will take nothing but will impress everybody."

In his first report on Wellington's activities immediately after his arrival, Talleyrand informed Louis XVIII that the Czar had visited the general the very morning following his arrival:

Alexander's first question was: "Isn't it true that everything is in a poor state in France?"—"Not at all. The King is highly popular, is very much respected, and acts with the greatest good sense."—"You couldn't have told me anything I would like to hear better. And the army?"—"It stands as ready against any aggressor from the outside and against any power whatever as it ever did," Wellington answered. He was having fun with the Czar. He then added: "Only in case of domestic troubles might it fail." This information, as Prince Czartoryski has told me, shook the emperor more than he dared show. It has surely helped the Czar to arrive at a quick decision on the Saxony problem, which, when Wellington arrived, was still beset with obstacles. These obstacles one may assume to have been removed.

All this is of a piece with Wellington's very snobbish behavior. Abbé Carpani reported:

Three days ago, Wellington was invited to dine at the Imperial Palace. He asked to be excused because of indisposition, then went to Count O'Reilly who, by reason of his intimate contacts with Murat's ministers, has not been invited at court for the past two or three years.

Mme. Grassini, the singer, continued to create quite a stir. Starhemberg had this to say about the subject:

The Duke of Wellington does not go out. The English told me yesterday: "He has a cold." Others, more concerned, speak of an incipient nervous fever. But so far there is no reason to believe this nonsense. He has brought a nurse along from Paris who will keep him company: I mean Mme. Grassini, who is in his retinue.

Abbé Carpani commented about his fellow countrywoman:

This Grassini woman was the sweetheart of the world. Beginning with the military police of Salò,[57] she graduated to the English princes of the blood royal and the freshly made emperors and kings. She is an amusing, pleasant, lively woman, an excellent actress, enjoys superb health, is more open-handed than stingy, and withal a good-natured person. She has never been known to engage in intrigue.

But Wellington also looked elsewhere for amorous conquests. Carpani reported about Princess Bagration:

The Princess started out by telling me that Wellington, at the masked ball, had made her a present of the Victory ribbon, which she showed to me.

[57] Apparently an allusion to the Battle of Salò (Italy), where the French defeated the Austrians in August, 1796.—Transl.

TADEUSZ KOSCIUSKO

Tadeusz Kosciusko, 1746–1817, Polish general and national hero, fought as Washington's adjutant in the American War of Independence. He headed the last Polish uprising against partition in 1794, defeated the Russians and relieved Warsaw, only to succumb at Maciejowice to superior Russian forces. Wounded, he was taken prisoner, but his alleged cry "Finis Poloniae" became a legend. Released in 1796, he went into exile. In 1815 he paid Vienna a short visit:

Under the pseudonym of Count Tadeusz Polski, Kosciusko, on a trip from Paris, registered at the Golden Ox in Vienna on May 30. He saw no one but Czartoryski, Lanskoronski, and Lubomirski. . . . He has aged greatly, no longer wears military or Polish dress. . . . At Baron Thugut's it was claimed that Alexander and Czartoryski let Kosciusko come to Poland to preach the gospel of the Russian emperor. Time will tell whose gospel he will preach when he arrives in the Duchy of Warsaw.

THE AUSTRIAN GENERALS

It would require volumes to describe the incompetence, cheerfulness, and bravery of the Austrian generals in the Coalition Wars. Beginning with Wurmser and Alvinczi, the record repeats with General Mack, who put down his arms at Ulm, to culminate in Schwarzenberg. Archduke Johann, also not known for his victories, served in the allied armies during the 1814 winter campaign. He wrote in his diary:

March 23, 1814: Once this war is over, I shall give a very terse summation of it. Our generals will make a poor showing. The North Germans will give us plenty to read about concerning this subject.

March 28: God grant an end soon, or the allies will reap precious little honor.

March 29: At last something—we pushed Napoleon back.

COURT BANKER LEOPOLD
EDLER VON HERZ

Leopold Edler von Herz was one of the few Jewish business-men who were ennobled during the reign of Franz II. He was a nephew of Baron Nathan von Arnstein and like him early revealed great financial talents. Gentz, his sponsor, introduced him to Metternich during the Wars of Liberation. Together with four other financial tycoons, he took part in winding up the British subsidies after the Battle of Leipzig. Herz was a suave, easy-going person who was welcome at all aristocratic gambling tables. The following agent's report reflects the anti-Semitism of the lower classes:

All eyes being on the Duke of Wellington and Prince Metternich, there is general comment about the fact that those two, joined by Lord Castlereagh and Lord Stewart, lunched with the Jew, banker Herz, on Thursday. This association is said to be the result of the late campaign when Herz was court banker and got to know all these gentlemen. They say Herz has the reputation of being the most unscrupulous of brokers, taking his cut in the most impertinent and culpable manner of each ticket sold in the lotteries run by the Bohemian nobles. They also say: "Metternich protects Herz because he owes him money."

JOHANN FRIEDRICH VON COTTA

Johann Friedrich von Cotta, 1764–1832, owner of the J. G. Cotta book firm in Tübingen, became Germany's most prominent publisher because of his friendship with Schiller and Goethe. The entire "modern" literature of the day appeared through Cotta. He therefore looked upon himself as the appointed representative of the German literary mind and appeared as such, together with Bertuch, at the Congress, primarily to do battle against censorship and the abuses of pirate printing. Hebenstreit reported on him:

I am now convinced that Cotta, the bookseller from Stuttgart, as deputy of the German booksellers, will formulate the resolution in favor of "universal freedom of the press" for the Congress to consider. This resolution and the one covering pirate printing are closely linked, the former being the foundation for the latter. If our government agrees to the latter but disallows the former, our book business is done for because nothing of any importance will be printed here, since Cotta pays well and will without hesitation persuade Viennese authors to work for him and him only. . . . Dannecker, the Stuttgart professor who came with him and stays with him at the same house, is known as a gifted sculptor. There seems no other point to his stay here than a desire to satisfy his curiosity and to advance the project for a monument in commemoration of the Battle of Leipzig, concerning which he has in the past already approached His Highness, Prince Metternich.

Hebenstreit supplied supplementary information:

Cotta from Stuttgart and Bertuch from Weimar, the delegates of the German book dealers, had an audience with His Highness, Prince Metternich, who assured them that just now was a most propitious moment for them to submit their proposals regarding copyright laws and universal freedom of the press. . . . Bertuch is much more open than Cotta. It flatters him to champion a cause that probably is important. Among others, he maintains contact with Prince Wrede and the Duchess of Oldenburg. Saxony's fate saddens him, though he knows no details of the matter.

JEAN-BAPTISTE ISABEY

Jean-Baptiste Isabey, 1767–1855, a pupil of David, was a famed portrait painter. He softened cold classicism into what was elegantly pleasing. To a large extent, his fame rested on his miniatures. De La Garde called him "the Congress-turned-painter," and, for a fact, he left hardly any of the Congress' greats unpainted. De La Garde said of him:

Soon we arrived at the artist's quarters in the Leopoldstadt district. A well-deserved reputation had preceded Isabey to Vienna. Introduced by the Duke de Sérent to Marie Antoinette, he had painted that unfortunate and beautiful woman when he was barely twenty. The Queen, who treated him with the greatest kindness, always referred to him as her "little Lorrain." Later Napoleon's court painter, he captured on canvas the features of every famous man in the Empire, as well as the most admired female beauties of the day. He is also known for having directed many of the festivities of that glittering, fast-paced period. In Vienna the European celebrities in a body stood in line to keep his brush busy, so much so that he hardly could carry out all commissions. The number of portraits he did at the time is astounding, proving his talent to be as prolific as it was pleasing. Each time that some new entertainment featuring the Congress was to be organized, it may be taken for granted that the presence of the artist who had staged Napoleon's coronation was put to effective use. Nothing was done without soliciting his advice.

Talleyrand, he said, had suggested he come to Vienna, and to this happy circumstance art owes an outstanding historical painting of a meeting of the plenipotentiaries attending the Congress. Napoleon's fall had robbed him of all positions. One day, when with Talleyrand, the man who was primarily responsible for his present unemployment, he complained bitterly over the consequences of the Restoration which had led to his ruin. Talleyrand, looking at an etching depicting the signing of the Treaty of Münster after the painting by Terborch, pointed to this, saying: "There is a congress assembling in Vienna. Go there." These words were a ray of hope for Isabey, and he quickly made up his mind. His decision to go to Vienna was in a most flattering way heartily endorsed by M. de Talleyrand. When Prince Eugène arrived for the Congress, one of his first visits was with Isabey. In his dubious position he was only too glad to see someone reminding him of his youth. More than once the painter, through his joyful recollections of earlier years, was able to banish the Prince's heavy thoughts. Sometime later Eugène also brought the Czar to Isabey. Isabey's conversation was stimulating and zestful.

He really came alive when he talked about the wonders he had created for Napoleon's coronation or of the house parties at Malmaison. Isabey was regally installed, as once was Benvenuto Cellini at the Louvre.

FRIEDRICH SCHLEGEL

Friedrich Schlegel, 1772–1829, classical philologist in his earlier years, was the founder of German romanticism. Married to Dorothea, née Mendelssohn, he wrote Lucinde, *the epochal novel that depicted the so-called "free love" of the romanticists. He studied Sanskrit in Paris and was a forerunner of Indology. In 1808 he converted to Catholicism. In Vienna he gave public lectures on* The History of Old and New Literature, *his chief literary work. He was a "war councillor" in Austrian service and as such officially took part in the Congress of Vienna. From 1815 to 1818 he was Austrian "legation councillor" in Frankfurt. The politicians and the military in Vienna did not take him quite seriously and denounced him as a schemer. Count Nostitz wrote about him in this spirit:*

Taking a look at the eccentrics and cutpurses of the Congress, I find, in addition to those readily identifiable by everybody, Friedrich Schlegel amongst them. Leaving Berlin for Vienna years ago, Schlegel took a position in the Austrian chancery and is now a renegade from his faith and former teaching. He deserves the opprobrium of apostasy, for it was not conviction that turned him toward Catholicism but, at best, possibly a spiritual voluptuousness that in no way however interferes with his more earthy desires. He has tailored Catholicism to suit himself, including its outward manifestations, for this holy man, quite in the manner of a freethinker, says that crawling on one's knees hurts. In addition to his Christian orthodoxy, he has a great political one, too, which he openly speaks about. A few days ago he said: "Frederick II should have been killed, for the Pope's ban authorized anyone regardless of rank to slay him." Whereupon a lady answered: "You had better guard your words, or people will not regard them any more, and this will bring you into complete disregard." [58] Of like hypocritical limitation are his current lectures on history and art, in which he so contradicts himself that he has Goethe outclassed by the pigmy Collin . . . Schlegel's wife, daughter of Moses Mendelssohn, also has turned Catholic and now practices bigotry with devotion and submissiveness. She means well, runs to all early masses, and is wrapped up in her lying, silly husband's piety.

Often, by the naïve especially, Schlegel and Humboldt were mentioned together, with the former compared to the latter. Thus, Bollmann, the American inventor, wrote a friend in Paris:

Of all the foreigners here Humboldt certainly is one of the most interesting. Every so often we gather at Gentz' house for select parties at which Humboldt is charm personified. Not that he shows much sentiment, but Schlegel, whom I also often see, exudes all the more for it. With the latter everything is inner revelation. Yet all too often the God that reveals itself is the old self-love that likes to clothe itself in noble words. I much prefer the bright, completely sane minds. But the most harmonious organisms—like that of a Goethe—lie in the middle of these extremes.

BEETHOVEN

Ludwig van Beethoven, 1770–1827, at the time of the Congress had reached the height of his fame but was still much attacked for his "modern" music. In this period fell the premieres of his Seventh Symphony, the "Wellington's Victory" Symphony, and Der glorreiche Augenblick. One of his most active sponsors was the Russian ambassador, Count Razumovsky. An agent reported about Beethoven:

Beethoven's academy of music has changed its regular meetings from Sunday to a weekday. . . . Yesterday's performance

[58] This play on words is more effective in the original German, where it is based on the homonyms *Acht* (ban) and *acht* (take care, beware, guard against).—Transl.

did not at all increase Beethoven's fame as a composer. There are actually anti- and pro-Beethoven factions forming. Opposed to Razumovsky, Apponyi, and Kraft, who idolize him, is a far greater number of experts who miss the music in the composer's compositions.

Ladies and Mistresses

*Never before—or after—have a group of statesmen and poli-
ticians, assembled solely and exclusively to deal with matters
of commonweal interest, labored so extensively and decisively
under the influence of women—not in Münster, nor in Rastatt;
not in Versailles, nor yet in San Francisco. Never before—or
after—have women shown such solidarity as at the Vienna
Congress, have had such communality of aims and methods of
attaining them, a communality that embraced all castes, classes,
and families, so that in the end there remained but little difference
between empress and cocotte, and even the best of circles took
no umbrage when the Danish king, half in fun, half seriously,
permitted his low-class mistress to call herself "queen." Never
before—or after—did a collection of members of one sex move
in such tight formation and so effortlessly from the past into
the future as did those ladies, would-be ladies, princesses, ad-
venturesses, ladies of the high aristocracy, and emigrants from
the lower nobility, who, to a body, having said farewell to the
ancien régime, set about consciously to adapt themselves to
bourgeois life and made their homes in it. But how would this
solidarity have been possible had there not been, on the opposing
front, devout admirers and swains, had others besides Prince
Metternich and Prince Talleyrand guided the affairs of the
Congress? Count Nostitz, in his diaries, gives us a charming
picture of the ladies' world of the Vienna of the time:*

Czar Alexander is paying more than ordinary attention to the local beauties, much to the annoyance of the Russian ladies. But there is no sultanic favoritism, and it must be fairly admitted that Viennese morals are not corrupted by the Russians. Though the polite conquerors, led by Chernichev, often enough have mounted an attack, their success has not been conspicuous, and many of the victors are later vanquished by their victims. Most moderate of all is the Czar, for whom a word and a glance seem to suffice. It is he who gallantly apostrophized six local beauties:

The coquette beauty:	Countess Caroline Széchenyi-Guilford
The banal beauty:	Sophie Zichy
The striking beauty:	Rosalie Esterházy
The celestial beauty:	Julie Zichy
The diabolic beauty:	Countess Saurau-Hunyady
The beauty who alone inspires true sentiment:	Gabrielle Auersperg

Besides these ladies, who surely rate among the most handsome of all, there are many others able to arouse feelings according to mutual desires and needs. To the budding beauties of the land belong the young Countesses Starhemberg, Wrbna, and others, who are as lively, delicate, and refreshing as walled-in city living, candlelight, and never-ending dancing permit. Newly arrived beauties have increased the number of the indigenous ones, of whom none abdicate or retire. Names that a decade ago were the toast of the town are still on the lips, if not in the hearts, of men, as for instance the Countess Lori Fuchs, the Princesses of Courland, etc. Poor Lori; she fights encroaching age, a fight that would be less desperate if at home the coffers were full of gold or full of paper money, which is even easier to spend. Her soirees are beginning to be less frequented. The Princesses of Courland I always disliked. They used to be just females who exploited their sex with all the passion of their blood. Youth, the vicissitudes of life, and the ease of new affaires made each of these pretty women equally interesting. But now their lively cavorting is confined within Austria's borders. At first their zest for life drove them to men; then cool calculation and a certain flexibility of mind made them seek out the company of women and also adapt to local conditions and local modes of thought and action, so that now one no longer knows what these ladies really are. Now feminine to a fault, now domineering; now circumspect, now sentimental; now a bit bigoted, now again frivolous: all this mixed into a stew of moods that makes one despair of them. Gone too is the lively interplay of feelings that kept these ladies center stage, and a drabness of taste makes them strangers to old friends. The Duchess of Sagan was the best, most intelligent, and most natural of the three, the one most steady in her attachments. For years now Prince Windischgrätz has been her lover, a liaison totally à la mode, without the least spice of any sacrifice, any indiscretion, any opposition, entirely quotidian and calm, something this lively and resolute woman was not accustomed to. Jeanne is leading a boring life with a Dutchman, Brel, who eight years ago was a fresh young knight in Vienna, but whose inborn lazy disposition, the easy life, and dull surroundings have brought to the point where he has lost all gumption and now lolls about on sofas and chairs like last year's Mardi Gras' masks. Pauline, after much playing the field on both their parts, has clung more and more tightly to Wallmoden, who in his phlegmatic furor loves her to distraction. Princess Bagration still maintains a salon where on fixed days people gather. A vivacious, pretty, grand lady, she is thus able to lend ever new patina to her charms. The young Princess Taxis, spouse of Paul Esterházy, is a new star in Vienna's firmament. She is a craving young Eve with hot eyes and Junoesque figure. She often seems bored, apparently with unfulfilled longing. When in this mood, she turns to young Karl Liechtenstein, whom her hand and eyes are never at a loss to find. When this young swain has recovered from the joys of the first surrender, aroused desire will find a way, and Paul Esterházy will enter into and be welcomed by that great fraternity of men [59] for which this young Methuselah is so splendidly readying himself with palsied limbs and dulling mind.

Among the foreign ladies, Countess Bernstorff is eye-catching

[59] i.e., cuckoldom.—Transl.

because of her height. She has youth on her side and the kind effect of candlelight but is entirely without grace, a Danish beanstalk. Concerning the English ladies there is much snickering over the strange get-ups of these hibernators who have sallied forth once more from their protective cave into the big, estranged city. They overdress in the most ridiculous and tasteless manner, and their behavior is wild and uninhibited. Lady Rumbold, wife of Sir Sidney Smith, has two most charming daughters, though they, also, are a strange breed with different dress and manners. But the younger is such an outstanding beauty that any nation would be proud to call her its own. The girl has a skin like white velvet struck by the first rays of the rising sun. Her teeth are like pearls, her mouth a rosebud, a foot as if made in Paris, a stature tall and voluptuous as in King Arthur's days, and a pair of eyes that constantly call: "Come hither!" Prince August of Prussia, with all the haste and zeal of his conceited ambition, did not fail to heed this call. The girl did not recognize the coin for the counterfeit that princes often use, and now, when much handling has taken off the mint sheen, she is inconsolable over the bad trade, because her own goods were genuine. This is good to know for the highest bidder who is in the market now. For, what with her liveliness and ardor, the girl is not likely to hide herself away in the empty little closet of her heart. Yesterday, at a ball given by Karl Zichy, I talked at length with mother and daughter, after the admiral had introduced himself. "Tell me on your conscience, sir. You were with Prince Louis Ferdinand. He must have been a very handsome man. Did he greatly resemble Prince August?"— "You are asking the wrong person. I was adjutant and friend of the late Prince Louis and am therefore paid to be partisan."— "But that shouldn't blind you to see, as all the world tells me, that the two looked very much alike."—"In that case I refer you to someone who knew the two as well as I did and who will tell you that Prince August is but a caricature of Prince Louis." That struck home. That evening at eight both father and mother made me welcome at their house.

Among the socialite dowagers the Russian emperor singled out the Countess Festetics, not for her own sake, but as mother of Countess Julie Zichy. In her own country she speaks Hungarian, in Vienna and wherever else fate might take her gross body, German. Laboriously, the Emperor struggled through the alien words and even more laboriously through the matron's utter shallowness. Recently she was very sad. "What is wrong?" the Emperor asked. "Oh, I must weep. I hear Your Majesty is about to make war on us. How terrible. . . ." Such simplicity, yet how truly and aptly spoken! If the old biddy is pumped about the subject of her talk with the Czar, she'll coyly say: "We discussed politics."

EMPRESS MARIA LUDOVICA

Empress Maria Ludovica, 1787–1816, third wife of Franz, was the daughter of Beatrice of Modena of the d'Este family. Tradition had it that she had an artistic vein and sponsored both theater and the arts at the Vienna Congress. She suffered greatly under her social obligations and but a year later succumbed to the curse of the imperial spouses that infested the dank and chill Imperial Palace: tuberculosis. Berthier and Goethe, Talleyrand and Grillparzer equally sang her praises:

She was a divine woman. Gladly would one have given one's life for her. . . . Hers was the gift to please and, as it were, the charm of a Frenchwoman. . . . She was very easy to get along with, carefree and gay, with lively eyes and ready conversation, original in all she said about the most divers subjects. She was the hostess par excellence of the most momentous assemblage of brains and beauties. Under her sway the regal splendor of the Imperial Palace came into its own again, as in the days of Charles VI. The elfin blonde floated like a fairy queen over the thronging Congress crowd, inventing as she went her very own style of vivacious majesty. Besides the large public affairs, there was many a more intimate gathering in her "chambers." Etiquette inevitably necessitated this, since not even the diplomatic corps was admitted to the huge imperial balls.

ELIZABETH, EMPRESS OF RUSSIA

Elizabeth, née Princess Louise Marie of Baden, 1779–1835, married to Alexander I in 1793, later accompanied the Czar to Taganrog where, in 1825, he died or disappeared. De La Garde wrote about her:

Next to the Austrian emperor sat the charming empress of Russia. This heavenly creature embodied everything needed to assure her own and her husband's happiness. Her features were ravishing, and her eyes reflected the purity of her soul. She wore her beautiful ashen hair shoulder length. Her figure was elegant, slim, and pliant, and her airy walk gave her away even in a mask. Coupled with a pleasant character was a quick mind, love for the arts, and a limitless generosity. Her porcelain daintiness, aristocratic bearing, and inexhaustible kindness made her beloved by all. From the very beginning neglected by a husband she adored, loneliness and sorrow had enveloped her in a sweet melancholy that gave a haunting echo to her voice and lent her every gesture an irresistible charm.

MARIE LOUISE, EMPRESS OF THE FRENCH

Marie Louise, 1791–1847, daughter of Emperor Franz and a pawn in Metternich's politics, in 1810 was married off to Napoleon, whom the very next year she presented with the longed-for heir to the throne. Still undecided in 1814, she finally found solace on a journey to the baths at Aix in the person of her companion, Count Neipperg, whom she married upon Napoleon's death. Mainly through the intervention of Czar Alexander the Vienna Congress awarded her the Duchies of Parma, Piacenza, and Guastalla for life. In 1834, after Neipperg's death, she married once more. This blonde, charming, sensuous woman was probably not nearly as simple as it was claimed she was. Her position at Schönbrunn and at the Imperial Court in Vienna was especially ticklish during the months of the Congress:

At Arnstein's and Hatzfeld's it was commented that the King of Württemberg immediately on arrival paid his respects to Marie Louise at Schönbrunn. Nothing would be more taste-less than for Empress Marie Louise to appear at the Schönbrunn ball on Tuesday, as she is bound to do. Our emperor, it was said, ought to exercise his parental authority and forbid her appearance, thus avoiding this scandal. *Nota bene*, the Empress Marie Louise has lost all public affection and respect. The Viennese do not like her any more at all.

When she returned to Vienna from France that summer, Marie Louise had all too openly put on French airs. Two weeks after her arrival another confidential agent's report noted:

Yesterday, Countess Colloredo-Crenville said: "At the mo-ment, Empress Marie Louise acts far more sensibly than prior to her trip to Aix. It has been a very long time since she had a letter from Napoleon. She doesn't mind at all, doesn't speak about it, doesn't mention Napoleon. She is resigned to her fate, her heart is back with her father and her childhood home. We were in Schönbrunn Saturday: myself, my daughter Crenville who is a friend of Her Majesty, and General Neipperg. Our meeting was very clandestine. The selection of the general as escort for the Empress was fortunate indeed."

Along the same line it was remarked in December:

Dr. Franck, the famous Viennese physician, bruits it about that General Neipperg pays court to Empress Marie Louise, who is pleased. Also, that the French court discusses this openly and also that young Napoleon is an extremely wicked, stubborn child.

Marie Louise's alleged unpopularity with the Viennese seems grossly exaggerated. Eipeldauer wrote about the Empress' return to Vienna:

God be praised and hallelujah, now all true patriots can sleep easy again, our most admired Princess of the House of Austria, the Empress of France, the one as who in anno ten sacrificed her-self so nobly for the good of all, has returned on May 21, half-past

six in the evening, all happy, hale, and hearty to Schönbrunn. . . .
We'd all been in Schönbrunn since five, awaiting her coming
like the Jews the Messiah. Soon as we got to the courtyard, where
a couple of thousand people had gathered already, why, there up
in the balcony we see who but our dearest archdukes to a man,
together with the Duke of Saxony-Teschen, standing up there
awaiting the arrival of the Empress, and here again the wonderful
humor of our most excellent princes came out again—because they
hadn't even put a rug over the iron railing on the balcony or
something, these good gentlemen each had to take out his
handkerchief and spread it over the railing so as they might once
in a while lean on their elbows in the long wait standing there. At
six a flourish sounded at the Schönbrunn guardhouse and we all
were thinking, there she's coming. But no, it was only a wagonful
of court ladies who right smartly drove right through our midst
right up to the main stairway. And why they sounded flourishes
already I'll not be knowing. Then for a while there was silence
once again. But around about half-past six, or maybe a minute
or two more, there go the flourishes again and all the important
folk they're gone from the balcony and we all know this is it,
and take our position. Sure enough in the far distance we hear
loud huzzahing. And then a Frenchy courier, green as grass, comes
galloping into the courtyard, and he's followed by our postmaster
in a red uniform and a lot of other gentlemen in uniform riding
in front and behind the coach, and there she was, the female
guardian angel of Austria, a little thinner (as well a woman
married these four years and having produced an offspring might
be) but oh much more pretty, if that's possible, than before, the
sweet little face like peaches and cream, fresh as a rose, a figure
like as made in a turner's workshop, and a foot, oh my, it's the
very model of a female foot in all the world, and all is so
fresh and healthy, the tears are coming to my eyes, and in the
private chambers of my heart I secretly thank the good Lord
for having so graciously protected a woman who as steadfastly as
her most illustrious parent sacrificed herself for the best of all
of us. . . . So there she sat, our beautiful Austrian Madam
Empress, in all her native friendliness, and then she held out

her right hand to the strange, the other Madam Empress, and our people throw their hats in the air and let go with a cheer that can be heard in the suburbs. . . . Then there's flourishes once more and that's for the coach bringing the young Prince of Parma.[60] His lady-in-waiting held him from the coach window so as the people can get a good look at him. Sir Cousin, the child looks positively like an Austrian angel, with a skin white as snow, great blue eyes, thick ashen curls that blow about his face, snow-white Austrian teeth—in short, the little princelet looks for all the world as if some genius cut him straight from one of those illuminated English cuts, and him such a lively and alert young master!

The desperate conflict in Marie Louise's heart over her alleged love for Napoleon and the new love for Count Neipperg created, above all, dynastic problems. As early as June, 1814, Archduke Johann noted in his diary:

If this marriage [61] should be null and void, then my niece was his mistress and the child is illegitimate. This, strictly interpreted, would have impossible consequences, and the child could never become an Austrian archduke. Let's hope things won't come to this pass, but that Napoleon will die. I hear anyway that he is negotiating with Murat and that he is beginning to arouse suspicion. In the end England will take a hand and prove the rumor true that has him deported to St. Helena. I don't understand how my niece can go to a far away spa [62] and leave her child here. Where is the sense in this, where a mother's love? Oh, enough, enough. How are we to understand all this? If something happens to the child, are we going to expose ourselves to the suspicion of foul play? Who the devil has so counseled my honest emperor?

Marie Louise was slowly beginning to let her heart make the decisions:

[60] The young Napoleon, Marie Louise's son.—Transl.
[61] Napoleon's to Marie Louise.
[62] He means Aix, no doubt.—Transl.

A person allegedly often with Countess Mitrovsky reports that Her Imperial Majesty, the Archduchess Marie Louise, had confessed to the Countess she had never loved anything about Napoleon except his greatness, that is, the splendor of the throne. Now she claimed to be so angry with him that she had vowed to make a pilgrimage on foot to Mariazell if she were saved from him.

Her affection for Neipperg was put under stress. The latter is with the Austrian army, fighting against Murat in Italy. A report said:

The Archduchess Marie Louise was recently overcome by tears. Her General Neipperg had arrived too late with his troops, and the Frenchman Frimont had put in a complaint about him. For this Neipperg received a very stiff reprimand, a fact Emperor Franz told the Archduchess at great length.

At the time of Napoleon's return to Paris, the Königsberger Zeitung of May, 1815, reported about a comment of Marie Louise's concerning the French people:

Personally, I did not want to marry Napoleon. But being a dutiful daughter, I heeded the pleas of a beloved father and sacrificed myself for my country. When thus auspiciously I arrived in France, the natural politesse of the French people possibly caused me to be too tolerant of the levity and instability of their character. I thought I had learned something about the nation. It fell away from Napoleon in his misfortune and recalled to the throne a prince it once cast off. But oh! Napoleon returns to France and the people abandon their king. What a miserable and disloyal nation! I shall never return there, and if it weren't for my son, to whom I shall devote my life, I would spend the rest of my days in a monastery.

GRAND DUCHESS CATHERINE OF RUSSIA

Grand Duchess Catherine Pavlovna, 1788–1819, was Czar Alexander's favorite sister. Her first marriage was to the Duke of

Oldenburg, who later died, and she maintained a small court at Tver,[63] *outstanding for its cultured and artistic atmosphere. In 1814 she accompanied the Czar to London and Paris and played an important diplomatic role. She also went with him to Vienna, where Archduke Karl fell in love with her. The marriage was foiled, however, by the dowager Czarina. Catherine subsequently fell in love with the Crown Prince of Württemberg, who married her and whose queen she became upon the death of his father. She died young of pneumonia, contracted, it is said, while out in the park, spying on her fickle husband. The Austrian secret police was not favorably impressed with her:*

This Oldenburg woman is an entirely different devil from the Czar. None in this family has a heart. In Russia army and public opinion are on her side, and it is said that without her Alexander would have never crossed the Rhine. One day this Oldenburg woman will play the Czar a nasty trick. The men and the army are with her and "before you know it she'll be sitting on the Russian throne." Such was said at Abbé Carpani's among intimate friends.

In Vienna it was the prospect of a marriage with the beloved Archduke Karl that occupied the public mind:

The Oldenburg woman is generally taken for a schemer and for being utterly false, even though at the same time she is recognized as possessing a good mind and political acumen as well, which instills in her a great desire to please and be noticed. The rumor of an impending marriage between Archduke Karl and the Grand Duchess is growing stale. The Italians—I should really say the Milanese—are enchanted over the possibility the Archduke might be appointed Viceroy of the Kingdom of Lombardy and maintain a grand court with her at Milan, something this great and beautiful country prizes above all.

We learn some of the details of the marriage plans and their frustration from the diary of Archduke Johann, who seemed not to have been entirely free of a personal interest in the matter:

[63] The current Kalinin.—Transl.

I seem to notice something I don't like: the Grand Duchess Catherine seems to be losing interest in Karl. Why, I don't know, but many little things point to it. Without directly saying so, I advised Karl to force the issue. He doesn't deserve to be kept guessing.

But Karl was no good at speaking for himself. After a talk between Catherine and Karl, Johann wrote in his diary:

The Grand Duchess must needs be dissatisfied with my brother. He did not declare himself, and the others have used this chance to put an end to the affair.

Bashfully Johann continued in his diary:

I know this woman, esteem her, and believe to know pretty well how she should be handled, something known to very few. I am truly sorry she didn't come into our family, With Karl it is all over; the law stands in Joseph's way; and, after what's happened, none of us others could do it. I could have had her for myself had I so desired. . . .

Besides the Crown Prince of Württemberg, who had entered upon the scene by this time, the figure of General Koller plays a role in this affair. Koller, an Austrian soldier-diplomat, obviously had been charged with a delicate mission concerning the Grand Duchess:

This Koller is there nearly every day. She blindly trusts him, taking him for God knows what. Koller is a soldier, is clever, and serves his emperor. He is being used to spy on the Grand Duchess and to insinuate desired actions to her. All mail goes through his hands, is opened, read, and delivered by him to the secret police. He, being the cleverer of the two, does what he will with her, she being none the wiser. I should have liked to warn her, but my hands are tied, and anyway, what's it to me? Koller plays a strange role, but he serves my master.

The role assigned to Archduke Karl in his relations with the Grand Duchess was somewhat questionable. Archduke Johann found this wrong:

She dismissed Karl, though in a friendly way. But why does she now demand of him the same devotion as before . . . ? How can she expect of him to play the swain, given no hope and after her statement . . . ? Or is she trying to use Karl as a shield against the machinations of the Crown Prince of Württemberg? I don't go along with this.

In 1815, when war was resumed, Archduke Johann, then at headquarters in Heidelberg, learned of the impending marriage between Catherine and the Crown Prince of Württemberg and also of brother Karl's engagement to Henriette of Nassau-Weilburg. Johann never saw much of a chance for Catherine's happiness:

The good girl will never know a happy moment.

Next, he summed up his judgment about the Grand Duchess and the whole involvement:

The grand duchess wanted to see Karl in an important position, not quietly here in Vienna. This didn't happen. The real reason the affair went wrong was that the Crown Prince of Württemberg wooed her. She fell in love with him and used Karl to lead him on. That explains everything.

To cap it all, "Cathou"—the Czar's tender nickname for her —from the very beginning was forced to share her husband's favors with Princess Bagration. Nor was the Crown Prince in general an overly attentive husband. When he returned to Stuttgart ahead of her, she wrote the most tender love letters to him:

All the news from Stuttgart is that there is a great rejoicing over your return, that the people adore you. . . . You cannot think how this enchants me. Should you succeed in calming the hotheads and in making them see reason, you'll have earned your place in heaven and served the country well. I am ever eager to believe the best where you are involved.

But the Crown Prince's only worry seemed to be to foil Catherine's plan to join him in the field:

You know my stubborn mind in such matters. . . . Women and war must never mix.

Four years later Archduke Johann dedicated a melancholy obituary note to her:

She later married the Crown Prince of Württemberg but was not very happy, was jealous, which partly may have led to her death. How often she may have let her mind go back to Austria. . . .

THE COURLAND LADIES

The designation "Courland ladies" refers to the three daughters of Dorothea, Duchess of Courland and Sagan, 1761–1820, a former Countess Medem, who, in her own rights a very gallant lady, married Peter, Duke of Courland in 1779 and became his widow in 1800. These daughters were: Wilhelmine, Duchess of Sagan, 1781–1839; Jeanne, 1783–1843; and Dorothea, Duchess of Talleyrand-Périgord, 1792–1862. Madame Sagan was first married to Prince Louis de Rohan, next to Prince Trubetskoi, and finally to Count von Schulenburg. Jeanne married Prince Acerenza-Pignatelli, and Dorothea the nephew of the great Talleyrand. Wilhelmine was Metternich's, Dorothea Talleyrand's mistress. The latter later became Duchess of Dino. All three were highly complex creatures, fit subjects for Count Nostitz' inimitable "rogues gallery of ladies." De La Garde, too, in his fulsome praise did more than justice to these untouchable super-courtesans and super-schemers:

And there . . . the Princesses of Courland: the beautiful Duchess of Sagan, passionately partisan for all that is heroic and great. Her divine beauty is not the least of her charms. In her sister, Countess Edmond de Périgord, her manner of walking, her gestures, her bearing, and the timbre of her voice unite to form a ravishing whole. In her face, in the totality of her person, is expressed that irresistible grace without which even perfect beauty is without effect. She is like a flower, unconscious of the scent she exudes. The last of these three Courland Graces, the enchanting Duchess of Acerenza, unites in herself everything we admire in the other two.

PRINCESS BAGRATION

Catherine Bagration, 1783–1856, was born into the Skavronsky family. A report by Countess Lou Thürheim contains the major points of her life:

Catherine Bagration was the daughter of Count Skavronsky and the great-niece of the Czarina Catherine I on her father's side, the great-niece of Potemkin on her mother's side. In 1804 she married the Russian general, Prince Peter Bagration. As early as 1802 an affair of Catherine with Prince Clement Metternich had led to the birth of a daughter, Clementine Bagration, who married Count Otto Blome in 1828. General Bagration was the idol of his troops and died of wounds received at Borodino. In 1830 Catherine married Sir Caradoc, later General Lord Howden. She visited Vienna once more, returned to Paris, and died there in 1856. The petite, charming little lady was related to the Czar's family and was one of those diplomatic sybils whose mission was to gain friends abroad for Russia's political aims. Metternich was her favorite lover, but others also (Gentz, for example) found a sympathetic ear with the lusty Russian lady. The familiar epithet applied in diplomatic circles to the Princess was "the beautiful nude angel" because of the deep décolleté she was in the habit of wearing. But to be close to her was an expensive affair. In 1802 (not yet married) she had a daughter by Metternich; in 1803 she preempted the Duke of Gloucester; Gentz saw her in Troppau in 1805 and wooed her; in 1806 she came to Dresden where she immediately began an affaire with Prince Louis Ferdinand, who went straight from her arms onto the battlefield and into his grave. From 1807 to 1814 she traveled abroad and, after the Congress of Vienna, went to Paris, where in 1852 (at age 69!) Count Hübner still saw her in a seductive situation.

Concerning Princess Bagration, I must tell of an incident

that fully exposes her perfidy. I have the story from the adjutant of the Crown Prince of Württemberg himself, who was an eye-witness. On the day of departure from Vienna, the adjutant—von Münchingen by name—sat next to his master in a coach that was taking them along the road to Purkersdorf. Both slept to compensate for the early hour of rising. Suddenly, someone shouted "Halt!" A lady tore open the coach door, peremptorily ordered the dumbfounded Münchingen to get out, quickly took his seat, and screamed at the coachman: "Get going!" All this took place in a few seconds; the Princess had managed one last rendezvous. But at the next halt the Crown Prince had her dismount and return to Vienna by public conveyance. However, the real meanness of the Princess lay in the fact that, entering the coach, she loudly called to the coachman to drive to the Princess Leopoldine Liechtenstein, a beautiful lady of spotless reputation to whom the Crown Prince was devoted and on whom Princess Bagration wanted to take revenge. Undoubtedly, the police reports about the incident named the innocent rival as the inceptor.

Countess Thürheim was slightly mistaken here. The report of a confidant also treated of the same adventure:

During dinner at court yesterday the story was told how the virtuous Princess Bagration had been recognized in her coach on the way back from Purkersdorf. . . . Mme. Bagration had looked pale and fatigued: she had escorted her Crown Prince of Württemberg as far as Purkersdorf. It is entirely possible that this tender leave-taking will result in the third illegitimate child of the virtuous Princess.

De La Garde saw only her more charming and entrancing sides:

The lady Bagration, who later became the toast of Paris, was exquisitely beautiful in those days, her beauty being enhanced by a head of golden hair and a pair of pale blue eyes. She had a young face, white as alabaster but suffused with a rosy hue, was stern of feature yet soft in expression, temperamental and entirely alluring. A touch of myopia made her glance appear unsure and bashful, and an oriental softness linked to Andalusian gracefulness lent an irresistible charm to her person and caused her to be the scintillating star of an evening's entertainment.

In Vienna her career began with the famous visit of Alexander, elsewhere described. Another agent's report referred to the same incident:

Visit of Alexander at Mme. Bagration's. The Princess did not at all mind mentioning the following to a confidant of hers. Speaking of Prince Metternich, Alexander tried to sound out the Princess' relationship to him, now that Metternich had apparently transferred his favors to Mme. Sagan. "Metternich," Alexander told the Princess, "never loved you, neither you nor the Sagan woman. Believe me, he is a cold fish who is quite incapable of love. Can't you see this plaster-of-Paris figure? He loves no one. . . ." Whereupon he proceeded to dissect several of the Austrian generals. . . . At yesterday's ball he noticeably singled out the Princess, with Sophie Zichy a close second. Though he danced the second dance with Mme. Sagan he neglected her for the rest of the evening. Aside from this, he appeared in an excellent mood. He had a long talk with Hardenberg, which took place in the princess' bedroom because Alexander had to shout at him.[64] It was noticed that the Czar paid no attention whatever to Princess Czartoryski and very little to Metternich.

In addition to the rivalry between Alexander and Metternich, Vienna society was titillated by that existing between Mme. Bagration and Mme. Sagan. Wise old Abbé Carpani wrote about this on October 2, 1814:

By a curious coincidence these two noisy foreigners, rivals as much in their loves as in their ambitions, live in the same house, a house which, shame to our aristocracy, caters to these high-born foreigners. Unless I miss my guess, the favors currently showered on Mme. Sagan by Metternich's and Talleyrand's frequent visits to her indicate that her salon has become the Austrian headquarters, while that of the Russians is with Princess Bagration.

[64] It will be recalled that Hardenberg was nearly deaf.—Transl.

Not that the rivalry between these two women was limited to Alexander and Metternich only. Other cavaliers also played a role:

Mme. Bagration, who, despite her jealousy of the Duchess of Sagan for the latter's insanely vainglorious love of Metternich, has started temporary love affairs with the two young Counts of Schönfeld and Schulenburg, has for several days been pursuing Prince Karl of Bavaria. Not without success, it seems, because he now spends hours on end with her, a matter the two Grand Duchesses much laughed about, together with Grand Duke Constantine, at Princess Esterházy's ball.

Confidential Agent *** mentioned the political ramifications:

The rivalry between the ladies Bagration and Sagan is more virulent than ever. The animosity and intrigue between them as concerns Metternich has reached crescendo stage. People are beginning to be indignant about the ladies' scandalous carryings-on, both from a moral and a political point of view. They are certain to play a role in the annals of the Congress of Vienna. Their influence on the Congress in a pro-Prusso-Russian direction is far too great, abetted and directed as it is by Humboldt.

As the affairs of the Congress progressed, this influence likewise progressed. Abbé Carpani, writing on February 5, 1815, said:

The Princess Bagration began by telling me how Wellington had presented her with the victory decoration he had received from a grateful nation and which he was wont to carry in his buttonhole. Then she told me how Metternich on the same evening had paid assiduous court to her, among other things having confided to her that Alexander's enmity had helped him greatly with the French, a fact he knew how to appreciate. "Confess," the Princess said to him, "it was easier for you to defeat Napoleon than it is now to decide on how to divide the spoils." "But that is precisely the reason," Metternich answered, "why I wanted to keep him on hand. That is the key to my politics, for I knew exactly how things would develop and that is why I wanted to hold on to him, but under guard."

It goes without saying that idle tongues were busy near such a personality:

Nearly every well-placed Viennese society lady disdains to associate with ill-reputed Princess Bagration, whereas the men swarm all over her. The Russian Grand Duke Constantine is one of her most frequent of visitors, though it is Baron Schönfeld who is said to be her declared lover.

Whether the following story is based on fact is a matter of surmise:

Recently, during a game of pledges at the home of Mme. Bagration, a daughter of Duke Starhemberg was present with her parents. During the play the girl went to a distant chamber with a Russian who locked the door behind them, whereupon the Duke broke down the door. They say the Bagration woman runs a whorehouse, a poor place for a mother to take her daughter.

Financially, the beauteous lady was predictably heading for disaster. The beginning was harmless, though indicative:

Since this lady (Bagration) plays a role in the political game, it behooves me to tell Your Excellency that she is in sore financial straits, so much so that creditors besiege her from all sides, and her own cook, who has so far paid from his own pocket, refuses to serve another meal unless he is reimbursed. She is completely penniless.

The next step was house arrest:

Everywhere I hear talk about the monetary trouble Princess Bagration is in. Now she has even been officially put under house arrest at the behest of her creditors. The public at large, which resents her undercutting the Austrian government with Czar Alexander, is enjoying her shame. . . . The rumor is this woman is pro-Napoleon and against making war against him, saying that it does not matter to Russia who sits on France's throne. . . . Her only friend is her companion, Aurora de Marassé, who has even refused an offer from the Empress to abandon her mistress.

And it was this loyal but talkative Marassé woman who sup-
plied Abbé Carpani with the details of her lady's debts:

Her debts stand at 21,801 ducats, 18,121 gulden, and 7,860 in
promissory notes. Banker Elkam has co-signed for another 7,000
ducats. All furnitures and other valuables have been sealed and
promissory notes issued in the name of her stepfather, Count
Litta. If they are honored, all may not be lost; otherwise milady
is headed for jail, she having exhausted all her resources. The
Duke of Serra-Capriola is to write Litta, as Carpani has also
promised to do. But this gentleman is very frugal and a great
egotist and even now is attempting to sell an estate of his step-
daughter's to get back the money he lent her last year. That is
the financial situation of this unhappy fool to whom all the world
paid court—and abandons now in her hour of need.

On July 1, 1815, a tersely simple report of an anonymous
agent to Minister of Police Hager reads:

The promissory notes which Princess Bagration sent to St.
Petersburg via the banker Elkam have bounced. Elkam is enraged
and the Princess has fits. This tragedy will soon end in the usual
legal action that the law permits creditors to take.

COUNTESS LAURA FUCHS-GALLENBERG

About this lady, de La Garde wrote:

On . . . I went to Countess Fuchs. Her salon was as usual
filled with guests, but luckily I still found a place next to Baron
Ompteda, a highly original character who explained to me: "The
salons have not changed at all. Especially this one has never
ceased to be the meeting place of the friends of our charming
'queen.' Never was a title earned more deservedly than this one
and never have her subjects rebelled against her yoke. Rarely has
a woman collected so many friends, but an even rarer talent of
hers is to so bind these friends together that they remain close no
matter what the distance between them. And no change in situation can estrange them. The keystone of her rule is: love me and
love each other. Our association lends authority to her sway; our

happiness guarantees its permanence. Indeed, I do not believe there exists in the whole world a more mild form of despotism nor laws more pleasant to live by. In her realm you will always find courtesy without hypocrisy, outspokenness without coarseness, a desire to please without attempt at flattery, consideration without constraint. Countess Laura is in complete harmony with herself, is ever true, ever kind. Her childlike face seems to mirror the goodness of her heart, in which dwells a certain gentleness no artfulness can imitate. Hers is a truly conciliatory spirit unalloyed by insipidness, which may well account for her remarkable influence over people."

Trust Count Nostitz to add his chilling commentary:

Countess Fuchs' indebtedness to Mme. Langes, the dressmaker, amounts to more than 10,000 gulden.

DUCHESS GABRIELE AUERSPERG-LOBKOWITZ

She was "the beauty who alone inspires true sentiment." Countess Thürheim writes about the lady's relationship with Alexander:

In the midst of the seductions and love affairs of the Congress, one cannot but admire the pure relationship that existed between Czar Alexander and the Duchess Gabriele A-L. Gabriele A. was a widow and enjoyed the reputation of a virtuous woman. Her beauty and her mind, on the other hand, were considered rather mediocre. Though barely twenty, she had been a widow for two years. Kind, simple and, despite her imperial conquest, modest, she held Alexander's heart in thrall not only during the entire Congress but also later. Many Viennese ladies, presumably unfamiliar with the tactics of resistance, declared that Alexander had never seriously laid siege to the lady's virtue, while others mockingly sneered that no credit was due the beauteous Gabriele, she being by nature cold and passionless. I am sure both are wrong. Partly I base my opinion on the fact that an attempt was made to force her bedroom door despite it being barred from the inside. The door held, whereupon the intruder simulated a robbery by taking a small porcelain vase from a neighboring salon. This caused a great stir and brought the whole police force into the act. This "robbery" showed a daring to the point of fool-hardiness. But since thieves are not in the habit of entering the palaces of princes, lurking before the doors of the princesses, then, instead of gold and silver, carrying off a small item, I, like everybody else, smiled at the robbery story. Nor did the police catch any thief, and the bedroom door remained closed. As concerns the lady's equanimity toward Alexander, the following incident indicates that the winsome widow suffered severe emotional upsets. On the day of Alexander's departure a lady friend surprised her on her knees in her boudoir, drowned in tears.

COUNTESS FIFI PÁLFFY-DE LIGNE

The Countess Thürheim related a charming anecdote about this lady:

"Alas, it isn't always conscience that bothers one, sometimes it is regret," said Countess Fifi Pálffy-de Ligne, speaking of her youth. Her husband was a most boring gentleman to whom, nonetheless, she remained loyally faithful, until one day a certain young Englishman fell so passionately in love with her that she found it nearly impossible to resist. Tortured by the situation, she confessed all to her husband. The latter, realizing the need for drastic measures, was able to effect the young man's immediate recall home. But more followed. On her swain's day of departure, poor Fifi's tears would not dry. To end the embarrassing scene, her spouse gave his permission to shed as many tears as she wished until midnight, at which time the sentimental outburst was to cease. Fifi took her husband's order literally: promptly at midnight she dried her eyes.

AURORA DE MARASSÉ

Baroness du Montet, in her Souvenirs, *wrote about Countess de Marassé:*

Poor Countess Aurora de Marassé was the daughter of a French general who, together with Dumouriez, abandoned his troops and fled to Austria. Aided by Emperor Franz, he lived in Temesvar where he died in 1805. His daughter, called Aurora by everyone, was beautiful and charming, a penniless emigrée, with no one to lean on, living recklessly. An honor graduate of the Brünn convent, she was introduced at court and readily received in the highest social circles. Although on familiar terms with the great, she was also friendly with the loosest of women and with those men most damaging to their reputation, such as Metternich and the Duke of Dietrichstein. Addressed as "Mrs." de Marassé because of her convent upbringing, she lived in the garret of the palace Palm as companion to Princess Bagration and a kind of governess to the latter's small daughter Clementine. In this garret she received, often while still abed, ambassadors, envoys and other high personages attending the Congress. Here she also listened to the pleas for help of servants out of work, happy to oblige without asking a penny in return. Protégée and protectress, wearing mended clothes but a beautiful diamond diadem in her hair, she was at times literally starving. She accepted costly presents from influential people, whose carriages and servants, unbeknownst to them, she would often use. Seen everywhere, ill, exhausted, ever beautiful, though with a yellow skin, pale of face, poor in posture, nothing prevented her from accosting the highest personages on familiar terms. She answered their poor jokes with dignity and great presence of mind, annoyed with them but never holding a grudge. The monarchs attending the Congress shook her hand in greeting. Aurora's garret abode often served as meeting place of the diplomats, who thereby thought to have outfoxed their surveillants. Yet her curious manner of life lacked refinement and all dignity, a fact she no doubt was bitterly aware of, though no one spoke ill of her or, worse, slandered her. . . . Nobody could understand how she earned her money. When the Courland ladies left, she came to me one morning, totally famished, begging me for a bowl of soup, having had no food since Wilhelmine de Sagan's departure twenty-four hours earlier. At last she achieved a position worthy of her when the ruling Duke of Saxe-Coburg appointed her chief lady-in-waiting to his new bride, who, possibly because Aurora's beauty aroused her jealousy, soon dismissed her again. Finally she was able to put an end to her emigrée's existence: in Aix-les-Bains she married the Count de Vanauson. Aurora stepped out of the environment of vice and depravity blameless and without blemish.

CAROLINE PICHLER

Caroline Pichler, 1769–1843, née Greiner, was exposed to the intellectual life as a child, meeting, as she did, Sonnenfels and van Swieten. She also at an early age showed poetic talent. In 1796 she married a civil servant and played hostess to men like Grill- parzer, the Schlegel brothers, Hormayr, but also to visiting digni- taries such as Mme. de Staël. Encouraged by Gibbon, she wrote the celebrated novel Agathokles, *praised even by Goethe, as well as plays based on patriotic, Pan-Germanic themes, such as* Heinrich von Hohenstaufen. *She felt German to the core, longing for a return to the Germany of the Middle Ages and the costumes of the time. In her* Memoirs *she wrote:*

Now that the struggle for German freedom had ended in success and the foreign yoke been cast off, hope arose in many a heart to see everything or nearly everything in the fatherland return to the good old days, and since at this time there was a far-flung and keen revival in the love of the romantic Middle Ages, a love kindled earlier by the Schlegel brothers, Tieck, the brothers Grimm, La Motte-Fouqué, etc., it was only natural that talk should get around to a German national costume that would have freed us from the inimical influence of French fashions. For many this thought became the dominant theme. During the carnival season there was a tournament at the Riding School which featured the cavaliers and their ladies in the gorgeous costumes of the Middle Ages and which lent even greater impetus to this thought. The contemporary male attire, compared to the dress of an earlier age, was considered colorless and ill-suited, and the desire to re- educate along the lines of an older pattern to include also a re- version to the feminine style of the times filled many a mind, as it did mine, with great love and longing. I wrote an article on the subject of female fashions, which Herr Bertuch saw fit to publish in his widely read fashion journal. Also, I had decided to attend, together with my daughter, a masked ball where everybody who was anybody would appear dressed in medieval period dresses. Here I intended to distribute a poem I had specially composed for the occasion, a poem that was to be an exhortation of our ancestresses, who had witnessed the tournament in great wonderment and who now requested their granddaughters to wear German dress:

> Oh lovely dress! Mindful of pious ages!
> We bow to you in joyous recognition!
> A happier time this very view presages,
> Your very look lets hope become fruition.
> But not in mummery and on the stages,
> No, living life must be your sole ambition.
> A German must in German dress resplend,
> No longer on the foreign fads depend.
> This should our princesses hand down to us
> In high regard for German womanhood,
> They, who have come as models down to us,
> Beloved, adored, the nation's common good.
> Not fashion's foolishness our only goal to us,
> But many a quiet virtue serve we would.
> A better spirit and more pious manners
> These are perhaps our fashion's banners.

Such were our plans, but, as frequently happened in those days, the day before the masquerade I had a fierce migraine headache again and there could be no question of a ball. However, the poem was published in a periodical.

FANNY VON ARNSTEIN

Fanny von Arnstein, 1758–1818, daughter of the master of the mint, Daniel Itzig of Berlin, married the Viennese banker Nathan Arnsteiner at an early age. He belonged to the small group of uncompromised Jewish bankers at the Vienna court and was later knighted as Baron von Arnstein. Fanny soon took the leading role in the battle for Jewish social emancipation. Until the day she died she retained her sympathy for Prussia and her religious faith. An enthusiastic champion of the liberty ideal in a conservative sense, she aided the Tyrolese with money and advice in their struggle against Napoleon. Throughout the Congress she opposed Napoleon and the French and favored Prussia. She maintained a large establishment, largely open to visiting Germans but also to neutrals like Cardinal Consalvi and many others. The book dealer Bertuch was among her many admirers. He wrote about her in his diaries:

Cotta and I have just returned from dinner with the Arnsteins, who are becoming more and more sympathetic to me. Baroness Arnstein is indeed a most worldly woman, full of sparkle, the perfect hostess. Her daughter, Mme. de Pereira, though not beautiful, is quite charming. There were twenty-two at table, among them the Duke of Acerenza-Pignatelli, several Swedish barons, the Italian poet Carpani, Wanda, Werner, Stegmann, Jordan, and others. I shall go there more often, for, as concerns refined sociability, their house probably ranks among the first in Vienna.

But the confidential agents were far from happy about one aspect of the social life in the Arnstein house—the sympathy for Prussia:

The ladies Arnstein and Eskeles are scandalously out to make pro-Prussian propaganda. They loudly complain about a censorship which permits publication in two Austrian papers of the English articles on the Saxon-Polish question and which permits the public sale of the pamphlet *Saxony and Prussia*. In short, these two ladies are scandalously pro-Prussian.

On the social level the Arnstein salon held its own against any aristocratic prototype. At Christmas, 1814, there was a surprise:

Following a Berlin custom, the Arnsteins day before yesterday gave a very large Christmas tree party. Present were Chancellor Hardenberg, the State Secretaries Jordan and Hoffmann, Prince Radziwill, Herr Bartholdi, and all converted and circumcised relatives of the host and hostess. Each guest received a present or souvenir from the tree. As in Berlin there was much singing of humorous songs, with Frau von Münch rendering some Punch-and-Judy numbers. Then there was an impromptu parade throughout the house, each guest carrying his gift from the tree. Prince Hardenberg was greatly entertained by it all. Humboldt didn't come.

The Arnsteins were ambitious:

Day before yesterday the Arnsteins presented *tableaux vivants* of the Müller wax figures.[65] No effort had been spared to make the show a success. It was. The room was filled to overflowing. Among those present were the Prussian princes, Cardinal Consalvi, Prince Trauttmansdorff, Prince Hardenberg, Prince Hesse-Homburg, Count Capo d'Istrias, Count Salmour, Count Keller, Count Solms, Count Degenfeld, Countess Coloredo-Crenville, Countess Bernstorff, and Abbé Carpani. Rumor had it that Fanny Arnstein had aimed at outdoing the *tableaux vivants* put on by the court. She succeeded.

There is more:

Yesterday the Arnsteins staged another wax figures production before distinguished company: Lord Wellington, accompanied by the Portuguese ambassador; Prince Beauharnais, together with M. Méjean; Cardinal Consalvi; M. de Labrador; Capo d'Istrias; Prince Hardenberg; Commander Ruffo; Count Saint-Marsan; Count Solms; the old Prince Metternich.

MME. SCHWARZ

Mme. Schwarz was the wife of a St. Petersburg banker and the mistress of Alexander I. The husband served Alexander in

[65] Comparable to the Mme. Tussaud exhibition in London.—Transl.

*daredevil financial exploits with (rather against) Denmark. The
Czar reimbursed him with huge and profitable Russian imports.
The Austrian agents kept a sharp eye on this couple, suspicious
even where there was no cause:*

For some time now we have had with us here a certain banker
Schwarz who, together with his beautiful young wife, stays at the
"Austrian Empress." Schwarz moved from St. Petersburg to Berlin
in 1813 and has been in Vienna since the opening of the Congress.
Already in St. Petersburg the woman had a clandestine affair with
Czar Alexander, which the public looked upon as one of his casual
liaisons. Only the Danish Cabinet knows that this "lady," together with her husband, is involved on Alexander's behalf in the
highest state intrigues. For this reason the Danish king secretly
commissioned his Chamberlain, von Scholten, to cultivate this
woman at whatever cost. In this Scholten wholly succeeded. Expensive gifts and above all his dashing figure have made him the
lady's favorite gallant, and now he tries, especially during the
languid hours of dalliance, to pump her about Alexander's conversation with her, the latter visiting her at least twice a week
and possibly giving her secret missions. The results have only
partly become known to me: Alexander often pokes fun at the
Emperor but even more at the Crown Prince. He also often expresses his annoyance over his confused behavior in Poland, saying that he had issued strict orders that Constantine was to expedite the organizing of the country and its army. He is supposed to
have given Mme. Schwarz a hint that her husband was to so
order his financial affairs in Berlin and Holland that in two
months' time he would no longer be involved in speculative ven-
tures. And in two months' time she was also to be in St. Petersburg. . . . A few days ago Alexander went to see her, completely
incognito of course. Still, despite the darkness, several people recognized and followed him to the gate of the "Austrian Empress,"
where they took up post. This enraged Alexander, who raved and
railed in harshest terms against Austria, and immediately on arrival he ordered Schwarz to take a stout stick and beat the people
off. But when Schwarz really went down, he tried, together with

the doorman, to disperse the people with kind words and without raising a ruckus.

Police Commissioner Göhausen was mobilized and in his turn reported:

For two days Mme. Schwarz has not been visited by the celebrated guest. She stays mostly at home during the day, her only company being the Hamburg merchant and money broker Lutteroth and the St. Petersburg merchant Schmidt. In the evening she has been twice to the theater. It is quite true that the Schwarz who is here now is her husband. She herself has volunteered that she shares Alexander's favors in St. Petersburg with a certain Mme. Schmidt, also at the moment at the "Austrian Empress." Alexander, she claims, in this regard does not seek out the highborn ladies of nobility but frequently visits her as well as Mme. Schmidt in St. Petersburg. She is very proud and vain about the Czar's favors and the thought of being his mistress. She has gone so far as to show off her vanity to the hotel director, saying how jealous the local ladies must be of her. She claims to have been in Paris last year and that she will remain in Vienna as long as Alexander does, but that she has no idea how long this will be. On another occasion she confided that she had received sizable presents from the Czar in the past but that, at the risk of at once losing his favors, she must never talk about official business and never ask for anything.

There was a rumor that Alexander gave Schwarz 400,000 gulden at the Imperial Palace. This reactivated von Scholten's interest in the lady. The report read:

Schwarz maintains liaison with a banker named Lippmann. All that I can guess at is that Alexander has secretly started something to undermine our credit badly. Schwarz has in fact said: "The rate of exchange will soon drop to one thousand."

Police Minister Hager was informed. Emperor Franz was alarmed. Göhausen sought the facts:

Schwarz has heavily engaged in speculation together with Trautenberg, has on several occasions even manipulated the rate of exchange. He has discussed his plans and projects at great length with confidential agent B., telling the latter that the exchange rate was bound to further deteriorate.

Göhausen added a new twist to the affair by a report that Schwarz did not come to Vienna at all for reasons of money speculation but to buy textiles. Now councillor Siber and Abbé Carpani got into the act. The new report was:

According to the latest information the Russian government did not commission Schwarz to influence the exchange rate. . . . Anstett has assured me of this and shown me that, despite Talleyrand's comment to the Austrian emperor to the effect this was just another method of conducting war, Alexander never intended to put the squeeze on Austria's foreign rate of exchange.

LA BIGOTTINI

Emilia Bigottini, 1783–1858, dancer at the Opéra Comique in Paris, according to rumor played the role of Goddess of Reason at the time of the Convention. She was the lady friend of many an important personage and the outstanding star of her time. The police were well informed about her:

The dancers Bigottini, Aimée Petite, and the two Aumers made such deep impressions on Prince Kaunitz, Count Trauttmansdorff, and Franz Pálffy that the latter Wednesday evening, when the dancing ensemble was at the theater, sent two vans to the hotel containing bedsteads, boxes, sofas, four deerskin-covered mattresses, and the like, all of the best quality and worth some 4,000 florins.

Count Pálffy for a time was obviously her declared lover and probably the father of her child. This, because of Pálffy's high position in the Hungarian nobility, embarrassed Emperor Franz. Police Minister Hager was required to submit several reports on the subject to his master:

Franz Pálffy's affaire with the Bigottini woman is coming to an end; at least it has cooled off considerably at the moment.

He wants to give her an annuity of 6,000 francs; she wants the capital at once or the assurance of an income for her daughter until her marriage day, her only worry in the world being this child. The brother preferred the income idea for Franz, considering it preferable for Pálffy to live in peace and quiet with a single woman, who incidentally was known for her loyalty to her chosen lovers, than to face recurring moves, with concomitant loss of fortune. Nothing could be arranged, however, and now all parties are at outs.

Eipeldauer writes about a famous Bigottini appearance in the Antony and Cleopatra *ballet:*

Ah, the pearl of the world is this Mam'selle Bigottini! Sir Cousin, that one dances like she was cavorting naked in a swimming pool, and when her part is done it's stupendous to behold how she disappears as if she'd never been there. And does she ever have control over her body, oh, my good gracious God Almighty! The prone positions full of expectant lust she assumes on a couch, oh dear, dear God, that's when the young and the not-so-young gents' eyes bulge, and when she suddenly flings herself at old Antony and wraps herself wholly around his body, why, a stone he would have been had he not promptly forgot wife and kiddies and died for love of her, as later there was much trouble in private houses over her act. . . . And a knowledge this person must have like an angel, for in 1792, when just a snip of a girl of fourteen or fifteen,[66] she played the famous role of the Goddess of Reason at the sansculotte parade entering Paris—but who knows if that's true.

Naturally, la Bigottini took part in all the larger public parties and balls:

Of the masked ball on the thirtieth it is said mostly men attended it, with few women present, and those of the loose type. The dancer Bigottini (pink mask) is reported to have sorely beset

[66] The inventors of Eipeldauer were mistaken. Born in 1783, la Bigottini could have only been nine at the time.—Transl.

the Russian czar, who then for some time talked in Russian with another mask and also with Beauharnais.

And then the sudden end:

There was great consternation over Demoiselle Bigottini's departure, who by the way has a law suit pending with the clothier Joel for a thousand ducats. Everybody is put out because all Viennese theaters are so very short of first-rate talent.

LA MOREL

Rosalie Morel, dates unknown, was the daughter of the Hussar Major Gany. Separated from her husband, allegedly a French army commissar, she was primus inter pares among Vienna's "gallant ladies," beautiful, chaste, and the mistress of the Grand Duke of Baden. Because she moved in such exalted circles, she was closely watched by the secret police, being suspected of espionage. Police Minister Hager reported to Emperor Franz about her:

Czar Alexander seemed greatly to enjoy the masked ball. He took quite an interest in the mask who was believed to be Countess Esterházy-Roisin. From two to half past three he and the King of Prussia were intrigued with a pair of black masks. Mme. Morel's beauty again caused quite a stir. She talked with Count Schönfeld and Prince Narishkin. Then Prince de Ligne took custody of her and stayed with her quite a while. The Grand Duke of Baden did not dare show up in the same room with her but did not cease stalking her and never left her out of eyesight.

Hager was set on removing la Morel from Vienna. But the Grand Duke could not interpose with him directly and was at last forced to appeal to the Chief Lord High Steward Trauttmansdorff to prevent this disaster. The pair's love idyll seemed to terminate suddenly. Anonymous sources, but also Count Benzel, reported:

Rumor has it that the Grand Duke of Baden is entirely at outs with the Morel woman (whose husband and children are living near Vienna) because of her all-too-flagrant unfaithfulness. . . . Yet at the latest masked ball, Karl of Baden stayed until four-thirty and exclusively near his beloved.

OTHER COCOTTES

The borderlines between the truly mundane, the occasional "loose" ladies, and several female members of high society were blurred during the time of the Congress. But it wasn't so much an insatiable lust for life and love that drove the young ladies into the arms of their divers lovers as a strongly developed business instinct, spurred perhaps by the fear of suffering once more under a financial debacle as the one that attended Austria's national bankruptcy of 1811. Of interest in this regard is an agent's report of November 26, 1814:

On St. Catherine's Day, Prince Rosenberg gave a plain luncheon in honor of his mistress Catherine Buchwieser, having also invited Mme. Aimée Petite and Chief Lord High Steward Count Trauttmansdorff, and the Munich dancer with her Count Rechberg. Mother Buchwieser's comment was: "My daughter has done a foolish thing to have taken up with Prince Rosenberg. She should have stayed with Prince Ghika. He paid better."

The most outstanding representatives of the "oldest profession" may be mentioned here: Mademoiselle Toussaint, who later called herself Countess Waffenberg, the official mistress of Ludwig, heir to the Prince of Hesse-Darmstadt; and Josephine Wolters from Cologne, allegedly the widow of a Frenchman killed in the Battle of Leipzig. She met the Czar's adjutant, Prince Volkonski, who smuggled her, dressed as a boy, into his quarters at the Imperial Palace. Then there were Wolter's girlfriend, Louise Schneider, who spent her evenings at the theater where she received a great many officers in her box, and, finally, the sisters Köppe, daughters of a civil servant. Best known of them was Johanna ("Gorgeous Jeanie"), married since 1810 to Count Desfours but soon divorced again. The authorities planned to employ this "ambassadress of Aphrodite" politically. In this the then incumbent French ambassador, Count Narbonne, and also Prince de Ligne played a certain role as early as 1813. The count's reception at the lady's house was not very friendly. An agent reported on this:

Count Narbonne saw her only once when de Ligne took him to her lodgings in the stables area. Here he was received in any but a friendly manner by her declared lover, Baron Karl von Mengen, a colonel of the Schwarzenberg Uhlans. Having just returned from a walk with the Countess, von Mengen in the presence of her two guests severely upbraided her for receiving the visits of strange men, snarling in leaving at de Ligne in a rather audible manner: "You ought to be ashamed to pimp for the Frenchie."

"Gorgeous Jeanie" was slated for permanent eviction from Vienna, an idea to which she violently objected in a petition to the police:

It is true that I live separated from my husband, but through no fault of mine. I am ready at any time to return to him, as soon as he gets rid of the mistress he keeps and installs me in all my rights as his wife, which includes furnishing with a suitable upkeep, something he has so far neglected to do.

After many an adventure, she came back to Vienna at the time of the Congress and now her star really rose. In a report of a post-Congress investigation of pandering we read:

It is known and documented that the business of pandering was most profitable for an Anna Heller during the Congress. Among the women and girls who nearly every day came to her place were: the Countess Desfours and the wife of the Court councillor Bablé, both living in the same house with her; the daughter of the former wine dealer Fischer; and a sister of Countess Desfours, Catherina Kepp, who was primarily engaged in writing and delivering the rendezvous letters. Convinced of ill-doings going on, Chief Commissioner von Pfleger had the lodgings of the Heller woman, the widow of a wholesale grocer, raided by the police. Several women, including especially the

Countess Desfours, but by chance no men, were found present. These women claimed to be either visiting with the Heller woman or to have come on business errands, which the latter also protested to be the case, adding that she was in the money-lending business. But in the end Anna Heller was made to admit that Countess Desfours had had trysts, once with Count Nako, another time with Count G . . . y in her quarters. She, the Heller woman, had been suitably rewarded by the Countess from the money the two cavaliers had paid.

Once again undergoing a short exile, Countess Desfours was soon back in Vienna. She took up a relationship with Gentz, who wrote in his diaries:

January 27, 1815. First rendezvous with a lady who is known under the name of Countess Desfours and whom I found very beautiful.

January 29. Rendezvous again with the lady from Friday. Her first name is Johanna. She gave me transports of joys I have not tasted for years.

A later note by von Schönholz reported that Countess Desfours allegedly turned pious and became the head of a "Magdalene House for Fallen Girls":

If all is on the up-and-up with this Magdalene colony—I was shown house and garden—there's no understanding why such a laudable undertaking is wrapped in secrecy. It leads to the most fantastic rumors. Thus, gruesome tales are told about the ascetic exercises the inmates are forced to undergo, that, for example, they are made to take ice-water baths to mortify the flesh and other similar nonsense. As head of this mysterious institute a certain Countess D. was mentioned.

Mavericks and Eccentrics

The composer Sigismund Ritter von Neukomm, 1778–1858, was born in Salzburg but lived mostly abroad. A pupil of Haydn, he early went to Paris where he continued to study under Cherubini and Spontini and became Talleyrand's protégé. He accompanied Talleyrand to the Congress. It was he who composed the requiem in honor of Louis XVI at St. Stephan's. In 1816 he was made a knight of the Legion of Honor. Neukomm was a highly prolific composer, creator of a total of 524 vocal compositions. His journeys took him as far as Brazil, and he never lost the reputation of working for the secret service. As early as October 26, 1814, an Austrian agent submitted a detailed report on him:

The musician Neukomm has been investigated some more. As reported before, he is the protégé of Talleyrand, who appreciates his talents and likes him for his quietly good-natured manners, as others do also. He was first asked by Talleyrand to write a mass in honor of the new king. Even though the top maestros fought for the honor, Talleyrand's protection was enough to give the nod to Neukomm, whose composition was chosen and who later received the Fleur-de-Lis order. Following this, Neukomm, generally described as a genial fellow, begged Talleyrand to take him to Vienna where he could see his old friends and where he could sponsor the musical training and career of his sister. Also, he planned to produce an operetta, composed in Paris, here, where he had begun his musical career and where his sweetheart of earlier years, Mme. Milder, would take on one of the parts. His particular concern was to pay his personal respects to his blind mother, still living in Salzburg, and to improve his sister's living conditions, both women depending on him for support. Neukomm still has some hopes of seeing his music produced in Vienna but has entirely given up the idea of bringing his sister there. He says he does not want her to work under the direction of the Jew Joel at an opera house he considers decadent. Joel is a rich lawyer and patron of the arts and said to be financially tied in with the Imperial Theaters. As is well known, Count Pálffy, not he, is the director. Because of all this, Neukomm will return with Talleyrand to Paris, where he will try to place his sister with the Paris Conservatory. In confidential talk he makes no bones about not liking France and advises every musician against going to Paris. His description of Talleyrand's character is rather odd. Often the latter will not utter a single word to the people around him in his study for two whole days. When he works alone, he often asks Neukomm to play the piano. Neukomm swears that at times he plays for two hours, not knowing if Talleyrand, who stands there, head bowed or writing, even hears him.

BOLLMANN

Dr. Justus Erich Bollmann was an American physician of German descent. He visited the Congress, where he soon gained access to the highest circles. His role as messenger from a new and better world has been mentioned. Bollmann's chief interest was his project of a steam-driven boat. In this capacity he had made contact with a certain Professor Hauff, who apparently in the end turned a deaf ear to Bollmann's proposal. This is revealed in an intercepted letter of Bollmann's to Hauff:

January 3, 1815. I have studied Your Excellency's letter of yesterday, and, if it pleases you, readily admit that in business matters I am rather stupid. Aside from that, I permit myself to mention that (1) I never discussed your model except when unavoidable; (2) that when I had to talk about it I always said the principle was right but the method of application to a working model is not feasible. This I consider to be so; this I know to be so. It may be foolish not to be able to or not to want to talk against one's own convictions, but such unfortunately is my habit. (3) The commission really left no doubt that none of the features of the model corresponds to the specifications. (4) The shrewd commentary of your clairvoyant privy councillor is most amusing to me. I am no more concerned with political affairs than the next political Viennese streetsweeper, have been neither "sent" nor "appointed" by anyone, owe no accounting about myself to a soul. Whatever your keen-eyed privy councillor may think, Prince Metternich, Count Stadion, and others of similar status know good and well what I am doing, what I want, what interests me. They do not take me for a politician, either in jackboots or in dancing shoes. But since I am considered to be such a dangerous or rather suspect person, Your Excellency will do well to sever all contact with me. Our courses have touched at several points and now must pursue their natural directions. Wishing you all the best, I remain Your Excellency's obedient E. Bollmann.

P.S. Be assured I shall not mention the model or the like ever again.

The same problem occupied Bollmann in a letter to a Mme. Reinhard in Paris, a letter also intercepted in Vienna:

There won't be any steamships on the Danube, I'm afraid, unless somebody takes a chance and sees if a concession would be granted. But who would do this? Professor Hauff thinks the only trouble is that his model is taken too lightly. I cannot say more than that I find the idea basically sound but the attempted execution quite impossible. Also, some half-wit has put the bug in his ear that his contact with me had been unfortunate since I was really a camouflaged politician. After that I had to tell him, of course, to go it alone. I hear he tries elsewhere now, claiming all powers of hell cannot stop him from getting the concession. He is pledging his honor. He wants the license for the

Rhine as well as The Netherlands. He is completely out of his mind through brooding, lack of money, and egotism.

Bollmann, the "camouflaged politician," did indeed discuss purely political questions with that aboveboard politician and general, Lafayette, in a letter to Paris for which a chiffon *turned up in Vienna. The letter was dated January 3, 1815:*

Now that war seems more likely than peace, Prussia and Russia have a definite advantage over their opponents because of their superior will to fight, meaning they are more capable, more eager, more filled with energy, etc. The young Prussians have developed a taste for war. They thirst after the warlike life, Hotspurs all of them. The Russians, on the other hand, have become used to the balmy climate and the looting. The Austrians seem far from coming out of their natural hibernation. France laughs at everyone. England is well aware that renewed war will be immeasurably expensive, meaning not only it must maintain its own armies but those of Austria as well. Thus, the future does not present a rosy picture.

THE GERMAN LEAGUE OF VIRTUE

The German Tugendbund,[67] a patriotic organization, was founded by Scharnhorst and Gneisenau in Königsberg, East Prussia, in 1811. The circle soon included such luminaries as Turnvater Jahn, Jena's Professor Luden, Ernst Moritz Arndt, and, as guiding spirit, the philosopher Fichte. At the Congress the "Bundists" sought in vain to gain an ear. The poet and confidential agent von Hebenstreit lectured on the Tugendbund *in Vienna:*

The "virtue merchants" at this critical stage—January, 1815— have run their course but live like sybarites. They take their noon meal either with Sperl in the Leopoldstadt or at the oriental eatery near the main customs building. Then they go to a café, to a room reserved for them. From seven to eight they gather in

[67] A secret society of German students, 1808–1816. The names mentioned are those of patriots hotly engaged in German moral rearmament after Napoleon's defeat.—Transl.

the "Three White Lions," where they imbibe much wine and eat oysters, and in the evening they frequent disreputable sections until ten or so. They are pretty well known and not noticed much anymore. Müller is still taken seriously because he is smart and doesn't exaggerate all the time. . . . At any rate, the contact with Alexander's personal physician, Willié, is no longer close and the Russians seem loath to hurt themselves by sponsoring the far-fetched interests of a few hotheads.

ZACHARIAS WERNER

The East Prussian playwright Zacharias Werner, 1768–1823, was the creator of the so-called "fate drama" such as The 24th of February. *Starting as a civil servant, he became a vagabond, wrote a series of "epic" dramas with undramatic scene sequences such as* Sons of the Valley *and* Martin Luther or the Solemnification of Power. *In 1810, in Rome, he converted to Catholicism. Goethe, in the same year, staged Werner's only full-fledged and meaningful tragedy—*The 24th of February—*in Weimar with great success. Werner came to Vienna for the Congress and enjoyed a great following as an evangelistic preacher. Opinion about him differs. The secret police dogged his footsteps but found nothing. Nostitz said he raged like a fool and talked like a coachman. The ladies were taken with him. De La Garde, together with Princess Suvorov, attended one of his sermons and wrote:*

Before Werner followed the footsteps of Massillon and Bossuet, he was a Lutheran and a dramatic poet. He wrote several successful dramas of decided romantic trend. Putting all his religious feelings into his dramatic talent, his goal was to present Lutheranism in its most telling colors. His conversion came as a result of an incident, at once poetic and epic. One evening he took a stroll around Vienna's cathedral, deeply lost in those dark broodings that are the hallmarks of German poets. Lost in admiration, he gazed at the imposing edifice and its Gothic towers whose highest pinnacle is lost in the clouds. Suddenly a door opened and there stepped forth a dignified priest in white robes, ac-

companied by two pages, on his way to offer a dying person
the final comforts of his religion. A torch threw a glimmering light
upon the path. Struck by the scene, the Lutheran poet involuntarily
stopped and watched the holy procession as it, like a mysterious
presence, slowly wended its way down the street and at last disappeared. He was deeply moved, his imagination stirred. This
simple act of an aged priest, on his way to administer the final
sacrament to a dying person, evoked the greatness and grandeur
of the Catholic religion in his mind's eye. From this moment on
Werner was a Catholic. He left Vienna and went to Rome where
he formally renounced his heresy in St. Peter's. After two years of
living in a monastery at the foot of Mt. Vesuvius, he returned to
Germany, exchanging the poet's corner for the pulpit. This abrupt
change in faith, his talent as a priest, his delivery, interspersed as
it is with the now brooding, now scintillating, flights of mind—
all this has made him highly fashionable. Whenever his turn to
preach comes up, the church is hardly able to accommodate the
crowd of the pious and the curious. His success as preacher has
caused the theater directors to reintroduce the author's plays, a
successful speculation. The same ears that in the morning had
rushed to miss no word of the latter-day St. Paul are seen in the
evening, Holy Script still fresh in mind, applauding the plays of
the saved heretic. Put out by this applause, Werner has felt compelled to use the pulpit to militate vociferously against his former
erring ways, which he would fain undo now if he but could. But,
poor fellow, the more he rants, the more titillating becomes the
contrast, leading to his ever-increasing popularity both as poet and
as preacher.

It was with great difficulty we found a place in the over-
crowded church. Princes could be seen, generals, ladies of rank
and, even more noteworthy, members of all faiths. The apostle
appeared, beginning his long sermon in German. I didn't understand a word of it but, presumably, was only one of many whom
curiosity had drawn and who nearly all were innocent of German.
Nonetheless, his sermon seemed to lose none of its effect: the
resonant voice of the speaker, his large emaciated pale face, his
sunken eyes, everything was in harmony with the cathedral, whose

vaults he made reverberate. Decorative as St. Stephan's cathedral looks from the outside, its interior is somber, and this very darkness, so conducive to the deepest meditation, gave the priest's delivery a sepulchral tinge. "Well," Princess Helene asked me in leaving, "what do you make of the preacher?" "I am hardly able to judge his ability to convey meaning. But to me his delivery was as of one possessed and has little kindled my interest in getting to know his dramatic works."

Friedrich von Schönholz, in his Traditionen, *highlighted another point in Werner's preaching: his obscenity:*

Zacharias Werner's love for smut and double meanings led him into trouble with several religious orders but did not stop him from practicing it with the Franciscans, where his skill at it became well-known. The story about the tongue, which, without naming it by name, he called in the most equivocal of phrase the "most dangerous piece of flesh," made the rounds throughout all Christendom as a homiletic scandal. Here is another story: One day I noticed scuttling down the pot-holed street an exceptionally emaciated figure in the habiliments of a secular priest, short surtout, breviary in left hand, an old umbrella in his right, his down-at-heel shoes tied with string across his insteps. The leathern features and deep-set eyes, the flying mane told me it was our famous Cain-raising priest. Following him closely, I came to the Franciscan church, where the congregation, mostly of the upper classes and female in sex, left no doubt what was about to transpire. About half an hour later, Zacharias did indeed appear in the pulpit, there once again to deflower his audience with his common, often coarse, zealousness, liberally applying cheap comedian tricks and scurrilous puns. This sin-swollen man, in bondage to the basest of lustful desires, sermonized about—continence! When he came to talk about ridding the flesh of lustful desires, he again told one of the little stories with which he always began: "But let me tell you a little story. There once was a king," he said, "who had a beautiful white horse, a white horse which had a marvelously strong tail"—putting, as he always did, lingering emphasis on the last word. "This king put up a prize: he who would pull out by the root the white horse's tail, to him the whole horse would be given. This brought to the scene many stout and strong lads who pulled and pulled to no avail. Then one day there came a wee bit of a man—a tailor of a man, who went to the tail and pulled one hair after the other," etc. The moral being, do with your sins as did the tailor with the horse's tail. Thus, as the tailor did the horse, you'll gain the heavenly kingdom. As soon as his, be it admitted, very earthy parable came to an end, he threw himself on his knees and shouted: "Let us pray the Holy Spirit for his blessing!" He then cradled his forehead in his hands, remaining thus silent until—he had thought out a way how to end his sermon, he being much too lazy to decide on one beforehand. Who recognized in this figure the creator of "Transfiguration of Force"? How is this lust for the obscene explained in this man turned Catholic priest? I recall a passage from one of his private letters to the Ligurian padre P. in which Werner explained the close relationship between lustfulness and devotion, one of his premises being that nature ever pours the most noble forces into the worst vessels. This idea, in relation to his own way of life, explains everything, and though there is doubt about the noble forces, there is none about the vessel, and here his self-criticism was right on target. About his conversion and his end I know only that Zacharias, after having rued, like Gresset on his deathbed, ever having written for the stage, died in the arms of one of the most skillful of priests of the Society of Jesus, the above padre P.—"reconciled with God and the world," as the latter assured me, not without smug satisfaction. But who reconciles the world's memory with one of its abortions?

Friedrich von Schlegel, in his collected works, told the story about the tongue:

In the end, little concerned with his listeners' peace of soul, he only sought to achieve effect through monstrousness of expression. It is even claimed he made bets he could with impunity present certain images from the pulpit. And he lived up to his boast in his sermon about the "teeny-weeny bit of flesh" that had brought all ills into the world and whose abomination he had hinted at in countless allusions. His listeners cast down their eyes in embarrassment. Suddenly Werner screamed: "Shall I name this 'teenyweeny bit of flesh?'" Deathly silence. "Shall I show it to you?" Agonizing pause. Then Werner stuck out—his tongue. Nervous giggling was the response.

SIR SIDNEY SMITH

Sir Sidney Smith, 1764–1840, retired English vice admiral, defender of St. Jean d'Acre, was a champion of the anti-slavery movement. De La Garde, in connection with Sir Sidney's famous picnic described earlier, gave some details about his life:

It wasn't only curiosity that drove Sir Sidney to attend the Congress: his aim went beyond nations to mankind as a whole. Though entirely without official mission, he was more active than nearly all representatives of the most influential powers. His plans did justice to his adventurous life, whose episodes were as picturesque as they were historical. A sailor from early youth and out of work since the American War of Independence, he went into Swedish service. Highly decorated after the famous sea battle of 1791, he soon after offered his services to the Turkish government. Recalled by royal proclamation to England a few months later, he joined Lord Hood in the blockade of Toulon. In 1796, lying off the coast of Le Havre, he seized a French raider, but a sudden calm foiled his plan to make off with it. A sailor secretly cut the anchor rope, and a rising tide carried the captured vessel up the Seine, forcing Smith to surrender to superior numbers. Taken to Paris, he was first imprisoned at Abbaye, later at the Temple. By means of faked orders of the Minister of Police, his friends effected his release, not itself a difficult task but one that later, under the walls of Acre,[68] served to foil the most momentous plans, possibly preventing a general uprising in the Orient. Who can still claim that great events have great causes! Returning to England, Smith was put in command of *Tiger*, a ship of eighty cannons, and ordered to patrol the coast

[68] Meant is Napoleon's sixty-one-day siege of 1799, successfully withstood by Turkish forces aided by Great Britain.—Transl.

of Egypt. Having bombarded Alexandria, he set sail for Syria, where the Turkish pasha decided on a defense of Acre, a decision based on Smith's presence and advice. It is a known fact that it was he who forced the lifting of the siege. This netted him a highly valuable gift from the sultan and from Napoleon the no less flattering comment: "This demon Sidney Smith has made Dame Fortune jilt me!" Returning to London, he was presented the key to that city as well as an expensive sword. Afterward, he sat in the House of Commons until the peace of Amiens was broken. Receiving a new command and raised to the rank of rear admiral in 1805, he set sail for the Mediterranean, where he blockaded and, in a few hours' time, took Capri. When, in 1807, Napoleon declared the end of the Braganza dynasty, Smith took the Prince Regent of Portugal and his family to Brazil. After that he was inactive. But the peaceful life was not to his taste, and the Congress of Vienna seemed to offer new opportunities to occupy his mind. He was one of the very first to arrive, calling himself the envoy of Gustavus IV, former King of Sweden, who, as Duke of Holstein, had commissioned him to regain the forcibly removed crown. He owed this signal mission to his earlier work in Sweden's service.

Count Nostitz also mentioned Sidney Smith briefly:

By look and speech Sir Sidney Smith is not the typical Englishman. His talk and his deeds are familiar to the world. Among the many decorations he wears, the most important one is the medal he received from the Bishop of Acre, after the defense of that fortification, with the words: "This medal is a gift of Richard Lionheart. I present it to a fellow countryman of his in token of gratitude for his presence in our city to which his king centuries ago also took his fame."

ANNA PRATASOV

Anna Stepanovna Pratasov, 1745–1826, an intimate of Catherine the Great whose éprouveuse *she was considered to be, was a "character" who is "disgusting and black like a Tahitian queen." De La Garde wrote about her:*

Among the curiosities of the day, largely because of the memories she evoked, was old Countess Pratasov, that declared favorite of Catherine II, who once held a position with the Empress of such utter intimacy that the English would not dare give a name to it. The Viennese talked of her as of a celebrity. I owed it to Prince de Ligne to lay eyes on this relict of a past age. "Our acquaintance," he told me, taking me to her one day, "dates back to a very ancient time when she, too, took that fairy-tale trip to the Crimea, not fortuitously, I should think, but because the Empress had become addicted to her: royal favor is often based on small things!" Entering the large living room, I observed a huge shape on the sofa. Gauged by the amount of trinkets she wore, she might have been an Indian idol. On her head, around her neck, covering her arms there was a veritable waterfall of glittering diamonds, bracelets, necklaces, ruby-studded medallions, tremendous earrings that reached down to her very shoulders. This jewelry display appeared to me some seventy years of age. On our entering the room she tried, in vain, to arise. She then offered the Prince her hand and, not without some trouble, made room for him beside her. Noticing me in the background, she addressed a few stereotyped, artificial, polite remarks to me that were very typical of her contemporary Russian society. Then began a long reminiscence of those beautiful Hermitage days of long ago. The past appeared enshrined as in a temple, the present a filthy thing. But the oddest thing of all was that the Prince seemed completely to have erased the thirty years since the Crimean trip and treated this wrinkled widow like a young girl, tenderly calling her "my little one" and "my child." The Countess on her part took his half-mocking gallantry in highly comical seriousness.

The Invisible Foe

Napoleon I, 1769–1821, the executor and executioner of the Revolution, Emperor of the French, King of Italy, protector of the Rhenish Confederacy, mediatizer of Switzerland, was victorious in over a hundred battles and skirmishes—but not in the last one. What was he doing, this beaten French emperor, at the time of the Congress? His journey through Provence in April, 1814, was fraught with peril because of the royalist bent of the populace. On April 25 the Emperor, in the guise of an auxiliary coachman, rode beside his coach:

April 26. Around one P.M. Napoleon stopped in La Calade at a large roadside inn. A half-hour later the foreign commissioners arrived. When they left their coach, Napoleon was awaiting them, head cradled in his hands. When they approached, he raised his head, looking like a man deeply worried and devoid of all hope. Seeing a crowd gathering, he abruptly arose and went inside, making sure all windows were securely bolted. During the meal the commissioners were considering the situation. They were aware that any new incidents must be avoided at all cost. . . . They procrastinated, and thus the whole day passed, it being impossible to go on until the Grande Place was cleared. At last, shortly after midnight, a troop of gendarmes cleared a path through the crowd and preparations for immediate departure were made. Napoleon was saddlesore and could no longer mount a horse. At the very last moment he decided to change his coachman's uniform for the dress of a foreigner. He borrowed Koller's uniform, Walburg-Truchsess' wig, Shuvalov's overcoat. To complete the camouflage, he entered the coach of the Russian commissar. Then, as an additional precaution, he sat down to the left of Shuvalov and gave the sign to start. Around one A.M. the imperial train moved off, the remainder of the trip passing quite uneventfully.

Napoleon, who continued to act the emperor on Elba, even maintaining a small guard, a court, and a deliberating body of "statesmen," was, especially in England, the object of intense curiosity. A report of the Austrian consul in Livorno, Gebhardt, contained some details:

Our neighbor on the island continues to draw a crowd. A British Member of Parliament, member of the opposition, spent four hours with him recently, hours in which the Emperor did not once mention the Empress Marie Louise but repeatedly and favorably spoke about the late Empress Josephine. "What," Napoleon asked the Englishman, "do you think of my financial system?" "I think it was very poor." "That," answered Napoleon, "I all too often became aware of myself. In this regard I was given very bad advice by my ministers." He protested to have become reconciled to his fate. Adventurer that he is, he has returned just about to the point where he started from. What hit him worst, as he put it, was Marshal Marmont's treason and disloyalty. "I had," he finally said, "a great goal, for which I would have sacrificed five million, as easily as five, people." He doesn't think much of the Bourbons, says there is not enough talent among the lot of them to rule the French and that there is bound to be another revolution. . . . When the great public divorce,[69] which some papers mention, takes place, then, I think, there will no longer be any reason to talk about this unfortunately very famous person.

There is another talk between Napoleon and a British traveler to Elba about which the Russian Ambassador in Paris,

[69] From Marie Louise.

Paul Bugyatin, wrote to the Russian Ambassador in Vienna, Count Nesselrode, in December, 1814. This missive fell into the hands of the Austrian secret police and was "processed" routinely. Since the official in charge had but limited time available, only the main points are extracted:

Napoleon: And the Congress?

Visitor: Nothing happens.

Napoleon: Metternich considers himself a diplomat. He is a liar, a tremendous liar. One lies once, twice, but never three times.

Visitor: But in this marriage business, Austria nevertheless. . . .

Napoleon: The Austrian court! Nothing is known about the marriage negotiations. I had meant to write my memoirs but will not do so. I'll just let the main facts be known. But the marriage. . . . I loved Josephine. I wept over her.

Visitor: She was very devoted to Your Majesty.

Napoleon: But in this marriage business, what low levels were not reached in them! Vienna was for all the world like a petit bourgeois marrying off his daughter to the Grand Duke.

Visitor: Did Your Majesty treat Her Majesty, Marie Louise, well?

Napoleon: Indeed I did! You want to know what this Congress does? Ignorance everywhere. Franz is impotent. Alexander is a rake, and little the world knows how false he is. The Prussian king considers himself a wise man and is nothing but a corporal. Yet, a good man, withal, a very good man. Somehow, they'll reach an agreement.

Visitor: And the British?

Napoleon: Do the English papers repeat the same inanities about me? Would I be respected in England?

Visitor: Indeed you would be.

Napoleon: But in England you treat men like you do your clothes.

The more disparate the opponents, the greater was the resistance to a peaceful settlement of all points of disagreement. A report of the Swedish envoy in Vienna said:

I am told that the Austrian consul in Civitavecchia has made a report to the effect that the Dey of Algiers in no way honors the military standards of the Isle of Elba and has even instructed his corsairs to capture Napoleon, should opportunity offer, and to take him to Algiers.

Later, that is at the end of January, 1815, other confidential reports reached Vienna, as, for example, that from the confidant Neustädter to the Bishop of Agram, Verhovacz:

The latest news is that Napoleon has stopped all construction on Elba and is trying to sell the cannons of the Porto Ferrajo fortress. This would seem to indicate he intends to leave Elba. An Englishman, returning from Elba, reports to have seen Napoleon taking daily coach rides, sitting alone in his open carriage, wearing a plain suit and reclining against the backrest. Opposite him sit two generals of his court, and behind the coach trail mamelukes, guards, officers and adjutants of the civil guard of Porto Ferrajo. He looks quite healthy and acknowledges each salute in a military manner. He has retained the imperial eagle in his standard.

What actually brought about Napoleon's escape from Elba, the primary causes of it, is to this day shrouded in mystery. His decision was probably partly influenced by the fear that, as a preventive measure, the Allies might yet transfer him to a more remote location:

Three days ago [70] at the Arnsteins' an Englishman appeared who had just returned from Italy and who created quite a stir. In January, this Englishman had been to Elba where Napoleon told him among other things: "The gentlemen in Vienna want to install me on St. Helena, but that will never happen. . . ."

The story of his departure from Elba, his daily, ever more triumphant return through Grenoble and Lyon to Paris, is known. How the news hit the princes and diplomats in Vienna like a bolt from the blue has been described. From Paris the correspondent of the Königsberger Zeitung reported:

[70] May 6, 1815.

Paris, March 29. The current ever-changing situation benefits first of all the portrait sellers, tailors, embroidery shops, and restaurant owners. Everybody admires the newly exhibited portraits of Marie Louise and the little King of Rome in the touching pose of a child praying for his father and for France. The changes in the uniforms keep a great many people busy, but the richest harvest is garnered by the messieurs Brilliote and Very.[71] Here the carousing, feasting, drinking, singing never cease. The Café Montansier, formerly a theater, has been in a state of bedlam for eight days. Several hundred guests push up against a table, on top of which one of them belts out songs about Napoleon, Marie Louise, the King of Rome, the imperial eagles. The audience supplies the chorus, and after a while the din rises to a pitch reminiscent of the first days of the Revolution.

Antoine-Marie, Count de Lavallette, first the adjutant, then the postmaster general of Napoleon, described the latter's entry into the Tuileries:

The top functionaries and civil servants of every rank were delighted to see the Bourbons take to their heels, being sure, as I am, that they are rid of them for good. Already the Bourbons' eleven-months' rulership seems nothing but a bad dream, lasting but a few hours. After I had reorganized the postal service according to Napoleon's wishes, I went into the Tuileries where I saw some five to six hundred half-pay officers embrace and congratulate each other on the prospect of seeing Napoleon again. Inside, the Emperor's two sisters-in-law, the Queens of Spain and Holland, were waiting in a state of deep emotion. Soon they were joined by their ladies-in-waiting and by those of the Empress. Everywhere the bees had been replaced by the lilies. But suddenly one of the ladies, as she carefully examined the huge carpet covering the floor of the throne room, discovered that one of the lilies had come loose. She tugged at it, and soon the bee appeared. Now all ladies fell to work and, amid much gaiety, the carpet resumed its imperial appearance in less than half an hour. . . . Vanguard officers, preceding Napoleon from Fountainbleau, told us about

[71] Two famous Paris restaurants.

the clogged roads, lined on both sides, choked from both sides, with huge mobs of peasants. Their enthusiasm is said to be boundless, and there is no saying when he will arrive. The hope is that he is not recognized for fear that an assassin's arm will reach him. But he and the Duke of Vicenza had had the good sense to jump into an old dilapidated coach with a roof on it. At last, about nine in the evening, this vehicle came to a halt at the iron gate near the Quai du Louvre. No sooner had he set foot on the ground than the shout went up: "Vive l'Empereur!" a tremendous shout, a shout to rend the heavens. It came from the half-pay officers who had crowded the entrance hall and stairwell in choking density. The Emperor wore his famous gray overcoat. I went to meet him, and the Duke of Vicenza called out to me: "For God's sake, clear a path for him through this crowd." He started to ascend the stairs. I walked one step ahead of him, backward, gazing at him in deep emotion, tears in my eyes. I was in such a state of blissfulness that I could only repeat, over and over again: "Oh! It is you! You are here! At last—You!" As for Napoleon, he walked slowly, with eyes closed, hands outstretched, as a blind man walks, showing his happiness only in his smile.

The Berlinische Nachrichten *reprinted the* Journal de Paris *article about the French reaction to the allies' manifesto that proscribed Napoleon an outlaw:*

The Paris paper . . . brings the following "Observations Concerning the Declaration of the Vienna Congress": The allied powers need not feel obliged to protect Louis XVIII on his throne, for in fact he is not sitting on the throne; they cannot desire to assist the nation, for the nation does not ask for assistance; they cannot wish to restore peace and order in France, for this peace has never been disturbed; nor, finally, are they compelled to take up arms in their own defense, for they are not attacked by us.

On April 4 Napoleon himself released a "Proclamation to the Sovereigns," which never reached the addressees. According to the Leipziger Zeitung *this proclamation read:*

My Esteemed Brother!

... The welfare and happiness of the French people required the establishment of the imperial throne. My most cherished thought is to apply this office to underpin the peace of Europe. Glory enough has been gathered under the flags of now this, now that of the various nations. Often enough great mishaps have followed great victories in the changing patterns of fate.

At this moment a splendid battle arena invites the sovereigns, and I am the first to enter it. After I have demonstrated to the world the art of fighting great battles, it will be a more pleasant sensation henceforth to know no other rivalry than that of obtaining the blessings of peace, no other race than the holy one for the happiness of the people. France eagerly and openly proclaims this to be the noble goal of all her wishes.

Less positive were the reports of the opposition in Paris. On the general atmosphere, Krüdener, a Russian diplomat, wrote to Minister Nesselrode in Vienna on May 5:

The news from Paris is uniformly in agreement about Napoleon's financial embarrassments, which at the moment have reached a climax and can no longer be hidden. Ready cash is the big problem. The mood is turning more and more against him, and the walls are constantly plastered with posters that urge his assassination. The Republican Party is dissatisfied with the constitution he pretends to establish. Even the army shows its annoyance over having been hoodwinked in the matter of the Archduchess Marie Louise and looks forward with little enthusiasm to a war it will be forced to fight on French soil against superior forces.

His great speech on the occasion of the so-called "May Field," [72] which Napoleon gave before the assembled army and the mass of the people and at which he also swore the oath on the new constitution, was one long justification of his past deeds. On June 2 the Moniteur *published a detailed report on this:*

[72] Mustering of men for military service.—Transl.

Description of the May Field assembly in Paris on June 1. Napoleon proceeded with a large entourage to the Military Academy, where the spectacle was to take place. First, mass was celebrated. Following mass, the members of the central deputation of the electoral colleges, some five hundred strong, approached Napoleon's throne, where they were introduced by the Lord Chancellor and where one of them, Dubois of Angers, elector and representative from the Maine-et-Loire Department, read an address in the name of the French people. Then the Lord Chancellor announced the result of the vote on the *Acte additional*, which modified the imperial constitution, to the effect that this act had been all but unanimously approved by the voters, there being but 4,206 ballots cast against it out of a total of 1,292,563 voting.[73] The first herald-at-arms then announced the act as passed. At this point Napoleon, with a pen handed him by his brother Joseph, signed the document, after the chief lord high steward had had a table placed before the throne. With the table again removed, Napoleon, seated and covered, gave a short speech in which he said: "My dear electors of the departmental and regional colleges! My dear deputies of the land and sea forces to this May Field! Emperor, consul, soldier, I owe everything to the people. In fortune, in misfortune, on the battlefield, at the councillors' table, on the throne and in exile, France and France only was ever the sole concern of my thoughts and actions. I, too, like the Athens king, sacrifice myself for my people in the hope of seeing the promise fulfilled that France will maintain her natural integrity, her honor, and her rights. What brought me back to the throne was the indignation at seeing these rights, hallowed by twenty-five victorious years, misinterpreted and forever lost; was the agonized cry of the ravished French glory; was the will of the nation. This throne is dear to me as symbol of the independence, the honor, and the rights of the people. Soldiers, when I traveled amid general rejoicing through the different provinces to reach my capital, I had reason to expect a prolonged period of peace. The various nations are bound by treaties which

[73] It should be noted only a small minority of Frenchmen had voted on the issue.—Transl.

their governments, of whatever stripe, have concluded. I called this May Field assembly. Soon I learned that the foreign powers are bent on making war on us. They are starting by enlarging the Kingdom of Holland, allotting all our northern border fortifications to that country as a protective wall. Furthermore, they seek to settle their disagreements by dividing Alsace and Lorraine among them. It became necessary to arm for war. At the same time, since I must expose my person to the fortunes of war and its battles, my primary concern had to be to give the nation a constitution. The people have accepted the proposal I submitted to them. Frenchmen, when we shall have repulsed these unwarranted attacks, when Europe has become convinced of the rights and the independence of 28,000,000 French people, a solemn law, passed in conformity with constitutional provisions, shall gather into a uniform whole all the still loose ends of our constitution. Frenchmen, you are returning to your provinces. Tell the people that through unity, energy, and perseverance we shall emerge victorious in this struggle of a great people against their oppressors, that future generations shall examine our present action, that a nation that loses its independence loses all. Tell them that the foreign princes aim their every attack against my person. Did I not know that they would ravish France, I would put my life, which they so bitterly resent, into their hands. But tell the people also that as long as the French people keep alive their love for me, a love of which they furnish me so many examples, our enemies' rage will remain impotent. Frenchmen, my will is the will of the people, my rights are their rights, my honor, my fame, my fortune can be nought else but France's honor, fame, and fortune."

Following this, the Lord Almoner, the Archbishop of Bourges, administered communion to a kneeling Napoleon, who took the following oath: "I swear to observe the constitution of the Empire and to see it observed by others." Then the Lord Chancellor swore the oath of fealty and obedience and the entire assembly repeated: "We swear it." After this act of swearing, a Te Deum was sung. This done, the presidents of the electoral colleges received eagle standards for the national guard units of the Departments. Then Napoleon went to the Champ de Mars, where, following a short address, he presented the eagle standards to the Paris national guard and to his own guard. "Defend them," he cried out. "Defend them with your life! Swear it!" "We swear it!" came back a unanimous shout. As finale, the entire body of troops, some 50,000 regulars and 27,000 national guardists, passed in review.

They marched, with a short detour at Ligny,[74] *directly to Waterloo. Three days after the battle, Count de Lavallette, still Napoleon's postmaster general, hurried to the Elysée Palace in Paris to see the Emperor. He wrote about this in his memoirs:*

He asked me into his study. No sooner did he catch sight of me than he came forward to meet me, laughing like an epileptic, a horrible laugh. "Oh my God," he uttered, gazing upward and pacing across the room several times. This emotional spasm lasted a very short time. He fought to regain his self-control and asked me what was going on in the Chamber of Deputies. I did not consider it my duty to hide from him that desperation had reached its highest peak there and that a majority seemed determined to ask for his abdication or, in the absence of his cooperation, pronounce it against his will. "What!" he cried out. "If they don't take action, the enemy will be at the gates within a week." "Ah!" he added, "I have spoiled them with so many victories. They can no longer tolerate a single day's misfortune. What is to become of this poor France? I did what I could for it." Whereupon he sighed deeply.

His last letter to his wife, Marie Louise, he had already written three months earlier. No answer ever came.

My dear Louise! I have written you frequently. Three days ago I sent Flahault to you. Now I am sending you someone to tell you that all looks very promising. I am adored here and in com-

[74] Napoleon's last victory, over the Prussians, on June 16, 1815, two days before Waterloo.—Transl.

plete control of the situation. Only you, my dear Louise, are missing, you and my son. Please, come to me immediately via Strasbourg. Let the messenger tell you about the current situation in France. Adieu, my friend. All yours,

Napoleon.

FINALE

The Future

The solution to the German problem—i.e., the creation of the German League—was probably the most outstanding achievement of the Congress, where "outstanding" is not meant to convey quality. The founders of the League were obsessed by a common, dimly felt, dread: a fear of the forces from "below." Agent ***, always well informed, wrote on April 27, 1815:

Baron Gagern, exalted as usual, speaks of nothing but the German National Assembly, while the Prussians and other diplomats see in this Germany's undoing. Their argument is that Germany must be "organized" from "above" by the Five or the Three (Austria-Prussia-Hanover-Bavaria-Württemberg), under no circumstances from "below"! This, they believe, would lead to rioting and general confusion. . . . Did not the Darmstadt grand ducal guard officers enthusiastically drink Napoleon's health eight days ago? Therefore, let there be no German "committee," but let the Five decide the fate of Germany's future. This is desired by the opposition.

Italy, the second trouble spot, received entirely different treatment, a treatment that paid no heed to national strivings or aspirations. Here, England, though behind the scenes, played a decisive role:

The English agent Johnson arrived in Vienna from London on September 29. This person, as well known in Vienna as any-

where, in a week's time will leave for Pisa for reasons of health.
While he undoubtedly is in need of rest, I think he chose the
place partly for political reasons. It is a known fact that he, in
1813, advised England to foment a national uprising in Italy by
invoking the shibboleth of freedom and independence. Johnson
also advised the British general Bentinck to conduct a feinting
maneuver by reassigning his troops from Spain to Italy, which
was actually done, though later than desirable. . . . Bentinck, accompanied by his wife, has recently returned to Italy where he
was soon afterward made commander-in-chief of all British forces
in the Mediterranean area. This leads me to assume that Johnson chose Pisa to be able to assist and advise his superior. The
fact is that since implementation of the above plan three battalions of Italian volunteers were fielded whose flags bore the inscription "For Italy's Freedom," Dall'Osi was appointed commander
of one of these battalions, all of which were recruited and supplied from the Genoa region. . . . Johnson spoke to me about
Italian independence, saying that there had been a time where
this idea needed encouragement but that now every effort must
be bent on maintaining peace in Europe.

*It goes without saying that the future of the vanquished, of
France that is, must be made part of the planning. But the most
powerful of the allies, Alexander himself, knows so little about
conditions in France that he in all seriousness considers the most
impossible solutions, such as, for example, instituting a regency
in a France allegedly abandoned by the Bourbons. An anonymous
agent reported on this subject in April, 1815:*

Not finding anyone at the Café Wohlfahrt, I paid a pre-
theater visit to the home of the Czar's personal physician, M.
Willié. We discussed the Bourbon dynasty and he told me that
Alexander didn't care who ruled in France provided it wasn't
Napoleon. The Czar, Willié said, realized that he could not prevail upon the French to live under the Bourbons, who are so lacking all talents for the military. France, according to Alexander,
ought to have a soldier-king, and the Archduke Karl, of the
House of Lorraine, and therefore acceptable to the French, would

be an ideal choice. The Czar saw no difficulty in getting the Bourbons to abdicate in favor of this Austrian hero, something they would never do for Napoleon.

Dalberg, too, was concerned over France's future and, especially, with plans for the imminent war against Napoleon. In the spring of 1815, from Vienna, he wrote his wife, who was apparently already in Paris:

Kesselstadt [deputy from the city of Mainz at the Congress] is on his way to see you. Great events are in the making, and I have reasons to believe that far-reaching military operations will start between May 10–12. There is no telling what may come to pass if there is now the least discord among the allies. Up to the present all is harmony. Bonaparte has torn off his mask: he is Mohammed at the head of an army of fanatics; he is a sword-wielding Robespierre on horseback, the champion of every Jacobin on earth. The sad business of this Congress is coming to an end and, judging by the results achieved, is as shoddy a piece of work as I have ever seen. France, no longer represented at the Congress, is meekly accepting its fate. Being an emigré in the truest sense of that word, I shall go to Munich. All I owned in Paris has been confiscated.

Württemberg's crown prince, also, was concerned about the outcome of the impending campaign and the future of France. From Stuttgart he wrote his fiancée, the Grand Duchess Catherine who had remained in Vienna, where his letter was promptly "intercepted":

Yesterday I met a well-informed person fresh from Paris. He has reconfirmed what I wrote you in my last letter. Napoleon is in absolute control, and anything reported to the contrary is just not true. Talleyrand is believed to side with him. There are several traitors in the King's suite, Clarke probably being one of them. Every Frenchman is a patriot now and, no matter what his party label, must be respected for it. They are determined to defend their fatherland from whatever danger threatens. Doubtless, in two months at the latest, the army will obey the magic summons and swell to some 400,000 strong. Though the national guard so far is disinterested and stands aloof, in the end it, too, will follow orders. The army is spoiling for a fight, wants to reconquer the lost provinces. This is the picture. On this there is agreement. But let there be no illusion that the walls will crumble of their own accord at the first trumpet sound, nor let us put any faith in a Frenchman as long as the issue is in doubt: they are and always will be traitors.

Austria, host to the Congress, was in the grips of sinister fears and dire forebodings. On this subject Agent *** reported in April:

The Austrian monarchy is looked upon as a quodlibet of nations and of heterogeneous provincial diets. The Austrian lands and peoples, though not yet ripe for Jacobinism, must with great caution be protected against foreign influence. Our armies abroad may become infected; foreign troops traversing our provinces may poison the minds of our troops. Each of our units entering France faces a severe test and is exposed to grave moral danger. I hear many a jeremiad expressed on this subject, hear many a sigh that if only our government would establish a kind of inquisitional control.

Police official Leurs, on December 22, 1814, submitted a report on Stefan Széchenyi, the Hungarian nobleman who later gained fame as statesman and reformer:

Count Széchenyi, a major in the Hussars, was twenty-two at the time and assigned aide-de-camp to the Bavarian king. During the late war he had been Prince Schwarzenberg's page. In 1813 he spent some time at the Red House Inn near Prague to recover from an illness. When fully recovered, he was wont to take his meals in the public dining room. Here one day, in my presence, he told his table companions, mostly Prussians, that Austria led a precarious, hand-to-mouth existence only. Despite its many advances and progressive outlook, the country cannot compete with the world around it because it is suffering from internal disintegration and, since its constituent parts are daily becoming more alien to each other and are more and more moving in divergent directions, will fall apart within the next century.

Schönholz saw the future as follows:

The winter of 1814–15 was precisely the right kind of time for spawning marauding bands. With the countryside denuded of all military forces, plunderers, deserters, and discharged soldiers averse to honest labor were everywhere. In addition, the dense woods on both banks of the Danube, from the Bohemian border to within a stone's throw of Vienna, offered an excellent refuge and base of operations. In no time the bandit chieftain Grasel had brought a force of nearly three hundred outlaws under his control. A third of this force was even mounted, and the whole band was organized on military lines. Strategically divided into subgroups, the gang was ruled with iron discipline and sworn to blind obedience. Murder was strictly out, the safety of travel was not to be endangered, the needy were to be succored, and only castles and public offices were to be looted, preferably of ready cash. . . . Grasel was nowhere and everywhere, his shadow was seen wherever the eye glanced.

It is Eipeldauer who draws the moral of the story:

As I was writing you, Dear Cousin, the other day now that this Mr. Bonaparte has been granted a dusting-off vacation from me (as the saying is here in the chancellery), and that's as how I should like for it to stay, for right now I don't have need for him so much because I've found a surrogate: there's a certain Grasel who's appeared as commander of a gang of outlaws and cutpurses and who's making in Austria as Napoleon in Europe, the only difference being Napoleon had himself 500,000 robbers and thieves to do his work and Grasel has only a handful of such kind of cutthroats.

Meantime, Napoleon had been vanquished and the finishing touches were being put to the document that summed up the achievements of the Vienna Congress:

The copyists of the Congress chanceries, all thirteen of them, daily fought a battle over how best to formulate the final version of the agreement that was to lay down the Congress' laborious toil. Clancartly never left the scriveners' offices anymore, spurring on the occupants to unheard-of heights of achievements. He kept the Prussian scribes busy from six in the morning to past midnight. Humboldt sat buried up to his neck in piles of Congress papers, a huge mass of files he was obliged to sort and pack for shipment. Traces of this battle of the scriveners are clearly in evidence in the Austrian copy, the writing being hurried. There are erasures and cross-outs, some even done in pencil. Also, the paper itself is of differing type and color.

On August 11, 1815, Lady Charlotte Fitzgerald wrote General Sir Charles Hastings how she and her husband had observed Napoleon go aboard the Northumberland *in Plymouth harbor:*

Napoleon was accorded the reception of only a lieutenant general aboard the *Northumberland!* He saluted the sentry on the gangway in a military manner and asked Lord Keith to introduce the ship's officers to him. If he sensed the peculiar situation, he gave no evidence of it. . . . Others may think this the end of his career: I am convinced he himself does not share this view. He looks for all the world like a bust made of marble and bronze, looks just as cold and immobile, seems totally divorced from human wisdom and human sorrow—but a marvelous man withal!

Postscript: Bonaparte's head is quite bald in the back. His figure and legs are good. I did not once look at Bertrand.[75] It is true that Mme. Bertrand did actually try to jump overboard. But this was mainly a theatrical gesture, help being so close at hand. The most awful silence reigned throughout the time it took to install Napoleon aboard ship. A pin could have been heard dropping into the sea.

A description of the bandit leader Grasel, caught and executed during this time, can well serve as a finale and as a signpost of the future:

[75] General Bertrand, who, with his wife, voluntarily accompanied Napoleon into exile.—Transl.

Here we have the case history of a talented but unlettered person who grew up to become an enemy of the social order, of the propertied class. In the military service he achieved maximum exploitation of his native intelligence, a full awareness of his latent powers. His soldiering exposed him to the various social classes and thus to a close look at the unequal distribution of wealth, a sight that enraged his susceptible mind. Stepping outside the constricting bounds of a world he believed in the wrong, and himself therefore in the right, he did not turn petty thief but, in full cognizance of his military superiority, bandit leader. As such he directed his daredevil exploits against the propertied class, which he saw as surfeited with power.

To rob the State and the rich in order to give to those he believed to be unjustly poor and oppressed: as far as he is concerned he sought nothing more than this untrammeled choice and freedom of action.

Though Grasel as a person left the stage, his name and spirit march on.

Chronology

Oct. 14	Germany's Big Five (Austria, Prussia, Hanover, Bavaria, Württemberg) meet on the German question.
Oct. 18	Prater parade and festival on anniversary of Battle of Leipzig.
Oct. 21–27	The monarchs visit Budapest.
Oct. 30	The Congress officially opens.
Nov./Dec.	Deadlock on the Polish-Saxon Question.
Nov. 8	Masked ball at Prince Metternich's.
Nov. 10	Prince Repnin, as Russian commandant, turns over Saxony's administration to Prussia.
Nov. 23	Grand tournament at Imperial Riding School.
Nov. 29	Beethoven concert.
Dec. 9	*Tableaux vivants* in grand ballroom. Performance of *The Pasha of Suresne*.
Dec. 12	Grand ball in Apollo ballroom.
Dec. 13	Prince de Ligne dies.
Dec. 24	Treaty of Ghent between United States and Great Britain.
Dec. 29	Sir Sidney Smith's picnic in the Augarten.
Dec. 30–31	Razumovsky palace destroyed by fire.

1815

Jan. 3	Secret treaty between Austria, England, France.
Jan. 21	Requiem mass for Louis XVI in St. Stephan's.
Jan. 22	Sleigh ride of the monarchs to Schönbrunn.

Jan. 28	Austria proposes Polish-Saxon solution.
Feb. 3	Wellington arrives in Vienna.
Feb. 10	The Saxony question resolved at last.
March 1	Napoleon lands at Cannes.
March 6	News of Napoleon's escape reaches Vienna.
March 13	Great powers declare Napoleon an outlaw.
March 25	Big Four conclude a military pact against Napoleon. Talleyrand joins them.
June 9	Signing of the agreement that concludes the Congress of Vienna at a solemn plenary session which is at the same time the first official meeting of the Congress.
June 18	Battle of Waterloo.
Nov. 20	Second Treaty of Paris.

Bibliography

Locale, time, and events promised a plethora of source material. This promise, though in a surprising and paradoxical manner, was amply fulfilled. It is less the contemporaneous correspondence, diaries, and memoirs that enable us to scrutinize the personalities and events of the day than rather the secret files of the Austrian police which, before they were destroyed, had been available in toto to Fournier and Weil when they later compiled their works. It is these reports of the police that, like a latter-day stenotypist at a court or business session or the even more modern tape recorder of current-day listening devices, accompany the various turns of events in their many details as well as their grand design, in their political as well as their human connotations.

Allgemeine Zeitung, Vienna.

Bartel, Paul. *Napoléon à l'île d'Elba.* Paris, 1935.

Berlinische Nachrichten, Berlin.

Bertuch, Carl. *Bertuchs Tagebuch vom Wiener Kongress,* ed. Hermann Freiherr von Egloffstein. Berlin, 1916. These are ingenuous but penetrating observations of the son of Germany's second most important (after Cotta) publisher. Bertuch, who died young, lived like his better-known father in Weimar and was highly thought of by Goethe.

Bibl, Victor. *Kaiser Franz*. Vienna, 1937. Though not entirely free of Nazi influence, this is a detailed and quite objective biography of Emperor Franz II.

Bourgoing, Freiherr von. *Vom Wiener Kongress*. Brünn, Munich, Vienna, 1943. A charming, comprehensive, but badly organized work by the renowned expert of the Austria of the day. The author, a conservative, is greatly impressed with the work accomplished by the Congress. His book contains many invaluable references and excerpts from contemporary sources.

Brett-James, Anthony. *The Hundred Days*. London, 1964. A valuable source reference.

Du Montet, Baroness Alexandrine de la Boutetière de Saint-Mars. *Souvenirs*, ed. Count de la Boutetière. Paris, 1904.

Eipeldauer. Letters of an ostensible farmer named Eipeldauer, written to his alleged cousin in Kakran from Vienna. 285 booklets in 43 vols. Vienna, 1785–1821. These are irregularly published broadsides, composed by one Joseph Richter (1748–1813) and continued after his death by Gewey, Bäuerle, Gleich, Weiss, and Anton Langer. These witty and very popular pamphlets, written on cheap paper in the Viennese patois, comment on every conceivable event, both of local and more general interest. The sound views and typical Viennese humor, as well as the slightly malicious sarcasm, expressed in these pamphlets caused them to be widely read in their day and have made them into a veritable gold mine for latter-day researchers.

Eynard, Jean Gabriel. *Au Congrès de Vienne. Journal de Jean Gabriel Eynard*. Paris, 1914. The author was a well-to-do Geneva banker who represented his city at the Congress. His account is especially detailed where it concerns his native Switzerland and France. His diary is reliable and slightly boring.

Fain, Baron. *Manuscrit de 1814*. Vienna, 1814.

Ferrero, Guglielmo. *Reconstruction. Talleyrand à Vienne*. Geneva, 1939. A short but critical work about the Congress. The author, an anti-fascist, lived in exile in Geneva. It is he who introduced the meaningful concept of legitimacy, as understood by Talleyrand, into modern historical writing about the Congress of Vienna.

Fournier, August. *Die Geheimpolizei auf dem Wiener Kongress*. Vienna, 1913. An exhaustive collection of confidential agents' reports from the days of the Congress and an incomparable source of information.

Gentz, Friedrich von. *Osterreichs Teilnahme an den Befreiungskriegen*. Selected and compiled by Alfons Freiherr von Klinkowström. Vienna, 1887.

———. *Staatschriften und Briefe*, ed. Hans von Eckhardt. Berlin, 1921.

———. *Tagebücher*, ed. August Fournier and Arnold Winkler. Zurich and Vienna, 1920. The "Secretary of the Congress" is as witty, capricious, and completely subjective in his writings as he was in real life. His psychological insight into the politics and love life of his master, Prince Metternich, is unsurpassed.

Goethe, Johann Wolfgang von. *Werke*. Vol. 27. Stuttgart, 1840.

Gräffer, Franz. *Kleine Wiener Memoiren zur Geschichte und Charakteristik Wiens und der Wiener*. Vienna, 1845. A rather unimportant but charming book of memoirs in the Biedermeier manner.

Grillparzer, Franz. *Werke*, ed. Stefan Hock, vol. XI (*Studien*). Berlin, 1927.

Hastings, Reginald Rawdon. *Report on the Manuscripts of the Late Reginald Rawdon Hastings*, ed. Francis Bickley. London, 1934.

Humboldt, Wilhelm von. *Wilhelm und Caroline von Humboldt in ihren Briefen*, ed. Anna von Sydow. Vol. IV. Berlin, 1910. True Prussian sentiment is reflected in this correspondence between Prussia's second delegate at the Congress and his wife. Humboldt sees little that is praiseworthy in the Austrian statesmen, least of all in Metternich.

Johann, Archduke of Austria. *Aus dem Tagebuch 1810–51*, ed. Dr. Franz von Krones. Innsbruck, 1891. The Austrian emperor's younger brother, favorite of the Alpine peoples, later (1848) German Imperial Administrator at the Frankfurt Diet, confronts the confusing events of the times with a sentient heart, a naïve but penetrating mind, and no firmness of purpose at all. His diary is both appealing and informative.

Königsberger Zeitung. Königsberg.

Lacourt-Gayet, Georges. *Talleyrand 1754–1838.* 4 vols. Paris, 1928–34.

La Garde, Count Auguste de. *Gemälde des Wiener Kongresses 1814–15.* From the French. Ed. Dr. Hans Effenberger. Vienna and Leipzig, 1912. Historical opinion varies about this most outstanding, most garrulous, and most amusing of memoirists. De La Garde was an adventurer with some rather unattractive traits. On occasion, he ran into trouble with the Viennese police. This, however, has little bearing on his literary qualifications. It is true that his knowledge of a number of events he describes was secondhand and his relations with many of the leading personalities he discusses were not intimate. Yet his closeness to one of the greats of the period, Prince de Ligne, all but makes up for this deficiency. There is no doubt of de Ligne being de La Garde's protector. Bourgoing's extremely harsh judgment of the latter is no doubt influenced by a certain competitive spirit—not to say professional jealousy. On page 251 of his book Bourgoing writes about de La Garde: "I have consulted his much overrated memoirs here only as concerns de Ligne, in whose house the author, a distant relative, was a frequent visitor. As the still extant police records show, de La Garde did not enjoy a good reputation. He, therefore, could not possibly have played the social role he has ascribed to himself. In the confidential files maintained by the police, and which Fournier, Weil, and myself examined before their destruction, Carpani is the only one who mentions him, once. It is obvious, therefore, that de La Garde had to base his description of social events that were by invitation only on hearsay. Besides this, it is not very likely that important personalities would engage in intimate conversation with a person of de La Garde's ill repute." This judgment seems to have far overshot the mark. There is no doubt that de La Garde was present at the major fetes, such as the tournament, the "peace" festival, and certain court balls, even if he did have to "crash the gates," as he often himself admits. It should also be remembered that Bourgoing, where it concerns standards of trustworthiness and

intimacy with "people of ill repute," applies the bourgeois morality of the nineteenth century to a period in which the frivolously
broadminded eighteenth century still set the rules.

Lavallette. *Mémoirs at Souvenirs du Comte de Lavallette, ancien
aide-de-camp de Napoléon, Directeur des Postes sous le Premier
Empire et pendant les Cents-Jours.* Paris, 1905. The postmaster
general's account of Napoleon's return to the Tuileries is of
touching impressiveness and one of the most moving stories of
this eventful epoch.

Leipziger Zeitung. Leipzig.

Leisching, Eduard. *Der Wiener Kongress. Culturgeschichte der bil-
denden Künste und das Kunstgewerbe, Theater-Musik in der
Zeit von 1800–25,* ed. Eduard Leisching. Vienna, 1898.

Ligne, Charles Joseph duc de. *Fragments d'histoire de ma vie.* 2 vols.
Paris, 1846.

Luckwaldt, Friedrich. *Das Zeitalter des Restauration* (Propyläen
Weltgeschichte), vol. VII. Berlin, 1929.

Mann, Golo. *Friedrich von Gentz.* Zurich, 1947.

Metternich, Prince. *Denkwürdigkeiten,* ed. Otto H. Brandt. 2 vols.
Munich, 1921. Of special interest in this penetrating and distinguished work is the account of the news of Napoleon's escape
reaching Vienna. These memoirs are pithy, somewhat vain, and
nearly always reliable.

Le Moniteur. Paris. This official newspaper, founded by Napoleon,
was known for its one-sided reporting and time-serving attitude
toward the Emperor. The war bulletins and all events concerning the Emperor and his family, especially, were ludicrously dis-
torted. Nevertheless, because of France's leading role in Europe,
Le Moniteur was often the only available news service.

Nicolson, Sir Harold. *The Congress of Vienna: A Study in Allied
Unity: 1812–1822.* New York, 1946.

Nostitz, Karl von. *Leben und Briefwechsel.* Dresden, Leipzig, 1848.
Nostitz, first in Prussian, then in Russian, service, adjutant and
friend of the renowned Prince Ferdinand of Prussia, general,
man of letters, and friend of the fair sex, knows how to depict a

panorama of events and personages entirely in consonance with his upbringing and beliefs, a panorama that leaves no doubt about his admiration for the military and his abomination of the politician.

Österreichisch-Kaiserliche privilegirte Wiener-Zeitung. Vienna. Then as now Austria's official gazette, this publication contains all official announcements, promotions, and civil service changes, but brings general news and supplies cultural fare as well.

Österreichischer Beobachter. Vienna.

Perts, Georg Heinrich. *Aus Steins Leben.* 2 vols. Berlin, 1856.

Pichler, Caroline. *Denkwürdigkeiten aus meinem Leben.* Vol. III. Vienna, 1844. This relatively unimportant woman and author (her main work was the novel *Agathokles,* praised by Goethe) founded a politico-literary salon that was to serve as the Vienna counterpart of the Berlin salons of Rahel Varnhagen von Ense and Henrietta Herz. (Both of these women played an active role in the cultural life of Berlin and all Germany. Their homes were meeting places of such intellectual giants as the brothers Humboldt, Engel, Gentz, Schadow, Fr. Schlegel, and Elisa von der Recke, among others—Transl.) Caroline Pichler's is the viewpoint of the then emerging staid bourgeoisie.

Schlegel, Friedrich von. *Sämtliche Werke.* Vol. I. Vienna, 1822.

Schönholz, Friedrich Anton von. *Traditionen zur Charakteristik Österreichs, seines Staats-und Volkslebens unter Franz I.,* ed. Gustav Gugitz. Munich, 1914. These are highly one-sided but amusing memoirs of a man whose very birth (illegitimate) and whose mother's private life caused him to harbor a certain resentment against the ruling social class, a resentment that is much in evidence in his often witty criticism and his always original observations.

Talleyrand-Périgord, Charles-Maurice de. *Correspondance inédite du prince de Talleyrand et du roi Louis XVIII pendant le congrès de Vienne,* ed. Pallain. Paris, 1881.

———. *Mémoires.* Publ. by the duc de Broglie. 5 vols. Paris, 1891–92. Talleyrand's letters, including those not meant to be published and therefore bearing the imprint of sincerity, in many places reveal the cunning, if highly gifted, nature of this greatest of all schemers at the Congress.

Thürheim, Countess Lulu. *Mein Leben. Erinnerungen aus Österreichs grosser Welt*. Publ. by René von Rhyn. 2 vols. Munich, 1913. Countess Thürheim, member of Vienna's high society and sister-in-law of Prince Razumovsky, in an often malicious, sometimes sentimental manner, deals mainly with the distaff side of the Congress. Her memoirs, always intriguing, border on the shocking.

Varnhagen von Ense, Karl August. *Denkwürdigkeiten des eigenen Lebens*. Vol. III. Leipzig, 1871. The literary style of this officer, diplomat, and writer is as volatile as was his nature. First in Austrian, then in Russian, service, he was infatuated with Vienna and the Viennese in an entirely un-Prussian fashion.

Weil, Commandant Maurice-Henri. *Les Dessous du Congrès de Vienne*. 2 vols. Paris, 1917. The French civil servant and scholar Weil published this entirely objective supplement to Fournier's work in the midst of the First World War. Weil's book contains all those secret documents which Fournier either left out entirely or treated negligently.

Index